362.8
B32   Bauer, Yehuda.
            My brother's keeper.

ISSUED TO

362.8
B32   Bauer, Yehuda.
            My brother's keeper.

Temple Israel Library
Minneapolis, Minn.

———

Please sign your full name on the above card.

Return books promptly to the Library or Temple Office.

Fines will be charged for overdue books or for damage or loss of same.

My Brother's Keeper

Yehuda Bauer

MY BROTHER'S KEEPER

A History of the American Jewish Joint Distribution Committee 1929–1939

THE JEWISH PUBLICATION SOCIETY OF AMERICA   *Philadelphia*

Contents

Tables

Preface

In 1962 I spent a few months in New York looking at material
dealing with the migration of Jews after the Second World War.
One of the main sources for this was the archive of the American
Jewish Joint Distribution Committee, known in the U. S. as JDC,
and among Jews everywhere as "the Joint." One day Moses A.
Leavitt, the late executive vice-chairman of JDC, called me into his
office and we began to speculate about the history of his organization. Was it just another Jewish group in North America, dealing
with overseas social work rather than the local Jewish community,
or was it something significantly different?

As time went on, Prof. Moshe Davis, head of the Institute of
Contemporary Jewry, and I reached the conclusion that in many
ways the history of JDC held the key to the story of European
Jewry in the first half of this century, at least in a number of areas.
Indeed, there were times when the history of JDC was, in effect,
the social and economic history of Jewish communities in the Old
World. The result of these thoughts crystallized into an agreement
between the institute and JDC to try to write a history of JDC's
attempts at rescue and rehabilitation of European Jewry between
the end of the 1920s and the dissolution of the displaced persons'
camps in postwar Europe, about 1951. The dates chosen reflected
two facts: in the archives of JDC there was a manuscript by Herman Bernstein, a journalist with close connections to JDC, relating

in detail the story of JDC between 1914 and the middle 1920s. No real historical writing can be attempted as yet for the period after 1951; the events are too recent.

The present volume deals with the first part of the period we are discussing, up to the outbreak of World War II. Two other volumes are projected, dealing with the periods 1939–45 and 1945–51. Each volume will be designed to stand alone and tell a meaningful story in its own right. However, there is an obvious link between them.

The story of European Jewry between the two world wars has not been written. Its outlines are clear and well-known: a speedy descent toward the horrors of the holocaust that befell the Jewish people during World War II. Yet more questions have been asked than answered, relating to the fate not only of German Jewry but also of Eastern European Jewry. The present volume is an attempt to deal with aspects of the social and economic history of European (including Russian) Jewry, as seen through the eyes of an American social aid agency—the largest agency of its kind in the world. The relations between American Jewry and Jewish communities abroad are dealt with, and I also hope to throw light on some of the international events that affected the fate of the Jewish people.

A generous grant by JDC made the research for this book possible. However, let me emphasize that no censorship was exercised by JDC on the content of the book, though advice and criticism were sought and given. The late Mr. Leavitt made the agreement with the Institute of Contemporary Jewry of the Hebrew University in Jerusalem, and the late Charles Jordan began to implement it. Both were of tremendous help in making the research possible. The present executive vice-chairman of JDC, Samuel L. Haber, saw the project through and in the course of doing so became a close adviser and, more important, a good friend. The friendly advice and interest of Edward M. M. Warburg, Louis Broido, Herbert Katzki, Gaynor I. Jacobson, and many others who allowed themselves to be interviewed and pestered with questions was invaluable. Miss Dorothy L. Speiser was the guide and guardian angel of the project, looking after all the practical matters as well as providing information from her tremendous store of knowledge. Special thanks are also due to my friend Irving Dickman, to Dr. Feiler and Miss Cantor of the JDC office, and Mrs. Mangiello, who served as my secretary in New York. Finally, and importantly, Mrs. Rose Klepfisz, JDC's archivist, and her co-workers smoothed the access to the thousands of files that had to be gone through; without her expert knowledge the research could not have been accomplished.

On the Israeli side, the Hebrew University allowed me to take two years off from my academic duties to do the necessary research. My friend and colleague, head of our institute, Prof. Moshe Davis, was in many ways the originator of the project and pushed me into undertaking it.

Y.B.

Kibbutz Shoval
Negev, Israel

My Brother's Keeper

Introduction

The First Fifteen Years[1]

In August 1914 a cable arrived in the office of Jacob H. Schiff, head of the banking house of Kuhn, Loeb & Co. It had been sent by the U. S. ambassador to Turkey, Henry Morgenthau, Sr., and it asked that $50,000 be sent to the Jews of Palestine, who were threatened with persecution and hunger as a result of the hostile attitude of the Turkish rulers of the country. The effect of World War I on the Jews of Europe and the Middle East was coming home to American Jewry.

Schiff brought the matter to the attention of his friends at the American Jewish Committee (AJC), founded in 1906 and dedicated not only to the protection of Jewish civil and religious rights all over the world, but also to an effort "to alleviate the consequences of persecution and to afford relief from calamities affecting Jews, wherever they occur." On August 31 the money was collected, with Schiff and the Zionist Provisional Committee (in effect, Nathan Straus) giving $12,500 each, and AJC voting the remaining $25,000.

American Jewry was more deeply divided in 1914 than it was to be in the coming two generations. Apart from the old division between the descendants of the Spanish and Portuguese (Sephardic) Jews and their German Jewish (Ashkenazic) brethren, there now existed the deep cleavage between German Jewry—from the middle and upper class, liberal, speedily adapting itself to the American way of life—and the masses of East European Jews who had been arriving in the New World since 1882. The latter were largely proletarian or lower middle class, and their spiritual outlook tended to be either Jewish Orthodox or, at the other extreme, socialist and antireligious. There was very little in common between those different kinds of Jews, except for the uncertain and ill-defined feeling that their common origin and cultural background should mean more to them than it actually did.

The German Jewish leadership of American Jewry was a highly sophisticated, intellectual group of men and women. The social elite at the top was made up of bankers, merchants, judges, lawyers, and doctors; they were well-bred, well-read, patrons of the arts and of sports, supporters and furtherers of a well-ordered democracy. Their philanthropy was sincere and well-meant. Most of them— there were some notable exceptions—kept some of the religious observances of their ancestors, or rather those of them that had not been discarded by the Jewish Reform movement. However, it appeared that their religion meant less and less to them as time went on.

In a sense their social obligation to their brethren (whom they awkwardly called "coreligionists," to emphasize the fact that there was really nothing in common between them except religion, or vestiges of it) was a kind of inherited trait. It had been transmitted to them from the customs and usages of their ancestors in the ghettos of Germany, where, a scant three generations before Morgenthau sent off his telegram to Schiff, life had produced the same kind of Jew as Eastern Europe did. In their efforts to "assimilate," that is, to become citizens of the world in which they lived, they often rationalized their aid to Jews as part of their concern for humanity as a whole. The common past put a moral obligation on them to help those Jews in backward Europe to reach the happy stage of equality—and therefore prosperity—that they themselves had attained. That, it was hoped, would be the end of the Jewish problem for Europe's Jews; it would also be the end of their own problem qua Jews, and it would no longer bother them. But in the meantime the obligation existed, and it had to be met honestly and openly.

The concern of German Jews in America for humanity in general and for Jews in particular was no pretense; on the contrary, their whole liberal background and education had developed in them a strong feeling of responsibility toward the poor and the underprivileged. Often the proportion of their money spent for general nonsectarian philanthropy exceeded the amounts reserved for their "coreligionists"; but even this was part of their strong, typically Jewish sense of a social and moral imperative, which appears to have set them apart as a group from other rich men in America. Their emphasis on nonsectarianism made their Jewishness stand out. Not that they hid it; they were aware of it, and most of them saw it distinctly as a matter of honor not to run away from it.

The American Jewish Committee was *the* organized expression of the German Jewish aristocracy of spirit, culture, and money. Its head was the undisputed leader of American Jewry until his death in 1929, Louis Marshall—lawyer, statesman, and thinker. The AJC that he led was by no means homogeneous in its political outlook. Apart from differences emanating from the American political scene, there were also divisions into Zionists and anti-Zionists. Judges Louis D. Brandeis and Julian W. Mack were to become the mainstays of American Zionism during the war. Others, especially Julius Rosenwald, the head of Sears Roebuck, followed German Jewish liberal tradition in seeing Judaism as a religious creed only, and rejecting all the implications of Jewish national identity. The majority of AJC tended to follow Marshall in his support of building up Palestine, whose great spiritual importance in Jewish history they admitted—as *a* place of refuge, not necessarily *the* place of refuge, for those Jews who wanted or were forced to go there. At the same time, they did everything they could to help Jews become nationals and equals in the countries of their residence, so that they would not have to look for places of refuge at all. Sooner or later, it was hoped, the dangerous notion of nationalism would disappear altogether.

These beliefs were held very sincerely, and yet this was the time —the summer of 1914—when the whole structure of nineteenth-century liberalism collapsed. The collapse was accompanied by a disaster that struck the Jewish people in the eastern and southeastern parts of Europe and the Middle East. Three empires and a kingdom—Russia, Austria-Hungary, Germany, and Romania— were involved in a deadly conflict, and out of the more than fifteen million Jews of the world, ten million lived in these countries. Within a very short time there were five hundred thousand Jewish refugees in the Russian interior, driven there by the czarist armies. Four hundred thousand more fled before the advancing Russians into the interior of the Austro-Hungarian Empire. Then German armies overran large areas of formerly Russian Poland. Some eight hundred townships and villages where Jews lived were hit and severely damaged, and about eighty thousand Jewish houses were destroyed.[2] Yet, significantly, the action of American Jewry was triggered by the alarming news that reached the U. S. regarding the fate of the eighty-five thousand Jews of Palestine.

The first to act were the Orthodox Jews of overwhelmingly East European origin. On October 4, 1914, they founded the Central Committee for the Relief of Jews Suffering through the War. The main officers of the committee were Leon Kamaiky, Harry Fischel, Harry Lucas, and Morris Engelman. But Orthodox Jewry could hardly carry the burden by itself. The leadership of the American Jewish Committee therefore convened a meeting of forty organizations which took place in New York on October 25, 1914. There a committee of five was elected: Oscar S. Straus, Louis D. Brandeis, Julian W. Mack, Harry Fischel (of the Central Committee), and Meyer London (of the socialists). This committee in turn asked one hundred prominent Jews from all walks of life to select officers for a new committee: the American Jewish Relief Committee (AJRC). Louis Marshall was chairman, Felix M. Warburg, treasurer, and Cyrus L. Sulzberger, secretary.

Contrary to expectations, however, the Orthodox group decided in the end not to join AJRC, and so on November 27, 1914, another body was established to distribute the funds collected separately by the two committees. At the suggestion of the new committee's comptroller, Harriet B. Lowenstein, Felix M. Warburg's secretary, it was called the Joint Distribution Committee. In August 1915 the socialists set up a third cooperating body, the People's Relief Committee, led by Meyer London, Sholem Asch, and others. More than half a century later, although the three original components are long since defunct, the organization's official name still remains the American Jewish Joint Distribution Committee; a tradition had been established and no one would think of changing the awkward name. "The Joint" had become a household word for many millions of Jews.

The demands on the young organization during the war years of 1914–18 were enormous. Local and state committees were organized in the U. S. and speakers such as Judah L. Magnes, Reform rabbi, pacifist, enfant terrible, and—later—president of the Hebrew University in Jerusalem, one of the great orators of his time, were sent to raise funds. By the end of 1915 some $1.5 million had been raised. This money was sent to Palestine aboard the coal steamer U.S.S. *Vulcan* in March 1915, along with nine hundred tons of food and medicines (55 percent of which went to the starving Jews, the rest being distributed on a nonsectarian basis under the supervision of the American consul). After long delays a second mercy ship, the U.S.S. *Des Moines,* reached Palestine in September 1916.

The Jewish aid society in Russia, EKOPO, received money from JDC to look after the refugees from the war areas, especially the ones who came from enemy (that is, Austrian) territory, who were forbidden by the czarist government to receive help from Russian Jewish institutions.

As for German-occupied Poland, the German Jewish aid society —Hilfsverein der deutschen Juden—established a special branch to aid the stricken Jews in that area. They served as JDC's agents there until America's entry into the war in 1917. JDC also sent Magnes and Dr. Alexander Dushkin to Poland to check allegations about the unjust distribution of funds (the two commissioners cleared the Hilfsverein committee). Both the accusation and the investigating commission were the first in a long line of similar events during the coming decades.

In the meantime, at the urging of friends of the Jewish people in the United States Senate, President Wilson set aside January 27, 1916, as Jewish Sufferers Relief Day. On that day about $1 million was collected. By the end of 1918 JDC had managed to collect over $16.5 million. This was done by perfecting fund-raising techniques, largely through the work of Jacob Billikopf, of the Kansas City Federation of Jewish Charities. The money was very carefully distributed in the areas of greatest suffering. As the war proceeded, large sums had to be sent to Austria and, after 1917, to those parts of Romania that could be reached.

After America's entry into the war the major problem was how to transfer money to areas under enemy control. From the start JDC insisted on full legality and cooperation with the State Department. Every step it took "had been taken only after consultation with and the approval of officials of the government, especially of the State Department."[3] With government approval a committee was set up in neutral Holland by the head of a Dutch bank; JDC sent Boris D. Bogen and Max Senior from America to represent it on the committee. This group then transferred the money received from the United States to Dutch diplomatic representatives in the stricken areas, who distributed it according to guidelines received from New York via Holland. Close to $2 million was thus channeled into German-occupied territory between the spring of 1917 and March 1918.

Despite all its efforts, especially in Russia, JDC was confronted with tremendous suffering when the war ended. Probably over a million Jews in Poland alone were homeless and were, quite literally, starving. Moreover, the creation of new nation-states—Poland, Lithuania, Latvia, Czechoslovakia, Romania, Yugoslavia,

Hungary, and Austria—and the Bolshevik Revolution caused further dislocation and local wars. The Jewish minorities, not knowing with whom to side and occupying an unenviable middle-class position in this postwar struggle of nations and revolutionary masses, became the butt of every slander and persecution.

Bloody pogroms instigated by Poles occurred in eastern Galicia and northeastern Poland. Even worse was the situation in the Ukraine, where Bolsheviks and their anti-Semitic White Russian opponents were struggling for control. Probably more than two hundred thousand Jews were killed or died in the 1918–21 epidemics in eastern Poland and the Ukraine; seventy-five thousand more were wounded. Suffering was especially grim during the futile Polish-Soviet war of 1920–21, fought over areas with large Jewish populations. The results were terrible. In Poland the total number of orphans after the war was estimated at seventy-five thousand. In the Ukraine it was said to be two hundred thousand. Sixty percent of the surviving children in Galicia alone suffered from tuberculosis. In the Ukraine five hundred Jewish communities had been abandoned, and about half a million Jews were economically ruined. With the suicide rate growing alarmingly and parents driven to desperation at the sight of starving children, some children were abandoned on the doorsteps of the relatively prosperous.[4]

The destruction of European Jewry during World War II has obliterated the memory of that first holocaust of the twentieth century in the wake of the first world conflict. Yet in pre-Auschwitz terms the experience was bad enough. Humanitarian groups such as JDC tried to respond in a suitable manner. After some misunderstandings had been cleared up, JDC joined in the efforts of the $100 million effort by the American Relief Administration (ARA), under Herbert Hoover, set up by Congress to help the people of Europe. JDC contributed $3.3 million, and in return JDC workers such as Boris D. Bogen were allowed to undertake aid missions to Jews in Eastern Europe as officials of ARA.

Financed by a tremendous fund-raising effort that yielded a total of $33.4 million for 1919–21, JDC established soup kitchens on a large scale, reconstructed and reequipped hospitals, established orphanages, and sent food in convoys of trucks to hundreds of towns and villages in Poland. It set up a tracing bureau to reunite families scattered by war and pestilence; it helped reestablish schools and institutions of higher learning, religious and secular. In 1919 the U.S.S. *Westward Ho* arrived in Poland with food; at the insistence of the Poles, the food was divided and handed out separately to Jewish and Polish recipients. Much of the money was spent on nonsectarian missions to the Polish countryside, because JDC was afraid of arousing anti-Semitism if it supplied only Jews (despite the fact that ARA did a great deal to save masses of Poles from the aftereffects of the hostilities). In June 1919 the U. S. ambassador in Poland arranged for official Polish recognition of JDC as a social agency operating in that country.

After the first two years of what was essentially emergency relief, the time came to take stock of the situation and decide on future policies. JDC had nominated Dr. Julius Goldman as its first European director at the end of 1919. Goldman tried to put some order into the operations and set down guiding principles for work in the various countries. Bogen, responsible for Poland and Russia, asked for and got the New York office's agreement to recruit social workers in America to help in Europe. In February 1920 Bogen arrived in Poland with 126 members of the first JDC Overseas Unit. Bogen also tried to bridge the deep ideological differences within East European Jewry and demanded that local committees be set up, from which he hoped a central committee for social work in Poland would ultimately emerge. This, unfortunately, did not happen, though in January 1921, when the Relief Conference for Congress Poland (the central part of that country) met in Warsaw, Bogen seemed well on the way to success. Local fund raising was also initiated in the spring of 1920; although financially insignificant (about $20,000 was raised in Poland in 1920), this was valuable in buttressing the morale of the population and preventing them from becoming the demoralized recipients of doles. Due largely to

Bogen's efforts, some local groups began to assume responsibility for palliative aid at the end of 1920.

Another vital service performed by JDC in Eastern Europe, especially in Poland, was the institution of a bureau for private remittances under Isidore Hershfield (who was succeeded by Samuel Golter). American relatives of Polish Jews could now transfer small sums of money to them and be reasonably sure that it would reach the desired destination. In addition to the considerable financial aid thus extended to Polish Jewry—$5,250,000 during the first eight months of 1920,[5] which was much more than the money spent on JDC's behalf in Poland—the effect on the morale of Polish Jews was tremendous.

Special efforts were devoted to child and orphan care, the settlement of the refugee question, and the development of medical facilities. In 1923 JDC founded an orphan care group called CENTOS,* which later developed into a general child care society. TOZ,† the medical society, had been founded in 1921. Both these organizations tended to become less and less dependent on direct JDC aid, though they never became completely self-supporting. During 1921 and 1922 JDC also managed to liquidate most of its work for the hundreds of thousands of refugees, arranging for the reception in temporary or permanent homes and helping establish local societies to deal with the problem.

In the cultural field, the JDC Cultural Committee in New York, under the chairmanship of Cyrus Adler, recommended in the summer of 1920 that schools in Eastern Europe be supported by allocating one-third of the monies raised by the Central Committee and the People's Relief Committee in their separate efforts. However, this arrangement was likely to give rise to a great deal of resentment, because the American Jewish socialists tended to support the secular, anti-Zionist Yiddishist schools, whereas the Or-

*Federation of Associations for the Care of Orphans in Poland.
†TOZ—Towarzystwo Ochrony Zdrowia Ludnosci Zydowskiej (Society for Safeguarding the Health of the Jewish Population).

thodox, of course, supported their own school system in Poland. This would have discriminated against the Hebrew and Zionist schools (the Tarbuth schools) which were then growing in strength and importance. Since AJRC was practically defunct by that time, JDC itself took over the responsibility of paying a suitable proportion of the monies to support schools and institutions that the Orthodox and the socialists did not wish to subsidize.

The end of the Russo-Polish war of 1920–21 also marked the last stages of emergency relief by JDC. Two Americans then in Poland, Dr. Charles D. Spivak and Elkan C. Voorsanger, supervised the dispatch of carloads of supplies to the stricken areas. JDC representatives on mercy missions also ventured into Polish-occupied areas in the Ukraine. On one such journey two JDC workers, Bernard Cantor and Prof. Israel Friedlander, were murdered by Ukrainians on July 5, 1920.

The approaching end of the period of emergency relief was marked by disagreements on the future organizational setup of JDC in Europe. Dr. Goldman, the European director, wanted to create an overall European Executive which would supervise JDC committees in the various countries. Bogen, on the other hand, preferred centralized control from New York and the administration of JDC funds by American country directors. In the end Goldman's concept was accepted and became the standard practice in the period between the wars. It was only later, after 1945, that nominating American country directors was adopted again, though without abolishing the European Executive, a basic JDC organizational tool that exists to this day.

Julius Goldman resigned at the end of 1920 and was succeeded by James A. Becker. Becker in turn was followed in 1921 by James N. Rosenberg, who served for one year. In 1924 Dr. Bernhard Kahn took over the post of JDC European director, which he was to hold for fourteen years.

Before he returned to America, Goldman proposed to JDC in New York that a decision be made to discontinue emergency relief, which was done on October 28, 1920, by the JDC Executive Committee. The date for the final liquidation of emergency programs was set for July 1, 1921. As expected, the decision caused a great uproar. A conference of representatives of Jewish aid committees meeting in Warsaw on February 20, 1921, protested the new policy and asked for a postponement, at least as far as eastern Poland was concerned, of six months. A decision to close down the JDC remittances department in Warsaw was also protested.

The situation in 1921 varied from country to country. There was no practical possibility of stopping emergency relief in Poland on the date determined in New York; but the trend was set, and though JDC never did actually stop emergency relief, its scope was very sharply reduced as the year drew to an end.

Lithuania was a different case altogether; JDC entered there only in 1919, when Sholem Asch, the famed Yiddish writer, went there on its behalf. He was followed by a committee from the German Hilfsverein, with whom JDC continued a very close relationship, composed of Dr. Bernhard Kahn, Dr. Arthur Hantke (a well-known German Zionist leader), and Dr. Meier Hildesheimer. A Lithuanian Jewish National Council was opposed there by a left-wing workers' committee. Successive American representatives tried to settle the local differences and help the suffering Jewish population, especially the thirty-five thousand refugees from Poland. Finally, with JDC's help, the Jewish People's Bank was developed, which in 1921 boasted of seventy-seven branches that granted loans at low rates of interest.

In Latvia, JDC operations started even later, in February 1920, when the first possibilities of transferring money there became known. JDC sent emergency relief to stricken Latvian Jews, many of whom had left the cities and had gone to the country because of lack of food. In Latvia and in Czechoslovakia—unlike Lithuania and Poland—central social aid committees were set up, largely due to the initiative of JDC. In Czechoslovakia a resident JDC representative, Henry G. Alsberg, was for a time in practical control of the Prague committee (Hilfskomité) of wealthy Jews. Under a new director, Slovakia and Subcarpathian Russia (in Czech initials,

PKR), the easternmost, poorest, Ruthenian-speaking section of the country, were made independent of the Prague committee in 1920. This was quite logical, because the Jews of Bohemia and Moravia, the western sections of Czechoslovakia, recovered very quickly and soon needed no more help.

In Austria the main problem was the close to 120,000 Jewish refugees crowded into Vienna at the close of the war. JDC sent Meyer Gillis and Max Pine to the starving city at the end of 1918. Before JDC help became effective, however, many of the refugees trekked home to Poland on their own initiative. The old Viennese social aid committee, the Israelitische Allianz zu Wien, did whatever it could to help those that remained. JDC sent close to $1 million to Vienna in 1919, to subsidize soup kitchens and provide medical and child care.

In Hungary the situation was still different. There, ARA's effective program for providing a minimum of aid was very cautiously supplemented by JDC funds for specific Jewish aims. A Hungarian Jewish committee, set up—as in other countries—with the full blessing of JDC, slowly took over specific Jewish tasks. The problem in Hungary was largely political. After the failure of the short-lived Communist regime under Béla Kun, a Jew, the White Hungarian government took a definitely anti-Semitic line, though in fact the Jews had perhaps suffered more than anyone else under Kun's government. The new reactionary regime deported twenty-two trainloads of Polish Jewish refugees back to Poland. In 1920 Hungary was the first postwar European government to institute a numerus clausus law, permitting only a low percentage of Jewish students to register at the universities. JDC, at any rate, ceased its operations there in 1921.

The situation of the Jews in Romania in the postwar period was even more complicated. While Jews had suffered relatively little in Old Romania (Walachia and Moldavia), complete chaos reigned in Bessarabia, Bucovina, and Transylvania, all of them provinces annexed by Romania from her Russian, Austrian, and Hungarian neighbors. Pioneer work was done there for JDC by Hettie Goldman and James A. Becker in 1919–20. The main results were the setting up of provincial central committees in Bessarabia, Bucovina, and Transylvania and the provision of emergency relief. After Becker, Alexander A. Landesco, himself a Romanian-born American Jew, was instrumental in establishing loan *kassas*— small cooperative banks lending money at very low rates of interest. Fifteen thousand refugees from Ukrainian pogroms also had to be supported, and this problem was dealt with by a local social worker, Noel Aronovici, who entered JDC service and was to become one of the central figures of JDC work in the whole interwar period. In February 1921 Landesco left Romania, having provided for the cessation of relief. Yet soon after his departure JDC had to intervene again when forty thousand Bessarabian Jews living within seven miles of the Russian border on the Dniester River were brutally expelled into Old Romania by government troops. In Transylvania the reduction in relief aid by JDC was made possible only through an increase in the remittances sent there by relatives in the U. S.

As we have seen, JDC was founded in response to a cry for help emanating from the Middle East. During the war Turkish Jewry received help via the Dutch Embassy at Istanbul, and after the war Aaron Teitelbaum of JDC supervised the administration of relief there and in Salonika, Greece, where an ancient Jewish community had been hard hit by a devastating fire in 1917. In Palestine a committee under Eliezer Hoofien, a Dutch Zionist who later was to be the head of Palestine Jewry's foremost banking institution, the Anglo-Palestine Bank, distributed funds under the auspices of the sympathetic Spanish consul, Señor Ballabar. During the war over $1.5 million was transferred by JDC, to deal with the problems of a community physically uprooted and evicted from their homes by the Turkish rulers. After the conquest of the country by the British, JDC asked David de Sola Pool, a member of the Zionist Commission then visiting Palestine, to act as its representative. Orphan committees, aid to a Zionist medical unit, support for the religious groups and their institutions, loan banks—all these swallowed very large funds: over \$3.2 million for the period 1918–21.

Additional efforts, smaller in scope but no less decisive for those involved, were made to help tens of thousands of stranded Jewish prisoners of war in Siberia in 1919–20. Dr. Frank F. Rosenblatt, the JDC representative, was the moving spirit in setting up a Siberian War Prisoners' Repatriation Fund, in which a number of organizations, including the American Red Cross, participated. Seven hundred thousand dollars was spent there by JDC. Other Jews stranded in Yokohama, of all places, were also helped to emigrate by a cooperative effort of JDC and the great Jewish emigration agency, Hebrew Immigrant Aid Society (HIAS). Others were helped in Iraq and Iran, and a group of scientists working with the Abyssinian Falashas, who are by some believed to be a lost Jewish tribe, were supported in their efforts.

In Europe, meanwhile, under Becker's directorship relief aid had been more or less terminated in 1921. The exception to this general rule was Germany, where sixty thousand East European Jews had immigrated, most of them after the 1918 armistice. When Germany underwent its catastrophic economic decline and runaway inflation, in 1922–24, JDC had to come to German Jewry's help. Its aid was concentrated on child care, and its contributions went partly to nonsectarian American efforts to aid German children generally. In this activity a very close and friendly cooperation developed between JDC and the American Friends Service Committee (AFSC) of the American Quaker community; this friendship between the two aid organizations was to yield important results during the catastrophes of the 1930s and the 1940s.

In New York, JDC set up a European Advisory Committee, headed by Louis Marshall, to cooperate closely with its European director. In its behalf Felix M. Warburg went to Europe in 1921 to investigate the situation. His report, together with the views submitted by Goldman and Becker, finally moved JDC to embark on a new policy in Europe: an attempt to help European Jewish communities to help themselves by supporting what was termed "reconstruction" activities. This was to be achieved by establishing each central committee in Europe on a secure, self-supporting basis. Where there were no central committees, functional organizations dealing with different aspects of social work would have to be made independent. This would finally allow JDC to withdraw and terminate its activities. On June 17, 1921, Herbert H. Lehman, chairman of the new Economic Reconstruction Committee, outlined these proposals to the JDC Executive Committee.

Parallel to Lehman's committee were other special committees, set up to deal with refugee problems (under David M. Bressler), orphans (under Solomon Lowenstein), and medical care (under Bernard Flexner); these now joined the older Cultural Committee under Cyrus Adler and thus a new organizational structure of JDC emerged, actually designed to lead it to the desired dissolution as speedily as possible. Budgets were itemized according to the different functions, and discretionary funds for the European director were cut to a minimum. A proper accounting system was supervised by the accounting firm of Loeb and Troper.

What was significant in this whole structure, beyond the practical technical points, was the complete and unquestioned authority of the laymen who provided the funds or directed their collection from others. Marshall, Warburg, Lehman, Lowenstein, Bressler, Flexner, Adler—these men determined what should be done. The professionals like Bogen or Senior, Dr. Rosen in Russia (of whom we shall speak later), and even Jacob Billikopf in America were important; they were treated in a gentlemanly way and listened to carefully and sympathetically, but in the end they were not the ones who determined policy.

In 1921–24, JDC collected over $20 million, hoping thereby to help Europe's Jews in a "once and for all" effort. But when Warburg went on another investigating trip in 1925, he found that JDC just could not abdicate its responsibility, at least not yet. An economic recession in Poland had caused the government there to founder in a series of contradictory economic policies, some of which were expressly directed against the Jews. A series of crop failures in Bessarabia and Bucovina did not improve the situation.

In the winter of 1925/6, 83 percent of the Jewish laborers in Warsaw were unemployed.[6] Warburg, returning from his investigation, suggested the creation of an "overseas chest." JDC and the Zionists cooperated in this venture at first (1925), but then the different aims of the two groups reasserted themselves. Faced with a Jewish American community that was becoming increasingly indifferent to disaster appeals, JDC nevertheless raised some $12.5 million in 1926–28 to continue its work in Europe.

At the end of the first decade after the war, fifteen years after its founding, JDC was still alive, though very reluctantly. It had always seen itself as a purely temporary organization to help the "coreligionists" in foreign parts get back on their feet economically. American Jews had to help the Jews abroad, certainly, but the proper place for philanthropy and social work was in the United States. Somewhat to its surprise, in 1929 JDC found itself in a world that had turned it into a permanent institution.

1

A Time of Crisis: 1929–1932

JDC has always prided itself on being a philanthropic organization run on business lines. Actual power in this organization rested not so much in its formal structure, its national council, its board of directors, or its Executive Committee, but rather in a small group of four or five individuals who actually made the necessary decisions and then had them ratified in the various committees, thus observing the rules of a kind of formal democracy and appeasing the traditional representatives of the religious as well as labor circles who had helped found the organization.

The chairman, a founder and outstanding figure in JDC during these early years, was Felix M. Warburg. A member of a family of German Jewish banking aristocrats, he had come from Hamburg as a young man and had married the daughter of Jacob H. Schiff, who had taken him into the firm of Kuhn, Loeb & Co.

Felix Warburg was a man of great sincerity and conviction, a fine, warm human being who was moved by a genuine feeling of compassion toward his fellowman, particularly toward his "coreligionists." Despite his parochial German Jewish background, he found no difficulty in dealing with and being sympathetic to the East European Jewish masses. As one of his associates put it many years later, to Warburg, "even Jews in Romania were human beings, a proposition which was not always accepted by everyone here." He had a very real concern for simply helping people, a concern that obviously was not based on any desire for status or social standing. His main motivation was an aristocratic yet somehow humble sense of noblesse oblige.

JDC was for Warburg "his" organization, and his rule was patriarchal and at times somewhat high-handed. As he and a few others tended to be responsible for the majority of funds raised for this organization, they saw no reason to be shy about implementing their own ideas without much parliamentary attention to the democratic structure. He had many compartments to his life. One was the bank, which was an obligation but neither a dominant interest nor a great satisfaction. He once described this aspect of his life as having taught him how to "draw the honey from even the sour flowers." His world of philanthropy was dominated by Jewish affairs, but did not prevent him from being a key figure in the nonsectarian settlement house programs, the Boy Scouts, the Red Cross, and so on, as well as one of the founders of the Federation of Jewish Philanthropies and the American Jewish Committee. He was deeply involved with cultural activities in New York, particularly in music and the various museums which he helped generously. Above all, he was a joyous, warm man who was constantly stimulated by his friends and associates, in return for which he supported them in their manifold activities.

He was not a good public speaker, but his warmth and intimacy, his straightforwardness, and his obvious lack of guile were refreshing. He was politically naive, and was very much astounded that he could not win over the Jewish political leaders to his way of thinking as simply as he had won over his colleagues on the domestic scene.

Paul Baerwald, also a banker, worked in JDC with Warburg and was a faithful supporter and friend of Warburg's. Baerwald was a far cry from Warburg, with his warm and engaging personality. A serious, rather shy man, Baerwald tended to be cautious and conservative where Warburg was innovative. Baerwald always desired to do what the powers that be considered "right"; he certainly had the courage of his convictions—but his convictions usually happened to coincide with the most conservative interpretation of any given situation. Baerwald was most convincing in person-to-person contact, where his overwhelming desire to do good and his great sincerity would stand out. As a chairman of JDC in the 1930s and after Warburg's death, he was a rather pale reflection of his predecessor.

Another individual of great importance in JDC was James N. Rosenberg, a lawyer whom Warburg had drawn into JDC. Rosenberg tended to be on the conservative side as well, but he was extreme and brash where Baerwald was cautious and shy. Rosenberg left an indelible mark on JDC. We shall have occasion to discuss his distaste of Zionism and its proponents; although he supported Warburg's attempts to come to terms with Chaim Weizmann, the Zionist leader, in the 1920s and the 1930s, he was in fact much more reserved and even hostile to Zionism than Warburg. On the other hand, Rosenberg's enthusiasm and tremendous drive were important factors in getting JDC involved with the great attempt to help with the economic and social problems of Russian Jews, which will be discussed later.

Joseph C. Hyman, the secretary, occupied a definitely inferior role, but he was very important as the actual executive head of the organization. Plans for fund raising and the overall budget were decided on in New York, but the real work of JDC was done in Europe. There, almost all decisions were placed in the hands of two individuals of great intellectual stature, Dr. Bernhard Kahn, head of the European office of JDC in Berlin, and Dr. Joseph A. Rosen, head of JDC's Russian work. We shall deal with Rosen in the discussion of the work done in Russia, but for the rest of Europe, Dr. Kahn was "Mr. Joint." The group of Jewish German-Americans, financiers and lawyers, who in fact ran JDC needed a man they could trust and who would interpret their ideas in the actual operations of JDC. Kahn was a German-educated Jew, a man Warburg could rely on. Born in Sweden of Lithuanian Jewish parents, he was a brilliant man, well-versed in Jewish law and lore, with a good knowledge of Hebrew and Yiddish. He spoke all the great European languages, was deeply steeped in German culture, and was an expert in economics, with a long record of work not only with JDC, but prior to the JDC with the Hilfsverein, the great German Jewish philanthropic organization. An early adherent of the Zionist movement, Kahn had been a delegate to the 1903 Zionist Congress that had rejected the proposal to direct Zionist endeavors temporarily to Uganda. He was a reserved man, outwardly rather cold and pedantic but deeply desirous of helping fellow Jews. He was the kind of man the JDC leadership was looking for. Utterly and absolutely reliable and responsible, extremely competent, he was sufficiently conservative and rigid to recommend him to the New York office of JDC, and at the same time a man of complete independence of mind, capable of a great deal of imaginative thinking, who happened to agree with the JDC group as to how the agency should be run. There was never the slightest trace of subservience about Kahn, never a suspicion that he was not at all times honest with himself and his office in New York. In fact, it even looked as though JDC was divided into three separate parts—the money-raising agency in America and two independent disbursing corporations: one under Kahn and the other under Rosen.

Warburg, Baerwald, Kahn, Rosen, Rosenberg, and Hyman— these men constituted the inner circle that determined JDC policy. Except for Hyman and Rosen, most of Warburg's lay associates in JDC work, members of the Executive Committee and Board of Directors, were of the German Jewish aristocracy in American Jewish life.

Up to his death in 1929, the towering personality of Louis Marshall provided a rallying point for these circles. There were close personal ties between the lay leaders of all the major American Jewish philanthropic and social organizations and the American Jewish Committee, disagreements on Zionism notwithstanding. Warburg and his friends belonged to that middle group in the argument on Zionism that centered around Marshall. Warburg never subscribed to Julius Rosenwald's anti-Zionism, though Rosenwald was the most important financial supporter of JDC.

Together with Marshall, Warburg lent his hand in the agreement with Weizmann that set up the Jewish Agency for Palestine in 1929. Warburg always remained basically faithful to this alliance with Weizmann, despite his non-Zionism and his very serious disagreements with the great Zionist leader. Palestine was not a matter of "only" to him, as it was with Weizmann, but of "also," and he and his circle did not adopt the Zionist attitude of "the judges" —Brandeis, Mack, Frankfurter—and their circle. Warburg never quite accepted the idea of Jewish nationalism, and he looked upon its representatives with a great deal of suspicion.

The 1920s was, generally speaking, a period of optimism—and not only in the United States. Distaste for war and, in America, a widespread feeling that the United States should never again get itself involved in European quarrels were accompanied by a fervent hope that the horrors of war, pestilence, and famine would now finally be conquered. It is therefore not surprising that JDC should have set up its Economic Reconstruction Committee under Herbert H. Lehman and endeavored to transform itself from a rescue and relief to a rehabilitation agency. At first, these efforts at reconstruction were directed primarily at Jewish life in Eastern Europe. The Jewish masses there were mainly composed of small traders and artisans, and an effort was made to provide them with cheap credit so that they would be able to compete with their non-Jewish neighbors. Therefore, cooperative loan *kassas* (banks) were set up, which received credits from JDC and others, collected share capital, invited savings deposits, and handed out credits at an interest rate lower than that charged by the banks. Healthy business principles demanded that short-term deposits not be accepted, that arrears in repayment of interest or capital of the loan be dealt with very strictly, and that credit be given only to credit-worthy people. Naturally, American credits granted to these *kassas* were to be repaid punctually and promptly. Generally speaking, the idea was that, with a few exceptions, East Europeans did not really understand business principles but they could be taught; this would enable them to rebuild their economy on a sound foundation.

There were certain principles which JDC carefully observed.

First of all, JDC was not a political organization. This meant that it could not get involved in any political argument with Jews or non-Jews and that it tried to be impartial to all Jewish factions. With the complications of Jewish political life, this was an ideal that was not easily attained, and naturally JDC had its sympathies and antipathies—because, in fact, JDC was Kahn and three or four people in New York. Nevertheless, despite these conditions JDC remained remarkably free of any political involvement and remarkably impartial in its operations, and it did manage to become recognized as probably the only really nonpartisan organization in Jewish life. This did not mean that JDC was nonpolitical in a European sense—that is, unconnected with the government. While there was no government intervention in its activities, JDC was careful to obtain Washington's consent for certain foreign programs. This was always given in a friendly but noncommittal form. Thus, when JDC was about to embark on a drastic expansion of its Russian work in early 1928, Louis Marshall wrote to Secretary of State Frank B. Kellogg, that "before we took any steps in this direction we communicated our plans to the Department of State and were assured that there was no reason why we should not carry on this work."

Kellogg replied on May 9. "I may say, however, that the Department sees no reason, from the point of view of national policy, to interpose any objection to your participation in the work of Jewish land settlement in Russia along the lines set forth in your letter." He added, however, that whatever JDC did in Russia was done at its own risk.[1]

Another JDC principle was its determination to help Jews to help themselves. It had come into existence as a relief agency, and despite hopes to the contrary, rescue and relief were always part of its operation. But the aim was neither relief nor rescue by themselves; the aim was to help Jews rebuild their lives as self-respecting, upright, independent human beings, who would neither rely on humiliating doles nor have to seek them. There was a definite feeling for the essential dignity of human existence, and this is perhaps one of the finest values upheld by JDC in its operations. Thus, Hyman wrote that "Dr. Kahn's policy has been to reconstruct, rehabilitate and make self-supporting those elements in the Jewish population which are physically and mentally capable of establishing themselves on a permanent self-supporting basis, in order that these people may eventually help their local social problem and bring assistance to the sick, deformed, defective, aged, etc."[2] At the same time, this was interpreted in a characteristic way: strict business principles had to be adhered to, and insistence on repayment of loans was emphasized in circumstances where at least an argument could have been made for a more lenient method of operation.

A third principle JDC always adhered to was "that Jews have a right to live in countries of their birth, or in a country of their adoption."[3] This was thought of as representing the American point of view of providing opportunity for all. Though undoubtedly influenced by American ideological concepts, this was in fact an old idea in Reform Judaism, brought over in 1848 by German Jews. This ideal was perhaps accepted at international conferences and talked about by statesmen all over the world, but it was strangely out of touch with the realities of Jewish existence. Admittedly, for a short period in the 1920s it seemed as though this concept might ultimately prevail, but later developments made it look completely unrealistic. In effect, it tended to cause JDC to view with some hesitation any movement tending to advance emigration projects as a solution to Jewish problems. Kahn "emphasized that the Jew must be helped where he is; the Russian Jewish question must be solved in Russia, the Palestine question in Palestine, the German-Jewish problem in Germany, etc."[4]

In practice, this attitude was untenable, and as the 1930s progressed and the rule of law and humanity regressed in Europe, JDC was forced to support emigration of Jews as the occasion demanded. The hope of the permanent settlement of the Jewish question in the various countries of residence, the basic dream of the permanence of Diaspora life in which Reform Judaism believed with fervor, had to be modified, in practice if not in principle. JDC showed a remarkable capacity to interpret its own tenets elastically, even to the point of negating them—a way of solving contradictions between theory and practice not unknown to Jewish tradition.

Finally, there was the assumption—not really clearly stated anywhere, but implied everywhere—that the help given by JDC entitled it to supervise closely the administration of such aid. At the same time, JDC always worked through local agencies or supported quasi-independent organizations to do specific jobs. A critic of JDC, Louis Berg, wrote in the *Menorah Journal* of June 1929 that "the leaders of JDC have never hidden their belief that the gigantic work of rehabilitating East European Jewry cannot be undertaken by the masses, but can best be performed by a few reliable and well-informed leaders, and a disciplined organization, within which there are no dissenting voices. Precisely as Mr. Louis Marshall said at this conference [in May 1929]: 'The work was so conducted that we would dispose of millions of dollars without a vote being taken.' "[5] While JDC was not a democratic mass organization, it did of course operate within proper statutory requirements. But, as with many organizations, the formal structure was carried by informal ties such as friendships, personal contacts, and so on, and formal decisions often merely finalized arrangements that had been previously agreed to. Berg saw the negative side of this procedure; but given the quasi-aristocratic character of JDC, there was an elasticity and an efficiency in its operations that was altogether admirable.

The desire to supervise the administration of aid efficiently without resorting to degrading methods of doles and relief seemed to contradict the policy of supporting and developing local agencies. In actual fact there was no hard-and-fast line. With a strong and independent community—German Jewry, for instance—supervision was minimal. In other places, JDC officials for all practical purposes administered not only the funds but the institutions supported by them, indirectly and sometimes even directly. This was bound to create bad feelings on occasion, and the cases had to be judged on their merits as they came up. However, JDC never ran a bureaucratic apparatus interfering with practically every aspect of Jewish life, such as other Jewish organizations (like the Jewish Colonization Association [ICA] in Argentina) were sometimes wont to do. Whatever the deviation from stated principle, the idea of helping Jews to help themselves, of authentic Jewish communal independence, was always upheld in the end. This made JDC, despite a great deal of criticism, an organization popular with the Jews all over crumbling Jewish Europe.

For most of the 1920s, as we have seen, JDC thought of itself as a temporary organization—reflecting the prevalent illusion of the permanency of Jewish economic reconstruction after the war. But when the conclusion could no longer be escaped that JDC would be needed for an appreciably longer period of time than had been originally anticipated, a decision was made in 1927 to reorganize JDC on a more permanent basis. In May 1929 a reorganization committee of eighteen was formed under Louis Marshall; this committee made its report on January 15, 1930, after his death. It was accepted and, after some minor modifications, resulted in the setting up of a new corporation registered in New York State on March 17, 1931, under the name of the American Jewish Joint Distribution Committee, Inc.

This new mood of stability was reflected in the fieldwork of JDC. In 1927–29 long-term reconstruction plans were considered, on the assumption that prosperity in the Western world would continue uninterrupted. The need for these reconstruction plans was obvious as far as the Jewish population of Poland, Romania, and other countries in Eastern Europe was concerned. There were a considerable number of these Jews in 1929: an estimated 2,850,000 in Poland (according to the 1921 census, or about 3,000,000 by 1929); some 260,000 in Lithuania and Latvia (according to censuses held in 1921 in Lithuania and 1925 in Latvia); in Romania an estimated 760,000 for 1925; in Czechoslovakia, between 350,000 and 400,-000; in Hungary, some 450,000. In all, some 5,000,000 Jews were living in these countries, or about 30 percent of all the Jews of the world (estimated at 15,000,000 in 1929).

Masses of Jews were living under the most unsettled circumstances, economic and political. After the crises of 1924–26, another general crop failure in 1928/9 all over Eastern Europe affected the economies of those countries. The Jewish middle class was still largely dependent on small trading operations involving the village-town relationship, and as peasants all over Eastern Europe became economically weaker, the Jewish position became increasingly precarious.

This also affected the political position of the Jews. Since the peasants formed the majority of the population in all these countries, the various governments made efforts to assuage them. Their direct economic relations with the Jews and their inability to pay the Jewish traders and artisans turned the peasant-Jewish relationship into political antagonism, expressed in nationalism and anti-Semitism among large sections of the population. While these tendencies had been ingrained among the population for centuries, they were virulently expressed when economic crisis and increased nationalism coincided in the late 1920s.

More deeply, this economic situation reflected the establishment of the nation-states in Eastern Europe after World War I. The Baltic states, Bessarabia, and most of Poland had been part of the prewar Russian market, with its tremendous possibilities for expansion. Galicia, Czechoslovakia, Hungary, Transylvania, and Bucovina had been part of another large political and economic entity, the Hapsburg Empire. Now, the huge market had been split up, and the successor states practiced economic nationalism and cutthroat competition. This was aggravated by Soviet dumping practices (selling goods in foreign markets below the cost of production, so as to obtain sorely needed foreign currency), which was also followed by other states (for example, the dumping of Czech shoes in the Baltic countries).

Jews, as small and medium-sized traders, suffered badly from these developments. The Lodz textile industry, set up to supply the

Russian market, now had to reorient itself to a small Polish market and tariff barriers in an economically divided Europe. The same thing happened with the wood industry. Economic nationalism turned into an attempt by some of the governments to run their own industries—a system of etatism or state capitalism, which met with singularly little success. But in the process of these experiments, government monopolies were established in trades where many Jews had worked before as entrepreneurs or employees. The new monopolies, whatever else they did, got rid of the Jewish employees as quickly as possible. This was especially true in Poland. Apart from this, sheer disorganization and lack of a stable currency, or, as in Romania, a corrupt and inefficient government bureaucracy, tended to lower standards of living and employment for the Jews.

In all these countries taxation was levied first on the traders and artisans—largely Jews. This was done because the government did not wish to antagonize the peasants on the one hand or the rich gentile landowning and merchant classes on the other. The Jews in Poland, though composing 10 percent of the population, paid 40 percent of the taxes. Having obtained these taxes, the government was reluctant to provide services to the Jews from whom such a large proportion of these monies had come. Subventions to Jewish institutions were ridiculously small, and no government plans were ever formulated to ease the Jewish economic problem in Poland, Romania, or the Baltic countries.

The economic problem came on top of anti-Semitic feelings. Modern nationalism saw the Jew as a foreigner and therefore an enemy. There were constant reports of anti-Jewish excesses, caused by economic factors, religious prejudice, or nationalist agitation. In October 1928 Polish factory workers went on strike at Lodz to protest the employment of Jews. A boycott against Jews was propagated by the National Democratic (Endek) opposition to the regime of Marshal Pilsudski, the Polish strong man. Ritual murder stories were spread in Lublin and Vilna in 1929. Attacks on the Jewish population occurred at Bialoczow and Zaleszczyki. A serious riot, involving the destruction of two synagogues, a Jewish editorial office, and some Jewish buildings, occurred in June 1929 at Lwów. Riots occurred at Volkovysk, in Lithuania, in the autumn of 1929, in which twenty Jews were injured. In Romania, anti-Jewish riots occurred constantly. In late 1929 there were riots at Chisme, near Ismail, and students held anti-Jewish meetings in Cluj and other places. The same pattern repeated itself, tediously and dangerously, in 1930, 1931, and 1932, even before the Nazi type of anti-Semitism had gained its major victory.

Discriminatory laws against Jews, a residue of czarist legislation, were in force in the formerly Russian part of Poland (Congress Poland) for thirteen years after the establishment of Polish independence, despite the fact that Poland had signed the 1919 Versailles Convention for the protection of national minorities. Under the law, Jewish patients were refused admittance to hospitals maintained by general taxes, and Jews were forbidden to rent state lands, punished for changing their names (from Jewish-sounding ones to Polish ones), forbidden to participate in village administration, liable to deportation to a certain distance from the borders "to prevent smuggling," and forbidden to engage in mining. These laws were not abolished until March 1931.

On the whole, the Polish government of Pilsudski's followers was not overtly or violently anti-Semitic, but since it did not enjoy the support of the majority of the population, it was afraid of antagonizing the anti-Jewish majority of peasant and town dwellers, and consequently did little to protect the Jews. Most of the Jewish parties—Zionists, Bundists,* and Yiddish Autonomists†— refused to be drawn into the circle of Pilsudski's supporters, and

*The Bund (Allgemeiner Yiddisher Arbeter-Bund), founded in 1898, was an anti-Zionist Jewish socialist party with a very large following in Poland.

†Yiddish Autonomists ("Folkists"), a middle- and lower-middle-class movement, aspired to the creation of Jewish national life on the basis of cultural autonomy in the Diaspora.

only the Orthodox Agudah* broke Jewish solidarity by becoming part of the government bloc. In return, the Agudah were granted an election law for Jewish communities that allowed them to influence elections by excluding anyone who had "publicly" expressed his disapproval of Jewish religion. This provision enabled the Agudah to exclude many of their opponents from Jewish community administration.

The Polish economic crisis of 1924–26 turned into a semipermanent depression, aggravated by the autarkic and nationalistic policies of the government. There was considerable administrative discrimination. Jews made up about one-third of the population in Warsaw, and they composed 27.3 percent of the Polish urban population generally. Yet their share in the municipal administration all over the country was only 3.4 percent in 1931. In Congress Poland only one Jew was employed in the postal services. Of the 4,342 employees of Warsaw's municipal trolley lines 2 were Jews, and among the 20,000 Warsaw city employees there were 50 Jews. In state administration and the courts the number of Jews came to 2 percent; in the police, customs, and prisons, to 0.18 percent.[6]

Jewish schools had to be maintained by Jews, and the government gave ridiculously small subsidies. Of the 300 million zloty budget of the Ministry of Education in 1930/1, Jewish schools got 242,000 zloty; later they got even less. Thus they had to support their own schools. At the same time, more and more Jewish students flocked to them, as the general schools tended to discriminate against Jews in every possible way. The number of Jewish students in Polish academic institutions between 1925 and 1931 decreased by 10 percent, while the number of students generally increased by 15 percent.[7]

Artisans had been subjected to restrictive regulations since 1927. The government was supposedly trying to modernize production,

---

*Agudat Yisrael was an ultra-Orthodox movement, anti-Zionist at first, then slowly becoming non-Zionist. A working-class section (Poalei Agudat Yisrael) in time became supporters of a radical Orthodox Zionism.

but these regulations had to do less with modernization than with nationalism and anti-Semitism. By a decree of December 12, 1927, every artisan was forced to pass tests in Polish history, geography, and language, as if that was a vital prerequisite for a Polish Jew who had been a satisfactory shoemaker for twenty or thirty years. The older people, who did not know Polish beyond what was needed for everyday use, who had never studied or showed interest in Polish geography or history, were now forced to go to school and undergo examinations. Licenses were introduced, both for artisans and for traders. For young people three years of apprenticeship with a master recognized by the authorities and another three years at a trade school were now required. For the 150,000 families of Jewish artisans this was a terrible calamity. The 345,000 smaller traders and peddlers now had to pay for licenses that they simply could not afford, and their position was no easier than that of the artisan.

The Jewish worker and employee in Poland did not fare any better. All but 440 of the 3,000 Jews who had formerly found a living in the tobacco industry were dismissed when tobacco became a government monopoly. The same thing occurred in the alcohol industry, where "in one of the largest distilleries, the administration categorically declared that it had received verbal instructions not to employ any Jews."[8] Six thousand Jews employed on the railways were dismissed in the late 1920s. The wood industry had employed 25,000 Jews, but by 1929 no Jews were working in the government-owned wood monopoly.

In 1931, according to Jacob Lestschinsky, the noted Jewish statistician, 48.86 percent of Polish Jews had an income of less than 50 zloty ($10) a week, 29.06 percent between 50 and 100 zloty, and only 17.25 percent over 100 zloty.[9] The result of all this was increasing misery. By 1929 between 25 and 30 percent of Polish Jews were living on the subsistence level. Something had to be done quickly.

An equally terrible situation prevailed in Romanian Bessarabia, Bucovina, and parts of northern Transylvania, as well as in Subcarpathian Russia. There, a primitive Jewish rural population lived among even more primitive local peasants and shepherds. In the late 1920s, as a result of the economic developments already briefly outlined, the anti-Semitic propaganda of Romanian nationalist students, supported by some German colonists, found a ready response. This was aggravated by famine resulting from crop failures in Bessarabia in 1928/9. The government was no help at all, though the new "peasant" regime of Juliu Maniu, installed in December 1928, promised that a firm line would be taken against the anti-Semites. The Jewish community itself was split. The Union of Hebrew Congregations and the Bucharest community (headed by Dr. Wilhelm Filderman, a friend of JDC) supported the Liberal party, which was defeated in the elections. Others, such as the Zionists, wanted to be independent, whereas the Agudists supported Maniu. The new government also passed a community law which was, in a way, parallel to the Polish law mentioned above, and was also inspired by Agudist rabbis.

The grimmest situation of all confronted JDC in northern Transylvania, in the areas of Máramarossziget and Satu-Mare. Extreme poverty reigned there, and the slightest economical and political upheaval could and did cause calamity.

This, then, was the situation confronting East European Jewry: newly developing nations engaged in the painful transition to a modern economy were determined to exclude the Jew from economic life. As the traditional middleman between town and country, the Jew no longer fitted into the economic picture. Excluded from the promise of economic advancement and from political influence, a stranger in language, religion, and cultural background, hated and despised, he was the first victim of every economic and social disturbance.

The activities of JDC in Eastern Europe were motivated by the desire to avoid relief work as much as possible; the relatively small sums could not, in any case, alleviate mass suffering. Work was therefore concentrated on reconstruction. This found expression in four aspects of JDC activities: medical work, education, child care, and the provision of cheap credits. (It was Dr. Kahn's principle not to engage in the latter work directly but to subsidize those organizations that were most effective at it.)

As far as the health program was concerned, JDC had founded TOZ in Poland in 1921. This group of medical workers and administrators ran their society on the basis of a dues-paying membership that controlled the organization, and they demanded certain minimal payment for a small part of their otherwise free services. Collections, government subsidies, and JDC subsidies made up the rest of their budget. By 1929 TOZ had 63 branches in Poland, with 14,854 members. It provided health education in the form of lectures, films, and publications. It ran summer camps ("colonies"), anti-TB clinics, dental clinics, and milk stations for children, and various school programs.[10]

In the other areas of Eastern Europe, JDC assisted in reviving the Russian Jewish health organization known as OSE.* Despite the fact that this old and well-established group was now cut off from its former base of operations in Russia, it continued after the war and was active in the Ukraine, the Baltic states, Danzig, Bessarabia, and Austria. In those countries it set up a system of health centers. However, it did not attain the singular importance there that TOZ had in Poland, and Kahn was apt to be rather critical of what he considered its conservatism. Nevertheless, OSE did very useful work in its own areas. As far as the care of children was concerned, JDC was instrumental in setting up in 1923 a child care federation of Poland, known as CENTOS, which engaged in social work with orphans and poor children, and cooperated with TOZ in summer camp programs and similar activities.

One of the direct achievements of JDC work in Poland was the establishment of a modern school for nurses in Warsaw by Amelia Grunwald in 1923. Miss Grunwald was an expert nurse and an efficient administrator who left her post in the United States to take

---

*OSE (OZE)—Obshchestvo Zdravookhraneniya Yevreyev (Society for the Protection of the Health of the Jews), founded in 1912.

over this venture. JDC spent some $95,000 on the school up to 1929 and, as a result, the government and the Warsaw municipality participated to an ever-increasing extent in the institute's budget. The school, which was attached to a municipal hospital treating mainly Jewish patients, had effected a significant change in the nursing profession in Poland generally. The nurse had been looked upon as a somewhat specialized servant of the doctor, but the school, along with another institution established by the Rockefeller Foundation, helped to transform her into a respected member of the medical profession. This found its expression not merely in a somewhat better economic position, but mainly in the social standing the nurse could now hope for. This achievement was a guide to the kind of pilot project JDC should engage in in other spheres of activity as well.

Schooling was another area where JDC, in its efforts at reconstruction, tried to maintain certain institutions so as to help build a generation of Jewish people who would be well adapted to the world around them without forgoing the kind of Jewish education the elders wanted for them. Subsidies usually came through the three original constituent organizations of JDC: the Orthodox Central Committee for the Relief of Jews Suffering through the War, the socialist People's Relief, and JDC itself, acting as AJRC. JDC's Cultural Committee was composed of representatives of these organizations, and the monies they sent were supposed to be divided according to a "key" that gave 55 percent to the Orthodox, 17.5 percent to labor (actually Yiddishist Culture) and 27.5 percent to all the rest (Tarbuth Hebrew schools, assimilationist schools, and some religious schools not supported by the Central Committee). This rather lopsided arrangement, which prevailed till the early 1930s, was a reflection of a European mentality rather than an American one, and superseded the arrangement of 1920 whereby each of the three groups supported, more or less independently, its own institutions. Government education was either inaccessible or anti-Jewish, or both; as a result, about half the Jewish pupils went to Jewish schools.[11]

However, the main effort of Dr. Kahn was directed toward

economic reconstruction. To this end, the Reconstruction Committee of JDC had joined forces in 1924 with ICA to establish the American Jewish Reconstruction Foundation, which was run by the two organizations with Kahn (for JDC) and Dr. Louis Oungre (for ICA) as managing directors. The governing body of the foundation was composed of six members from each of the two founding organizations, and eight members who were supposed to be responsible Jewish leaders representing the Jews of Poland, Lithuania, and Bessarabia. The list included some labor representatives, some representatives of merchant circles, an Orthodox Jew, and a Palestine Zionist. But both the Orthodox member (Jacob Trockenheim) and the Zionist (Berl Locker) failed to put in appearances at the foundation council meetings.

The main task of the foundation was conceived to be the establishment of cooperative credit institutions known as "loan *kassas.*" These *kassas* would call for the payment of share capital, accept savings and deposits (to a certain extent), and lend money at a reasonably low rate of interest, mainly to Jewish merchants and artisans. The idea behind this movement was that the merchants —actually petty traders—and artisans, who constituted the overwhelming majority of the Jewish population in Poland and East European countries, were suffering from a lack of cheap credit. If financed in a conservative and businesslike way, they would not only be able to compete with non-Jews, but would also regain their self-respect as useful members of their community. With the help of political bodies, including some of the Zionists and the Bundists,

---

T A B L E 1
Kassas *of the Reconstruction Foundation*

Year	No. of *kassas*	No. of members	New foundation investments (net)
1929	747	310,000	$246,000
1930	768	321,000	$865,000

a central federation known as the Verband was set up to exercise control over individual *kassas,* and a bank was established to serve as the financial instrument. This economic movement was undoubtedly popular.

Well over a third of the Jewish population in Poland were reached by the *kassas.* The loans were small, averaging about $50, and were usually repaid on time; cases of defaulting debtors were relatively few. However, these *kassas* only reached that portion of the Jewish population that was still credit-worthy, if only to a limited degree; it was quite clear that the poorer groups could not be included in this venture. Yet ICA did not see its way clear to supporting something akin to relief for these people.

Kahn, representing JDC, looked for some kind of solution, and in 1926 he established in Poland a series of institutions with the traditional name of Free Loan, or Gemiluth Chessed, *kassas.* *Gemiluth chessed* (giving of mercy) was the traditional term for almsgiving. However, in the nineteenth and early twentieth centuries the term was expanded to include interest-free loans. Kahn now enlarged on this notion and established credit societies that would grant very small loans in large numbers at a nominal rate of interest, or no interest at all. Here again share capital was invited, but the low-interest JDC credits covered a much greater part of the needs of these *kassas* than they did of the loan *kassas.*

The Free Loan *kassas* apparently filled a crying need. By 1930 there were 545 of them in Poland, with 100,000 members. The total resources came to $1.1 million, of which $665,000 had been invested by JDC. A traditional concept had successfully been adapted to a modern situation, and as a result the popularity of the Joint among Polish Jews increased considerably.

All these ventures alleviated Jewish suffering to a considerable degree, and were vastly important in the lives of the millions of Jews in Poland. However, Kahn was too much of a realist not to see that he had not really touched the core of the Jewish economic problem. The *kassas* were really no more than an instrument to soften the economic blows from which the Jews were suffering to an ever-increasing degree. It was quite obvious that the poorest of the poor—a third of Polish Jewry—could not benefit even from the Free Loan *kassas*. To spend the precious dollars for outright relief would not only be degrading but also futile. Could anything be done to change the situation and give Poland's Jews a real chance to rebuild their economic lives?

Kahn very clearly thought that with purposeful action on the part of American Jewry, Polish Jewry could be so changed as to adapt itself to the society now emerging in Poland. In the summer of 1929 he appeared before the leadership of JDC in Zurich, while the Jewish Agency discussions were being held there, to propose a plan for the industrialization of Polish Jewry. There were several aspects to Kahn's plan. He thought that Poland was going to be industrialized and that anti-Semitism would not be powerful enough to blind Polish statesmen to the interdependence of Polish Jewry and the Polish economy. Therefore, it might be possible to interest the government in a scheme that would integrate the Jews into the economy. He assumed that there would be a steady stream of American money at the rate of about $1.1 million yearly for five years; properly applied, this not very large sum could work wonders. Also, Kahn considered emigration to be no solution and felt that the problems of Polish Jews would have to be solved in Poland. Another assumption was that the program would be implemented by American Jewry acting through JDC—in fact, through Kahn. He does not seem to have considered the possibility of any participation in planning or direction by Polish Jews themselves. He also insisted with great clarity and conviction that no planning was possible except on a minimal five-year basis, with funds that would insure the fulfillment of that first stage. This is what had been done for Russia, and Kahn obviously relied on the experience gained there in his attempt to deal with Polish Jewry.

Given these assumptions, Kahn proceeded to outline his plan.

We must try to create a healthier economic structure of the Jewish masses and do away with the present competition among the various classes of Jews, create an economic situation which is so constructed that the various groups can rely on one another: the workman on the artisan, the tradesman on the industrialist, etc., in which the individual parts supplement one another economically.

But a sudden radical change of the economic structure is not possible. The chief occupation of the Jews will be the same for many years to come. Industry, trade, commerce, crafts, professions, in which 70–80 percent of the Jews are employed, will continue to be the basis of their earnings.

These professions must be regulated, competition decreased in the smaller industries, and production adjusted. Trade is not systematic, there is no order or calculation in business, the crafts are one-sided, some branches overcrowded, there is too little variety and not enough specialization, and lastly the artisans have not had sufficient training and are using old-fashioned methods.

When we talk about the "restratification of the masses" we must not only try to create new professions in which a large number of Jews can be employed, but also rearrange all professions. Great numbers will be excluded in industrial branches and trade, although we are going to do everything possible to maintain the Jewish economic position in trade and industry. Those who are thus excluded may find positions as employees.

A regeneration of Jewish trade and industry will bring about normal conditions for employees. Everywhere now employees are taking the place of the independent small tradesman and industrialist. The number of employees is increasing rapidly, much more rapidly in proportion than the number of laborers. . . .

Another means of adjusting larger masses of Jews to the new economic order is to be found in industrialization. As yet, there are comparatively few Jewish factory workmen and industrial laborers. The workmen whom we had were in most cases home workmen, who did work at home for factories and workshops and worked in small workshops. They are not mechanics. The progress of the machine has left these workmen unemployed, prevents more Jewish workmen from obtaining employment. Artisans too must find employment in shops where machines are in use if they wish to secure any employment at all.

It is well known that the Jewish workman, especially the Jewish industrial worker and factory worker, is unemployed. It is further known that the masses of Jewish workers are not mechanics and that in "the shifting of the masses" it is absolutely necessary to place larger groups of Jewish workmen in industry and factories.

With our small means we have made a start in Lodz. Here, together with Jewish manufacturers, we have taken over a small textile factory in which we employ workmen and are placing Jewish weavers at machine work, who, after a short period of training, go out into Jewish factories, so that there is a continual training of Jewish workmen going on. . . .

If we are able to continue the organizing of this work, I believe that after a few years we will have strengthened the position of the Jews to such an extent that a gradual prosperity for them will set in.[12]

The financial requirements were very modest; apart from Kahn's normal budget, which would go into very much the same type of work as before, he would require $625,000 annually to proceed with a minimum program embodying his proposals: mainly, the organization of factories operated by Jewish employers who would train Jewish youngsters to become factory workers.

Kahn's industrialization plan was an imaginative attempt to tackle the economic problem of the Jewish masses by modern means and in line with the developing economy of Eastern Europe. It was bold, it was based on a set of hard facts, and it would be in the hands of a first-class administrator and economic expert. But the plan never got off the ground because at the end of 1929 the Great Depression set in. However, it is doubtful whether the plan had any real chance to succeed. It assumed too blandly that anti-Semitism was an economic phenomenon, that if Polish Jewry was helped, then the benefits accruing to Polish society would neutralize anti-Jewish feeling among the population and the government alike. Without the help—or at least the benevolent neutrality—of the Polish government, it was unthinkable that the project could succeed.

More important, the project assumed that one could remold the Jewish economy in Poland without at the same time remolding the Polish economy as well. This seems to have been a fallacy—and JDC was not really strong enough, even in a time of prosperity, to tackle the whole of Poland. Also, Kahn thought that by proper export arrangements Jewish production would find a market. This was an assumption based on the existence of boom conditions in the U. S. and elsewhere. But in Europe, 1929 was not a very good year, and we have already mentioned the crop failures in the East that had diminished the purchasing power of the peasantry. If the position of the peasantry was not improved, who would buy the Jewish products—or any other products for that matter? The success of the economic absorption of Soviet Jewry a couple of years later was a good guideline to the possibilities in other countries. In Soviet Russia the solution of the economic problem came when Jews were accepted as laborers in a swiftly expanding economy suffering from a labor shortage. Without an expanding economy, however, it is difficult to see how Kahn's industrialization plan could have worked in Poland. Yet this has to be remembered: of all those who made an effort to find a solution to the Polish Jewish problem, Kahn came nearest to a positive and practical approach. It was not his fault that his program never materialized.

The Great Depression that started in America in 1929 was a major turning point in world history generally, and in Jewish history in particular. Just as JDC was about to become a permanent fund-raising organization, with serious financial commitments designed to contribute materially to a radical improvement in the conditions of the Jewish masses in Europe, it found itself swept off its feet by an economic disaster that threatened to cut off its financial basis in the United States; and this at a time when the conditions of European Jews were seriously deteriorating. It must be borne in mind that Eastern Europe had been suffering from a local economic depression even prior to the major disaster emanating from America. The condition of the Jews there had prompted the regeneration and mobilization of JDC resources just described, but there was no comparison between the plight of Polish Jews in 1932 and in 1928. Bad as the situation in 1928 was, in 1932 it was incomparably worse. At the same time, the income from collections in the United States reduced the JDC budget to $340,000 in 1932.*

At the end of 1929, owing, no doubt, to the better relationships

---

*See the Appendix for a table of JDC income and expenditure during this period.

prevailing between Zionists and non-Zionists as a result of the establishment of the Jewish Agency, an Allied Jewish Appeal was launched for $6 million, $3.5 million of which was earmarked for JDC. In fact, however, the JDC share of the monies collected in 1930 was a mere $1,632,288. The strains of a campaign conducted in an atmosphere of gloom were too much for a united fund-raising effort, and in 1931 the Zionists and JDC conducted separate appeals. The $740,000 collected in 1931 and the $385,000 collected in 1932 were inadequate to the point of disaster.

Warburg was associated with the Jewish Agency, as well as with JDC, but not even he could improve the collections for either of the appeals. In the face of these developments, budgets had to be cut drastically—no more industrialization plans, no more expansion. The contribution of JDC to Free Loan *kassas,* child care, and medical aid became minimal, and often only symbolic.

At this juncture, opinions were divided into two camps. James N. Rosenberg thought that JDC was no more than a disbursing agency of American Jewry. If American Jewry could not or would not provide JDC with funds, JDC should close down and merely maintain a skeleton staff in New York against the possibility of reviving the organization whenever the funds collected justified it. He repeatedly expressed this opinion in 1931 and 1932. The other point of view was expressed by Kahn, Warburg, and Baerwald. They maintained that a complete cessation of funds from America would not only destroy the Jewish institutions that had been built up at such tremendous expense after World War I, but that these institutions, once closed down, would never be rebuilt. These differences of opinion were resolved in favor of the stand taken by Warburg, and JDC continued to supply dollars in driblets to the starved Jewish institutions in Eastern Europe.

The crisis and its consequences did not, however, materially affect the Reconstruction Foundation work, as this was done with a fairly large amount of capital that was at least partly used as a revolving fund; credits were granted to the foundation loan *kassas,* and repayments on these loans and credits were coming in regularly. JDC itself was doing the same thing with the Free Loan *kassas,* but on a much smaller scale. Thus, the foundation's activities now assumed major proportions, and its relations with Eastern European Jewry became very important.

In 1930–32 a struggle developed between the Reconstruction Foundation and the leadership of the loan *kassas'* central institutions in Poland: their bank and the Verband. Ostensibly the disagreements were economic and financial: the Verband was not supervising the work of the *kassas* to Kahn's satisfaction and tried to free itself from the foundation's supervision as much as it could. As a result, its affairs were mismanaged. More important, the bank, (in effect run by the members of the Verband) had become an ordinary banking institution charging high rates of interest; it also tried to free itself from Kahn's meticulous control by rather doubtful procedures. In these it failed miserably. In addition, practices were uncovered that were dangerously close to being corrupt. The bank had loaned money to private individuals who could not pay it back and had practiced what amounted to a misappropriation of funds entrusted to it by the loan *kassas.* In the end, after many attempts at saving the situation, Kahn was forced to insist on the liquidation of the bank.

But this was a financial crisis on the surface only. In reality, it was a crisis of confidence between representatives of Polish Jewry and JDC. Kahn had managed only with difficulty to persuade his ICA friends to set up the bank, and its liquidation was accompanied by many "I told you so"s on the part of JDC's more conservative partners in the Reconstruction Foundation.

The Zionist and Bundist press attacked Kahn personally, and some of these attacks were printed in America. Kahn was accused of being a cold bureaucrat, of not having come to the aid of the bank when it still could have been saved, of refusing to consider the fate of the *kassas* themselves if the bank was liquidated, and of superciliousness toward the Jews of Poland. These accusations were factually quite incorrect, but, as the Warsaw paper *Hajnt* put it, Kahn would probably win a court action but might not do well in front of a jury—in other words, though Kahn was legally right, his policy could be questioned on moral grounds.

Should he have insisted on a strict attitude toward the Polish Jewish organizations (to which, of course, he was fully entitled), or should he have taken a softer line and thus saved the prestige and self-confidence of the people he was dealing with? On the whole, it seems that he was trying to do the best he could with a critical Dr. Louis Oungre at his side and a woefully inadequate supply of money. After the failure of his industrialization plan, he was determined to take drastic steps to avoid wasting the little money he had. Also, he was out to imbue the Polish Jews with a realization that only correct business methods and solid banking operations could help them. There had to be casualties on that road, and Kahn judged it to be in the best interests of Polish Jews themselves to pay the price. Right or wrong, he was convinced that it was not the crisis that had been the cause of the difficulties of the bank and of some of the *kassas,* but weak leadership and bad business methods.

As a result of Kahn's policies, the loan *kassas* of the Reconstruction Foundation and the Free Loan *kassas* of JDC maintained themselves on the whole, despite the withdrawal from them of one-half of the 60 million zloty in deposits in 1931.

The *kassas* saved the money of many Jews who lost their deposits when important banks in Poland collapsed during the depression. What could be saved of Poland's Jewish middle class—and

T A B L E   2
Development of Loan Kassas *and Free Loan* Kassas *in Poland*

		Loan *kassas*			Free Loan *kassas*		
	No. of	No. of	Credits granted	No. of	No. of	Credits granted	No. of
Year	*kassas*	members	(in millions of $)	*kassas*	members	(in millions of $)	loans
1930	768	321,000	16	545	100,000	1.2	180,000
1931	756	313,000	13				
1932	744	295,000	12	664	100,000	1.8	164,000

not very much could be saved—was achieved largely through the *kassas*. This, of course, did not even begin to touch the core of the problem of Polish Jewry, but it was all the Reconstruction Foundation and JDC could do at the moment.

Another question must be asked at this point: What were the methods by which this relative stability was achieved? The answer is that the methods were occasionally rather grim. As we have noted, there were *kassas* not only in Poland, but in other countries as well. In Romania, for instance, in 1930 there were eighty-six loan *kassas* with sixty-four thousand members; in 1933 the same number of *kassas* had fifty-four thousand members. In Romania, and especially in Bessarabia and Bucovina, the conditions of Jewish life were as hard as in Poland. There, too, the Reconstruction Foundation opposed the acceptance of deposits by the *kassas*, especially of short-term withdrawable deposits. Any infringement of that rule brought an immediate breaking of relations with the foundation.[13]

This general situation was clear, not only to Kahn and Oungre, but also to members of the Reconstruction Foundation's council, including the representatives of East European Jews. One of these was the famous Bundist leader Victor Alter. Alter led a rebellion against the foundation at about the same time (1931) that the difficulties with the Verband and the bank started. Alter objected to the high-handed methods of Kahn and Oungre. His attitude was very simple: the funds collected in America for the needy Jewish population in Eastern Europe undoubtedly belonged to that population. The foundation was considered to be an intermediary for the disbursement of funds, the administration of which properly belonged to representatives of East European Jews.

On March 12, 1930, Alter submitted a memorandum to Kahn in which he stated that the chief task of the Reconstruction Foundation was to prepare the ground in Poland for what he termed "healthy economic activity." However, he pointed out that the foundation's concentration on loan *kassas* did not produce the hoped-for results. "Were the lack of credits the main obstacle in the economic activity of the Jewish population or the principal cause of its depressed economic condition—then the credit *kassas* would be of permanent constructive importance. Unfortunately, this is not so, and the experience of the past years has proved that despite the growth of the credit *kassas,* the economic position of the Jewish population (including the petty traders and artisans) has become much worse." He thought that since the Jewish small trade was in a very bad way, and since the situation moreover was being aggravated by cutthroat competition among the Jewish traders themselves, there was no possibility that this segment of the population would be able to establish itself on a sound business basis. On the contrary, he said, the only solution for this vast mass of people would be to reduce the number of small traders and shift some of them to other walks of life.

The situation of the artisans was, in his opinion, similar. The only solution for the Jewish problem in general terms, Alter thought, "is to have a part of them attempt to capture fields of industrial activity in which they are not represented as yet and to have the other part raise their technical standards, so that they may be able to meet the extreme competition." The larger the number of workers who would enter industry, especially large-scale industry, the better. Since many Jewish employers refused to employ Jewish workers, the institutions connected with the Reconstruction Foundation should grant credit only to those persons or companies who employed Jewish workmen and employees. The credits were to be in proportion to the number of Jewish workers and employees occupied in the undertaking. The foundation should help create establishments that employed Jews, and assist in finding new markets for them.

These proposals were submitted at a time when personal relations between Alter and Kahn had deteriorated considerably. Alter was a politician, an excellent speaker, and a very difficult man. In ICA and JDC he saw capitalist organizations that did not really understand the Jewish workingman, and he hoped to change their aims with the help of his labor friends in the United States, Bundist and even Zionist. But he met with a rebuff. Hyman and Baerwald did not have to work hard to convince the American labor leaders; Charney B. Vladeck, Alexander Kahn, Bernard Zuckerman, and Meyer Gillis agreed with JDC's view that Dr. Kahn's authority must be upheld, that JDC was responsible to the Jews of America for the way the money was used, and that it could not become a simple disbursing organization providing monies to Jewish political leaders in Poland for their economic programs. They expressed this view in a cable sent to Alter on June 11, 1931.[14] Also, many were convinced by Kahn's practical answers. Kahn's contention was that

the foundation was created in order to secure, strengthen, and extend what was already in existence. The foundation is the administrator of a fund that must always be so applied as to guarantee the maintenance of the institutions which we have created, or now support, but that can only be accomplished if the repayment of the monies advanced is made as certain as possible. The foundation cannot make investments that are essentially experimental and therefore do not offer great possibility of being returned. Mr. Alter's criticism of the credit cooperatives must be challenged by the fact that the extension and strengthening of the credit cooperatives' systems in Poland, just as in all other Eastern European countries, has accomplished a great deal in maintaining the economic positions of the Jewish masses.[15]

Kahn also said that something had already been done to strengthen working-class institutions and producers' cooperatives, but that the result of these attempts left much to be desired. He considered the industrialization program advanced by Alter to be an experiment that could not be justified to the Reconstruction Foundation's council.

Matters came to a head. In August 1931 Oungre and Kahn declared that if Alter remained on the foundation's council they would not carry on. Alter had urged, they said, that the foundation "limit itself virtually to labor cooperative work" (which was not true), and had introduced a vote of censure against them. Leonard L. Cohen, the ICA representative, who was president of the foundation, declared himself to be reluctant to preside at meetings where Alter was present, and ICA members generally thought that the experiment of having representatives of East European Jewry participate in running the foundation had misfired. With difficulty they were convinced by JDC not to change the system of administration of the foundation, and to carry on "with one or two of the obstreperous 'C' members removed." On December 16, 1931, Alter finally submitted a letter of resignation that was intended for publication. All contact was severed between himself and the foundation.

Ironically, Alter's proposal was substantially the same as what Kahn had suggested in 1929; in fact, the two proposals are almost identical. And lest we think that by 1931 Kahn either was convinced that his own 1929 plan was premature or had changed his mind, here are his words to a JDC Executive Committee meeting on November 11, 1931—just about when the Alter controversy was at its peak. He described his 1929 plan as an extensive program "of industrialization of the Jewish masses, a specialization, and thereby a vitalization of Jewish craftmanship, an extensive induction into agricultural pursuits, a revival of ruined Jewish industries, the protection of deteriorating business enterprises, instruction of manual workers for the factories; in a word, a general resuscitation of all economic vocations that still have a means of livelihood, or the introduction of new and timely vocations for the Jewish masses." Then, he said, "a frost fell on a night in spring. In the midst of our negotiations with the Polish authorities, I received a telegram from the Joint Distribution Committee warning me not to proceed further" because of the economic depression that had set in. Now, in 1931, he was still in favor of starting something along the the lines that he had suggested in 1929 and stated that he could get some kind of program started with half a million dollars yearly.

It seems quite clear that Kahn objected to Alter, rather than to his policy. This may have been because of a conviction that to succeed, an industrialization plan would have to be implemented not by the supposedly quarreling, hairsplitting theorists of Eastern Europe but by the seasoned businessmen of the West.[16]

It must not be thought that, because of the crisis, Kahn worked only with the *kassas*. Fully realizing how essential it was to make maximum use of every dollar, he decided to concentrate on work for children. Of the paltry sums he had at his disposal, in 1932 he gave 62 percent to the various schemes to feed children, establish summer camps for them, and pay for vocational training and trade schools. Of the total budget of the Polish child care organization centers, JDC contributed only 17.57 percent of the money; but this was decisive. There were 8,386 children under constant care in 1932; 3,053 were trained in vocational schools; 20,050 were sent to 152 summer camps. In a situation where, for example, 73 percent of the Jewish children in Lodz belonged to families living in only one room (83 percent of these rooms had no plumbing), JDC gave money for feeding children in the schools. During the winter of 1931/2 an average of 32,000 children were fed monthly. In Subcarpathia 2,800 children were fed in a famine that broke out there in the spring of 1932; the same was done with 12,607 children in the Máramaros district.

At the same time, Kahn continued to subsidize ORT,* TOZ, and OSE, all of which received small and inadequate sums. He continued to object to handing out money for relief, though he changed his policy at least as far as the children and some of the health institutions were concerned. He said, "I could spend less than 20 percent on relief if I did not from time to time get admonitions from New York that I should do more relief work." His policy came into sharp focus in a little incident that occurred in early 1930, when Hyman was pressed by Romanian Jews in New York to do something for a soup kitchen in Czernowitz at the Morgenroit Institute. After some rather angry correspondence, Kahn finally wrote: "I have promised $300 for the kitchen at the Morgenroit Institute,

*Organization for Rehabilitation through Training—the English rendering of the original Russian name.

since you evidently place importance on this for campaign purposes. Of course, I must also give something to the Poalei Zion,
which likewise has a kitchen. I only hope that these forced subventions will not spread to the whole of Bucovina."[17]

While in this instance—and many others—pressure by contributors made Hyman urge a more lenient policy on Kahn, it was
undoubtedly a matter of principle with Hyman to press for the
allocation of a larger proportion of funds for relief. "In the case of
the work of the OSE and the TOZ and the Child Care Federation
of Poland, it was necessary, in view of the unusual suffering and
very bad economic conditions, to go much more slowly in absolute
and rigid insistence" on the nonrelief policy than Kahn was doing.[18]

Even Kahn relented in 1931. Quite apart from the depression
and anti-Semitic outbreaks, there were natural and man-made
calamities. A fire destroyed much of Saloniki's Jewish quarter in
June 1931. There were floods in Vilna and a fire at Plungiany. On
July 4, 1931, anti-Semitic peasants set fire to the largely Jewish
townlet of Borsa in Transylvania. This came on top of the most
acute suffering in Poland and Romania. Kahn reported that half
or more of the employable Jews in Poland were out of work, and
that one hundred thousand families (which included seventy-five
thousand children) were "on the verge of starvation."[19] Seventy
thousand Jewish merchants, and twelve thousand industrialists
were reported to have closed their doors.[20] Jews were starving in
Poland "as in periods of the worst famines."[21]

The situation in Romania was deteriorating rapidly. The government was actively encouraging Romanians to compete with Jews,
and Maniu's government had an ax to grind against Filderman and
the Zionists, who had not supported it politically. The crop failures
already mentioned completely disorganized the administration; a
JDC report on Romania declared that the country was "faced with
complete collapse."[22] Government employees and the army received salaries for only one month between December 31, 1931,
and June 1932. Agricultural prices were one-quarter of the 1929
level. Filderman, who had continued to carry his public burden

with the active encouragement of Kahn, was near collapse himself. "The teachers," he wrote on December 5, 1932, "held a meeting and decided not to carry on teaching. Their salaries have not been paid for 4½ months. . . . The same applies to the rabbis. The milk vendors refused to supply milk to the [Jewish] hospitals."

The peasants, especially in Bessarabia and Bucovina, refused to pay their debts after 1930. They argued that they were selling to the Jews too cheaply and buying from them too dearly. Peasant unrest was thus turned against the Jews by anti-Semitic agitators, such as the notorious Professor Cuza and others. Anti-Jewish riots were the order of the day. The Old Romanian provinces, Moldavia and Walachia, which up to then had been relatively prosperous, now suffered as much as the others.

In the face of all this, Kahn declared that "today I am a convert to relief work in some measure. We cannot silently and unmoved pass by the spectacle of suffering of the Jewish masses. At least we must give some help to the starving Jewish children; we must give some subventions to the Jewish institutions that, without our help, will never survive the crisis."

While Hyman agreed with this, there were others who pondered whether this was the right approach. James N. Rosenberg wrote to Paul Baerwald on July 27, 1932: "If I were the recipient of charity I would sooner starve to death and be done with it than starve slowly over six months." Similarly, Baerwald wrote that

we know that there are numbers of Jewish people in Poland who live in misery. It is doubtful if even large sums would be effective in bringing about a big change in their condition. Does everybody agree that a more liberal support for the Jews in Poland would definitely work for their ultimate benefit? Will not the Jewish people in Poland by sheer necessity be forced to a quicker recognition on their part that their own best policy is a greater attempt to become part of the political and social structure of Poland instead of keeping up their isolation?[23]

Only an assimilated Western Jew could possibly have written these lines of utter incomprehension about the nature of Polish Jewry, words reflecting a mood that was dangerous for Kahn's work. He must have sensed the pessimistic atmosphere, which was amply augmented by his own gloomy reports. As David A. Brown wrote in the *American Hebrew and Jewish Tribune:* "We might just as well have tried to scoop out with a soup spoon the water rushing into a leaky boat as to attempt to solve the Jewish problem in Poland."[24] Kahn himself reported that "the need in Eastern and Central Europe is acute, overwhelming, desperate, hope is dying."[25]

While it was true that Kahn felt that he should report the situation as it was, it was equally true that he had to encourage his own organization to carry on in its task. He praised JDC for its past work,[26] but he emphasized that it would take a long time, a generation and more, to accomplish a restratification of the lopsided Jewish economic structure. The Eastern Jews had been caught by the crisis in the midst of a process of economic rebuilding that JDC had inaugurated. If JDC now stopped work, long years of endeavor would be lost. On another occasion he said that if JDC were to cease work, the result would be calamitous in every sense of the word.[27] Jews would be even more pauperized than before. The economic rehabilitation that had just begun would be endangered, and despair would engender radicalism and Communism among the younger Jewish generation if no help came from the outside. He cautioned that the fate of East European Jews would never be an isolated one, and a demoralized, despised Jewry in Europe would mean disaster for all Jews, including those in America. Kahn believed that in time Eastern Europe would take on some shape that would enable the Jews to live under fair conditions. Siberia (sic!) might ultimately become a haven of refuge for Polish Jewry, but in the meantime JDC's help had to continue. Kahn was supported by, among others, Morris D. Waldman of the American Jewish Committee. Despite everything Kahn's position was positive, even optimistic, in tone.

Of course, larger plans had to remain on paper in the meantime, and the economic restratification that Kahn talked about had never really gone beyond the planning stage. Attention had to be concentrated on immediate ways of helping Polish Jews. One of these was intervention with the government of Poland. This was not really JDC's province, but that of the American Jewish Committee. In late 1930, following an interview given by Tytus Filipowicz, the Polish minister to Washington, protracted negotiations began with the American Jewish Committee, during which the committee tried to obtain some concessions from the Polish government. These efforts were of no avail. Although the government had accumulated a reserve of 464 million zloty in gold, in accordance with the prevailing economic doctrine they refused to part with it. Also, in April 1930 the Sejm, the Polish parliament controlled by the opposition, had been dissolved. Immediately afterward the peasants' groups organized in a powerful new political body, which was certainly not pro-Jewish. In this precarious situation the government could not be bothered about the unpopular Jews.

On the other hand, the attitude of JDC was a mixed one of respect for authority—any kind of authority—and distrust. As Warburg wrote to the Polish minister, Stojowski: "Whatever the government decides to do must be satisfactory to us and we are watching with a great deal of interest."[28] While appreciating the efforts of the Polish government in behalf of the Jews, he hoped that, practically at least, the government monopolies would be thrown open to Jewish employment. In fact, the government did just the opposite. Yielding (not quite unwillingly, it appears) to its anti-Semitic critics, it paid less to the Jews and extracted more from them.[29] On the political scene, by manipulations and rigging the Jews were deprived more and more of their representation in the Sejm, except for the Agudists, who cooperated with the government.

The other way of reacting to the crisis lay in a tightening of belts, a rigorous policy toward the *kassas*. In the last resort, what else could JDC and the Reconstruction Foundation do?

In this crisis situation the various agencies supported by the JDC did not obtain what they thought they should. OSE and ORT tried at one time or another to get additional allocations from JDC by using friends or contacts in America who were in positions of influence. OSE was not really powerful enough to prevail, but ORT had an American Committee; some of the members of the JDC Executive, such as Alexander Kahn, one of the great American Jewish labor leaders, and Henry Moskowitz were also members of the ORT American Committee. ORT had received considerable subsidies from the JDC.[30]

ORT had also founded and now operated the Machine Tool Supply Company, to supply European branches of ORT with tools and machines. JDC also used these services for its operations in Russia. When the depression came, the company got into trouble and was faced with an ever-increasing accumulation of debts. Since ORT had very few reserves of its own, it asked JDC to grant it more money. After a great deal of pressure, they were allocated 7 percent of the 1931 budget ($68,000), at a time when all JDC staff salaries were cut, part of the staff were dismissed, and JDC generally was cutting down on all activities.

This served to show that JDC was vulnerable to pressure from contributors and members of its own committees who might represent outside influences. Kahn and Hyman, especially the latter, were by no means happy with this state of affairs. On one occasion Hyman wrote to ORT that "first, the obligations of JDC to you were embodied in a written agreement; second, we have lived up to our agreement; and third, we have no money."[31] But for once he had no choice. ORT got its appropriation and it was far larger than what it normally should have received.

Bernhard Kahn was, as we have seen, a man of penetrating intelligence. It is therefore not in the least surprising that he should have commented on the rise of the Nazi movement with more than ordinary perspicacity. In a remarkable speech at the home of James N. Rosenberg on December 14, 1930, he analyzed the Nazi electoral victory of 1930, which made them the second largest party in the German Reichstag. Then he dealt with the hope of many Jews that the Hitlerian movement would not amount to much more than did the anti-Semitic movement in Germany in the 1890s. He warned against such a comparison: "The anti-Semitism in Germany today is more dangerous than the former outbreaks of this Jew-hatred."

This new movement fed on both the economic misery and the political unrest resulting from World War I. However, Kahn said, "there is no possibility of disenfranchising German Jews if the Hitlerites should form part of the government. It may be that then some of the Jewish immigrants, or the foreign Jews, would suffer. There would be some expulsion of foreign Jews, of whom there are 100,000 in Germany," but even these would be "partly protected" by their governments, not because of a love of Jews but because these states had a "bone to pick with Germany." If the anti-Semites came to power, Kahn surmised, "there may be no pogroms (although even these are possible)," but the Jews would be driven out of positions in the political and administrative apparatus. A number of Jews were already moving out of Germany, and the economic squeeze that the Jews could expect if the present trend continued would cause misery and the desire to leave. The great danger was that the Nazis might gain control of the provincial governments, especially in Prussia. Even today, Kahn said, "the atmosphere is almost intolerable. The situation of the German Jews is very critical" and JDC could soon expect calls for help from Germany. Kahn saw a clear connection between the anti-Semites in Germany and anti-Semitic outbreaks in Eastern Europe: "The teaching of anti-Semitism goes out from Germany."

As the Nazis gained in influence, Kahn became increasingly worried. In the course of an address to a group of rabbis a year after the Rosenberg meeting, he again returned to this theme.[32] This time he expressed the fear that the danger in Germany was considerably greater than what he had feared a year previously. Nevertheless, he expected economic discrimination rather than "medieval persecutions."

The same opinion is found in his letter to Cyrus Adler and others on February 2, 1932.[33] He assumed that if elections were held now, the Nazis would get 180 to 190 seats (actually, they got 230 in the July 1932 elections). They might come to power if they allied themselves with right-wing groups, such as Alfred Hugenberg's German National People's party or even the Catholic Center party, but these conservative allies would not allow Jew-baiting. "It would be a different matter if with a government of Nazis and others, the Nazis were to seize absolute power by a coup d'etat and maintain it. Then it would of course depend on who the president would be at that time"—surely an amazingly accurate description of what actually happened a year later.

There were one hundred thousand foreign and stateless Jews in Germany, Kahn said, forty-two thousand of whom were Polish and fourteen thousand were Austrian. The Nazis would probably turn first against these. But Kahn was no longer as sanguine as he had been previously regarding the possibility of foreign governments intervening in behalf of their Jewish citizens. Laws would be enacted, ostensibly against trades but actually directed against the Jews. There would probably be no pogroms unless the Nazis achieved power through an overthrow of the government. While "medieval persecution" was not envisaged, the Jews would nevertheless suffer a great deal. Therefore, refugees had to be expected from Germany. The point of this letter to Cyrus Adler was that quiet preparations should now be made (in April 1932!) to meet such an emergency.

The year 1932 began on this note, and this extremely discouraging situation continued throughout the year. East European Jewry was starving, unemployed, desperate. "The record of Jewish insolvency and even suicide is a tragic one," Hyman wrote.[34] German Jewry was faced with a frightening tide of rising Nazism, and American Jewry was struck by a depression that seemed to make any attempt to collect money illusory. Yet something had to be done to save European Jewry. "My big brother must be with me if his strength shall be of any use to me. His shouting from far away would not help much."[35] Then in January 1933 Hitler came to power.

2

Agro-Joint

Operations of JDC in Soviet Russia began with the entry into Russia of the American Relief Administration (ARA) in 1920/1. After war, revolution, and bloody civil strife, Russia had emerged as a starving country, battered into economic destitution, her trained labor force scattered, her railways torn up, and her bridges demolished. In the Ukraine, where a sizable proportion of the 2,750,000 Russian Jews lived, the terrible pogroms already mentioned caused a wave of horror to spread among American Jews and a corresponding desire to help. JDC, as an American philanthropic organization, rushed to the aid of Russian Jewry.

By an agreement with ARA, $4 million was spent on Jewish relief up to 1922. This entailed soup kitchens, care for orphans, and other palliative measures taken under the direction of Boris D. Bogen, the JDC representative in Eastern Europe. After intervention by James N. Rosenberg in August 1921, Col. William N. Haskell, who cooperated with Herbert Hoover on the ARA program, invited Dr. Joseph A. Rosen to join ARA as JDC representative in Russia.

Rosen had a checkered history: he had fled from Siberia, where he had been exiled as a revolutionary with Menshevik leanings, and had come to the United States in 1903. By profession he was an agronomist, and he completed his training in the U. S. He developed a new variety of winter rye and had become an agricultural expert of international renown by the time he went to Russia. Rosen was a man of tremendous willpower and seems to have had a very impressive personality. While personally very modest, he possessed at the same time an overriding ambition to do whatever he could to save the Jews in Russia from starvation and degradation. In Russia he met Dr. Lubarsky, an agronomist friend with whom he had worked prior to the war, and engaged his services for JDC.

The problem facing the Soviet regime in Russia after the confiscation of the nobility's lands immediately following the Bolshevik Revolution was both grim and simple. Russia's main export prior to the war had been grain. This export surplus had come from large farms owned by the landowners or the state. After the revolution these lands had been divided up into small parcels and given to the vast masses of Russian peasants, to buy their support for the Bolshevik regime. These peasants, who previously had gone hungry within sight of the aristocratic palaces, produced very little more now than they had before. The grain surpluses now went to increase slightly the food rations of the Russian peasantry. Who would now provide food for the Russian cities and grain for export to pay for essential industrial goods? The result of the agrarian revolution was that the Soviet regime was faced with the necessity of either forgoing any industrial expansion, which would run counter to the very base of its ideology, or else create large agricultural holdings to produce the necessary surpluses.

In the early 1920s this situation caused a serious imbalance in the food production of the country; drought in certain areas could create a serious shortage of bread for the whole country. This was exacerbated by the destruction of the country's transportation system. In 1921 and 1922 situations such as these had created food shortages and mass starvation. This affected everyone, but the situation of the Jewish population, concentrated in the Ukraine and White Russia in small townships and large villages, was especially precarious.

Rosen thought of a way to increase food production without actually increasing the acreage sown. This could not be achieved by the traditional methods of sowing wheat or barley, especially since the seed was lacking owing to the droughts. With full Soviet support, therefore, Rosen began the importation of seed corn from the United States, and 2.7 million acres in the Ukraine were sown with that crop. It is hard to gauge the importance of this intervention, but it is a fact that after that, Rosen enjoyed the confidence and respect of the Soviet leadership. His second very significant action was taken in 1923/4, when JDC started its reconstruction activities in Russia. In order to help the Jewish colonies then existing and the new colonies he was about to establish, Rosen imported eighty-six tractors, complete with spare parts and mechanics to work them. These were the first modern tractors that Russia had seen since the war, and Rosen's stock with the Soviet leadership rose accordingly.

In the meantime ARA had ceased its operations, and since December 1922 JDC had been working in the Soviet Union by special agreement with the government. The phase of palliative relief was passing; in 1921 the government had introduced the new economic policies (NEP), designed to give the country an opportunity to regain some of its strength by a partial restoration of capitalism (under careful government surveillance) before any further socialization was attempted. Trading was permitted now, and small shops could employ a limited number of workers. In agriculture the difference between the poor, the average, and the "rich" peasant—the kulak—grew. The Jewish trader and artisan could therefore hope for at least some respite and a chance, however slender, to earn his living.

Nevertheless, the situation was very difficult. Starvation or extreme poverty prevailed in many parts of White Russia and the Ukraine, where many Jews were still living in the shtetlach, the small towns of what had been the Jewish Pale of Settlement under the czarist regime. Rosen suggested that a large-scale colonization program be started to save thousands of Jews from degrading poverty by taking them out of the little towns, where most of them would have no work in any case.

There had been Jewish agricultural colonies in Russia ever since

the period of Alexander I, in the early nineteenth century. Prior
to 1914 some fifteen thousand families lived in them. After the fog
of war had lifted, about ten thousand families still lived in what
now came to be called the "old" colonies in White Russia and the
Ukraine. Help was extended to them, and, by agreement with the
Soviet government, new colonies were founded. Up to 1924 some
five hundred families were so settled under an experimental program. The experiment was held to be successful, and on July 17,
1924, the American Jewish Joint Agricultural Corporation (Agro-
Joint) was founded. Rosen became its president. Financial control
was vested in a number of trustees appointed by JDC, who held
all the stock in the new corporation.

Under Rosen's direction, 5,646 families were settled between
1924 and 1928, some in the Ukraine, some in the Crimea. This
settlement work was done in conjunction with two organizations:
COMZET, the government-sponsored committee for settling Jews
on land, and OZET, a quasi-voluntary organization to recruit and
screen candidates for settlement. The head of COMZET was a
non-Jewish vice-premier of the Russian Soviet Socialist Republic,
Peter Smidovich, a man who was very much interested in the
success of the venture. He was influential in obtaining the government's agreement to the Jewish settlement of a large tract of land
in the Crimea; as much as one million acres were set aside for use
by Jewish settlers. It seems that this agreement was not accepted
with enthusiasm by some Jewish Communists, especially by those
who ran the Jewish section of the Communist party, known as the
Yevsektsia. One feels a constant undercurrent of opposition to the
very idea of a foreign capitalist organization being allowed to engage in agricultural settlement in Russia.

It was probably owing to this attitude that the local Yevsektsia
in White Russia made an attempt to have agricultural settlement
directed there. At the same time, in 1924/5, other settlement possibilities were investigated in the upper Volga region and the northern Caucasus.[1]

It is an indubitable fact that the settlements in the Crimea founded by the Agro-Joint included a number of Zionist colonies settled by people who saw the Crimea as a stepping-stone on the road to Palestine. There were some thirteen of these with Hebrew names, some of them—like Tel Chai (there were two separate settlements by that name), Mishmar, Khaklai, Avoda, Kheruth, Maaian, Kadimah—having distinct Palestine-centered connotations. In 1928 there were 112 Agro-Joint colonies in the Ukraine and 105 in the Crimea. In addition to these, Agro-Joint also helped other colonies with occasional loans or by other means.

ICA renewed its support of the establishment of agricultural colonies as well, also dealing with some of the older colonies, where work had been started in prewar days. By 1928 ICA had settled 1,769 new Jewish families on the soil, and by 1930/1 they had spent some $4 million on this venture.

The period of the NEP was not accompanied by any easing of the economic situation of the Jews, except for a small group of traders—the so-called NEPmen. The number of Jews employed as workers in factories had not grown significantly since prewar days, when it had been a mere forty-six thousand. According to 1926 figures, which included some 80 percent of the Jewish population, only 14.7 percent of the Jews were factory workers; 23 percent were employees, 23.9 percent were artisans, 14.2 percent were traders, and 16.8 percent were defined as having no definite occupation, being permanently unemployed or "miscellaneous";[2] 5.9 percent of the Jews were peasants.

The Soviet government deprived of civil rights all those whom it defined as its class enemies. These people were called *lishentsy*. They were not allowed to occupy any administrative position, they were excluded from all social and medical services, and their children could not go to state schools. This category included all those who were not "productively occupied." Apart from traders and people of ill-defined occupation, Jewish artisans were also included in this category of déclassés because they employed one apprentice or more. Since many of the employees were out of work, a large proportion of the Jewish population were in dire straits. Dr. Ezechiel A. Grower, a close associate of Rosen's and a member of the Agro-Joint board, estimated the number of Jewish déclassés at 830,000.

The attitude of the Soviet regime was not tinged by anti-Semitism at that time; but it just so happened that the Jews had been the traditional middle class in Russia, and the Russians' new policies were directed against the middle class. Jewish Communists, who tended to be more "orthodox" than their non-Jewish comrades, bore down heavily on their fellow Jews.

At this juncture Russia came forward with the idea of a vast expansion of the Jewish colonization scheme and offered the Jews large tracts of land, especially in the Crimea. In 1927/8 it was obviously interested in transforming the Jewish population into a productive and loyal force. It also needed grain, and the establishment and encouragement of state farms (sovkhozy), which were set up on state lands, had so far not been very successful. Moreover, Soviet Russia needed American dollars very badly, and an arrangement with JDC meant not only a contribution to the solution of the pressing Jewish problem, but also an influx of both hard currency and valuable machinery, of which the Soviets were very short.

One of the social problems that Rosen desired to help solve in an expanded program of land settlement was the question of the *lishentsy*. "The Jewish masses in Russia," said Rosen, "whether they wish it or not, must remain in their country." The most constructive plan for adapting large numbers of Jews to the new conditions in Russia had been found to be agricultural settlement, whereas by contrast, the position of the tradesmen and middlemen in the present economic structure of Russia was utterly hopeless.[3] In the colonies, according to Soviet law, the *lishenets* would be allowed to regain his civil rights by the simple process of becoming a peasant, a productive member of the society. This was also in the best interests of the government, and again a mutual understanding could easily be reached. The achievements up to 1928 seemed to warrant this expansion of the program.[4]

It appears that by the end of 1928 the Agro-Joint had settled about six thousand Jewish families in its colonies. Some ten thousand more were living in the old colonies, and an additional few thousand were being supported by ICA, ORT, and Ozet. Some twelve to fifteen thousand other holdings seem to have been of the kind that would normally be described as garden or vegetable plots. The total population of the Jewish colonies was therefore about one hundred thousand.

Early in 1928 Rosen put the proposal to enlarge colonization activities before the JDC leadership. This came at a time when the economic prosperity in the United States, present and future, was not in doubt, at least not in business circles. The business of the United States was indeed business, and investment capital was looking for outlets. Philanthropy was flourishing too, and the rich families of German Jewish descent were following a modern version of a very ancient Jewish tradition by giving generously (from money partly deducted from their taxes) to various good causes. They were liberals in the 1848 tradition, dues-paying members of important Reform synagogues, who hoped that nationalism was dying and would be replaced by equality of opportunity and brotherhood of man; and they felt that Jews ought to be loyal and equal citizens of their respective countries. A Rousseauean and romantic tradition made them especially enthusiastic about agricultural schemes. This was applied to the Russian situation, and the fact that the government was Bolshevik made no difference. Provided the leadership was sincere and the Jews would really be granted equality of opportunity, the project was likely to be accepted.

James N. Rosenberg wrote in 1926 that

considering how much money the JDC has spent in the past 10 years, and how small a proportion went to Russia, I maintain that Russia stands first. If we fail to continue this work for the Jews in Russia, it will be an incalculably tragic Jewish defeat. The Jews whom we have helped, and are helping in the other portions of Europe, have had a bad enough time, but which of them have gone through anything like the tragedy of the last century, as the Jews of Russia? Kishineff, the terrible Gomel pogroms, the Beiliss case, the World War, military occupations, civil war, revolt, Petlura, Denikin, bandits, pestilence, famine. The Spanish Inquisition and the bondage in Egypt were second to these. Today these Jews feel a hope. They feel that hope through colonization, and it is their only hope. It is voiced pathetically, but with noble dignity and without any cheap asking for money anywhere. Nowhere have I been pestered or begged for money. They have simply described the situation to me. If we fail these Jews, it will be a collapse of dreadful significance.[5]

There was no possibility of emigration, and in 1925 Rosen called it a "mockery to talk about emigration."[6] Add to that the power of Rosen's personality, his intimate knowledge of Russia, his humanitarianism, his agricultural expertise, his business acumen and simple common sense—and the outcome was clear. Felix M. Warburg for one, was a faithful Rosen admirer: "Looking back upon the work during the last few years, I feel that the Russian experiment has been the one original piece of work for social improvement that has been done, but whenever I try to tell you that I admire you tremendously for what you have done, you blush and change the subject."[7]

The major financial power in the circle of JDC's friends was Julius Rosenwald, the anti-Zionist Chicago millionaire who was the architect of the Sears Roebuck empire. Rosenwald, who hated ostentatiousness, was determined to use his money to good purpose, according to his lights. He agreed to provide five-eighths of any sum that might be collected for the Russian venture. The ultimate goal was $10 million for ten years, but the immediate aim was the collection of $8 million; by late 1928, some $7.1 million had been subscribed, Julius Rosenwald pledging $5 million (provided the ceiling of $8 million in subscriptions was reached), Warburg $1 million, and the Rockefeller Foundation $500,000 as an outright gift. The money did not come out of JDC collections, but by private arrangement from a limited number of large subscribers who were canvassed quietly by a handful of key individuals. This procedure was used so as to avoid a head-on clash with the Zionists and their supporters, as well as to prevent a public discussion. In a letter dated October 4, 1928, Rosenberg claimed that there was no contradiction between supporting settlement in Palestine and in supporting it in Russia.[8] "Both movements deserved support. The colonization in Russia has resulted in over 100,000 Jews going to the soil, where most of them are already self-supporting farmers." But Rosenberg added a significant comment: "Those who know the situation in Palestine realistically must all agree that it is impossible to have a rapid, large-scale colonization in Palestine." In the meantime, Rosenberg claimed, Jews in Russia must be saved from starvation and ruin.

In preparing to weather the expected storm of opposition, JDC attempted to enlist the support of ICA for this new program. In the summer of 1928, Rosenberg initiated an attempt to get ICA to contribute $1 million to the new scheme, without, of course, attaining any control over the actual operation. It seems that ICA was negotiating in Moscow at the same time that Rosen was. But the conservative ICA directorate did not carry the matter any further, and nothing came of the attempt to gain ICA's support for the venture.

The money was acquired by a new company that was formed for that purpose—the American Society for Jewish Farm Settlements in Russia (AMSOJEFS). JDC appointed a Board of Directors for that fund-raising organization, and James N. Rosenberg became chairman. On January 21, 1929, an agreement was signed with the Soviet government that provided that until 1935 AMSOJEFS was to advance $900,000 yearly for the agreed purpose of settling Jews on the land. This money was seen as a loan, and in return AMSOJEFS would receive USSR government bonds bearing 5 percent interest. In addition, $100,000 a year would be paid for so-called nonreturnable expenses (not as a loan), such as administrative outlays. For its part, the Soviet government guaranteed to put up 500,000 rubles for the Agro-Joint settlements each year and place this budget at the disposal of the Agro-Joint.

There were several unique features about this agreement. In

1921 the Soviet government had, under Lenin, offered concessions in Soviet Russia for the exploitation and development of mines, forests, and other natural resources. But there had been little response from an anti-Soviet West.

Now, with the Agro-Joint, the Soviets reverted to their earlier offer. However, not only did they pledge to return almost all of the amount loaned to them in dollars or gold and to pay interest, but they actually appropriated sums in Russian money to be administered by a foreign organization. The reasons for this attitude can only be guessed: a desperate shortage of foreign currency, a wish to foster good relations with rich American interests, a genuine desire to promote Jewish colonization, and the chance to import seeds and machinery with the money thus advanced. Yet, it must be added, this liberal policy was possible only in 1928/9, before the full weight of the five-year plans descended on the Soviet Union.

The quarrel between the factions in the Communist party had reached its height in the late 1920s. The left wing, advocating a working-class dictatorship over the peasants (who had to be subjected to expropriation in order to provide the wherewithal for a rise in the proletariat's standard of living), had suffered a defeat. Trotsky was exiled to Soviet Asia in 1927 and left the Soviet Union in 1929. The worker-peasant coalition, the *smychka,* advocated by Lenin, remained the official policy of the party. Rosen, closely following the events in Moscow, cabled in 1928 that Stalin's influence was waning, that the collectives were a passing fad, and that the Right would increase its influence.[9] Under these conditions, it seemed safe to enter into an agreement with the Soviet government in the hope that no great upheavals were in prospect.

Rosen's views were also reflected in a communication by Joseph C. Hyman to Morris D. Waldman of the American Jewish Committee: "Irrespective of the attempts made elsewhere for collectivization, I am very definitely of the opinion that, so far as the Crimea goes, where the bulk of our Society work and future operations are concerned, the collectivization experiment will not work real hardships on our colonies."[10]

The possibility that masses of Jews would be absorbed into Soviet industry, an obvious result of Soviet industrialization if it succeeded, was hardly considered. In fact, Dr. Grower said that most Jews would have to become artisans *(kustars)* because it was obvious that the majority of the Jews could not possibly become workers.[11] In a sense, the policy of JDC in Russia was to follow rather closely the example of JDC work in Poland under Dr. Kahn.

All these intentions and preparations were overthrown by two events—the launching of the first five-year plan in Russia and the economic crisis in the United States. Rosen's prediction had proved wrong. The Right—Bukharin, Tomski, Rykov—had become weaker, and Stalin's center group adopted an audacious and brilliant plan for Soviet Russia to pull herself out of her economic difficulties by her own bootstraps. The background and aims of the five-year plan have been related too often to bear repetition. However, it should be emphasized that the original concept did not envisage a sudden transition to collectivization, but planned for a gradual transformation, with 25 percent of Soviet Russian farmers' families being brought into cooperatives by 1932/3. The farmers were to be convinced by propaganda, and at the same time there were to be enforced grain collections that would permit the country to buy abroad the machinery and expertise to enable them develop vast heavy industry projects in Gorky, Stalingrad, Kharkov, and other places. These new factories would include tractor-producing plants (Stalingrad and Kharkov) that would supply machinery to the collective and state farms and thus insure a higher salable grain yield. This in turn would increase exports, and the industrialization of the country would proceed.

There were several preconditions for the success of this venture, one of the chief ones being relative price stability in the capitalist world. This condition could not be met: the 1929 depression began in the United States more or less at the same time (October) that the first large-scale steps to implement the five-year plan in Russia were being taken. The depression spread quickly to other countries. It caused a catastrophic fall in all prices, but industrial prices fell less than those of agricultural products. Russia now had to export more grain to buy the same amount of machinery. Moreover, control by the Communist party over their enthusiastic agents sent out into the field was far from complete. They were in fanatic competition with each other, and class warfare was practiced in the villages by teams of agents (mostly young party members from the towns, students, and even high school pupils). The kulaks were driven out, subjected to expropriation, exiled, arrested, beaten up.

All this did not affect the new Agro-Joint colonies to any great degree, because they had accepted certain cooperative practices from the outset. There were even some communes that practiced a far greater degree of collectivity than the cooperative villages (kolkhozy) set up by the party. But in the old Jewish colonies kulaks had to be found—even if there were none. An ICA representative gives us a description of such proceedings in a report he wrote to his organization:

This liquidation is entrusted first to a special delegation of communistic workmen sent to all the corners of Russia. This delegation, composed of three persons, arrives at the colony, assembles the poor elements, keeps them shut in all night, and, at 5 o'clock in the morning ordinarily, sends them into the houses of colonists designated in advance. Veritable platoons of execution are thus formed, going to the houses of the "kulaki" carrying communist flags and singing the Internationale. Arriving on the spot, always at 5 o'clock in the morning, they proceed to the complete expropriation of all that belongs to the designated victim, carry off all the furniture, tear from those asleep, old people as well as children, the very sheets of their beds to the very last pillow, leaving the old people and the children on the bare floor and leaving for the needs of the family hardly enough flour—should there be any—only for three days. Mostly, the "kulaki" are expelled from their houses and obliged to leave the district within three days. The "kulak" is robbed of all his goods and, in three-quarters of the cases, is far from being an exploiter, is far from having employed hired help, being in all a more industrious and laborious colonist than the others. He may also be designated as a "kulak" for having at a time long past been engaged in some commerce or other in addition to agriculture.[12]

The result was disastrous. Between October 1929 and March 1930 some fourteen million Russian peasant holdings were united in collectives, mostly against the peasants' will. Of these peasants, only the poorer elements were interested in the kolkhozy. Many of the others, forced to enter the collectives, killed off their draft animals and other livestock because from now on the state would be looking after them in any case. A very high proportion of the livestock was literally eaten up. Stalin intervened in this situation, and, in an article in *Pravda* on March 2, 1930, laid down a new line, or rather a retreat from the original concept: collectives were to be voluntary and people could leave them freely. The result was that about ten million peasant families left the kolkhozy between March and May. The enmity toward the collectives and toward the government was such that the peasants, the Ukrainian peasants especially, deeply resented any persons who, for whatever reason, stayed on in their collectives.

The period of collectivization coincided with the beginning of the expansion of Jewish agricultural settlement by the AMSOJEFS and the Agro-Joint. In 1929 seventy-nine new groups were settled in the Crimea and three more in the Ukraine. The total number of families settled was 2,276.[13]

Rosen watched the scene anxiously; his personal sympathies were Menshevik, and he had a great deal of criticism of the regime. Naturally, he tended to exaggerate the influence of the Right, with whom he found common language, and this tended to warp his judgment. He had not believed that Stalin would win, and this had also been the belief of many of Rosen's Menshevik friends, who had cooperated with the Bolsheviks in the hope that the latter would modify their policies as time went on. By now Russia had risen from the depths of economic disaster and recovered its position prior to World War I. The Menshevik and other socialist opponents of the Communist party who had remained in Russia and had cooperated with the regime had played a significant role in this achievement. Now, however, the five-year plan, decried as unrealistic and adventurous, had actually been inaugurated, and Rosen

was extremely apprehensive about the outcome, both for Russia
and for Russian Jewry.

On January 24, 1930, Rosen cabled that general conditions in
Russia had become very difficult. The Stalin group was in complete
control and had adopted a decidedly left-wing policy, whose main
features were the complete liquidation of the NEP—amounting to
a complete eradication of all private business by means of excessive
taxation, confiscation of property, arrests, and exile. The plan
would put a strain on investments in government industries, with
results that were still to be proven; there would be an ostensibly
voluntary, but in reality forcible, collectivization of millions of
poor and middle-class peasants, combined with ruthless extermination of the "richer" kulaks. This, said Rosen, would affect Jews
comparatively little, as there were practically no kulaks among the
settlers and very few among the old colonists. Under the new policy
a great number of people had been deprived of voting rights and
were now classed as *lishentsy;* as such, they received no bread cards
and were being expelled from the cooperatives. While the government had at least a 50 percent chance of succeeding in the collectivization drive, there was real danger of serious peasant disturbances
and perhaps even civil war. Rosen reported discussing these matters with "our colleagues and Jewish leaders" (sic!) in Russia. His
conclusion was that the Agro-Joint's work must continue, because
its very presence in Russia was extremely important.

Rosen had achieved practical results with his interventions with
government and party officials. One was the restoration of the
voting rights of former petty traders and artisans who had employed one workman. This would affect at least 50 percent of the
Jewish *lishentsy,* automatically eliminating all legal restrictions for
them. Other Jewish groups of *lishentsy* would be accepted for land
settlement practically without restriction and would be admitted
into cooperatives with various degrees of limitation; however, neither they nor their children would be accepted in government
factories. Moreover, emigration would be made easier for *lishentsy*
who could secure visas and prepaid tickets from abroad.[14]

Here, Rosen scored a major victory over his leftist opponents among the Jewish Communists. On June 5, 1930, the government did actually publish a decree that in effect restored to about half of the Jewish *lishentsy* their basic civil rights. The presence of the Agro-Joint seemed justified even if only on the general grounds of acting as a defensive shield for the Jewish masses.

The situation looked very grim nevertheless. Boris Smolar, the Jewish Telegraphic Agency (JTA) journalist who happened to be in Russia at that time, cabled on November 24, 1929, that "notwithstanding their loyalty," four of the Jewish colonists in the Crimea

were nevertheless arrested and sentenced to three years' jail each [and] their property confiscated, leaving only the property mortaged by the Agro-Joint which according to law cannot be confiscated. . . . The local population assured me [that] even government officials are aware that [the] arrested submitted all [the surplus grain] they could. However, arrest was made with [the] purpose of showing neighboring non-Jewish peasants that also Jews are arrested.

There was no thought of opposing the government's policy. Rosen pointed out that

with reference to the collectivization policy, we will be obliged to fall in line. It would be impossible and inadvisable to carry on Jewish colonization work under a different system from the general government policy. The fate of the German colonists who were turned back from the borders after unsuccessful attempts to get out of the country and who were permitted to continue their farming methods without collectivization can teach us a good lesson. Their position now is much worse than before. They are being ostracized, are considered enemies of the government and of the country, and do not receive any assistance from the government or any credits from the government agricultural banks, etc.[15]

On the contrary—extremist elements, who wanted to end all foreign participation in the colonization work, managed to more or less force the Agro-Joint out of the Kherson district in the Ukraine, where a number of its colonies were situated.

Smolar reported that "in the Kherson region, which is now 100 percent collectivized, the Agro-Joint now limits itself to finishing its buildings . . . while agricultural supervision there is done by [a] state agronomist who eliminates [the] Agro-Joint. This resulted in Agro-Joint closing its central office in Kherson." Smolar's contention was that "it remained to the Agro-Joint to either reorganize its methods to follow the collectivization line being dominated by the state or limit itself exclusively to bringing new déclassés from [the] shtetlach on the soil, settling them on collective principles, and leaving them to the government, since the collectives are supposed to be provided for by the government."[16]

Despite the fact that practically no expulsion of kulaks had taken place in Agro-Joint colonies, the effects of forceful grain collection and collectivization were similar to those in other villages. Rosen's statement on November 12, 1931, admitted that the collectivization "had driven out a good many people from the colonies,"[17] although this had been denied by him (and as a result by JDC in New York) at the time the collectivization actually took place.

Some basic differences, however, appeared immediately after Stalin's famous article (March 2, 1930). Basically, as we have seen, the Jewish colonies had been in the habit of practicing cooperative principles. They had done this before the collectivization drive, though the original aim undoubtedly was the establishment of small private farms. After the collectivization drive many of the Jewish collectives remained in existence, and the Jewish farmers hesitated to leave them. We have no record of the decisions and arguments that must have taken place on this question in the colonies, but most probably the arguments were of a pragmatic nature. The colonies had at least as great a chance as kolkhozy as they had had when they were private villages. The new post-March regulations permitted the individual peasant to retain not only his house, but a cow, a small garden and vegetable plot, and a few livestock as well. The full utilization of Agro-Joint tractors and other modern machinery was conditional upon the existence of a large farming area and a rational division of work. On top of that, the government, despite its temporary tactical withdrawal, wanted the collectives to succeed; it gave fiscal concessions and provided cheap seed and other advantages. Generally, the Jewish farmer was not as intimately bound up with his property as his non-Jewish neighbor was. In short, the Jewish colonies by and large remained collectivized.

Rosen cabled on May 27, 1930, that the general situation was much improved, compared to the January–March period. While a deficiency of commodities, especially of foodstuffs, was felt keenly, three factors helped improve the situation: the partial abandonment of left-wing policies, the generally good crop outlook for 1930, and a marked progress in industrial development, resulting in the almost complete disappearance of unemployment for even slightly skilled labor. Rosen claimed to have definite information that the left wing of the party was preparing a new attack at the coming Communist party conference. This might cause new troubles, but the chances were that the right wing would triumph. Therefore, he felt, Agro-Joint could safely go ahead with its projects. Moreover, Rosen was trying to get Smidovich to oust and to punish the government officials who had shown excessive zeal during the collectivization drive and had caused havoc, especially in the Kherson area.

The *Chicago Daily Tribune,* which on August 18, 1931, had declared that the colonies had been "destroyed by the Soviet government, which had decreed that all individual Jewish farmers must be united in communal agricultural establishments," was therefore quite off the mark. Rosen himself tended to be sceptical regarding the chances of the kolkhozy while the fierce drive for collectivization was carried on in Russia. It also seems that he was not quite aware of the tremendous force of the government and the bureaucracy that supported the drive. His view, expressed on February 13, 1930, was that "if it does succeed, everything will be fine. On the other hand, if it doesn't, and there are more chances that it won't, there will be two results. They will have to retreat, and the right wing will come into power and change the policy; or it might result in a civil war."[18]

His view changed after the March article by Stalin, which put an end to the forcible collectivization. This apparently caused him to agree to Lubarsky's going out to the Ukraine to help decollectivize the colonies. There he met not only with determined Communist opposition—on April 12, 1930, Merezhin, vice-president of COMZET, attacked him personally in an article in the Jewish Communist paper *Emes*—but also, as we have seen, with a reluctance on the part of some of the Jewish farmers to leave the kolkhozy. Others, of course, joined in the general exodus from the collectives. Smolar reported on April 9, 1930, that in the Krivoi Rog region Jewish colonists forcibly took away from the collectives not only their cows but also horses, which was illegal.[19] His cable of May 31, 1930, on the other hand, related the sad story of the Jewish colony of Ingulets near Krivoi Rog, where Ukrainian peasants burned down the Jewish colony because the Jews had not abandoned their kolkhoz.[20]

Rosen himself appears to have been torn between two opposing emotions. One was that "the idea of collectivization in the production of grain is a perfectly sound one,"[21] and the other was abhorrence at the method by which this aim had been achieved. Rosen was, after all, a socialist. His sympathy with many aspects of the Soviet regime was real, and the cooperative or collective principles in agriculture were very dear to his heart. In this he was by no means unique. Mirkin of ICA, in the report already quoted, went so far as to say: "I must say that all our agronomists and our officials . . . are unanimous in recognizing that collectivization has had only favorable results for our activity and for the colonists themselves."[22]

The Ukrainian peasants took their time in rejoining the collectives they had precipitately left after March 1930. But slowly they were forced back by economic pressures: they were taxed much harder as individual peasants than as collective farmers, they had few draft animals and livestock left, and they simply could not maintain themselves outside the collectives. The Jewish colonies prospered by comparison. Their livestock had been damaged to a much lesser degree, their method of working of land did not materially change, and they—especially the Agro-Joint colonies—came out of the collectivization drive relatively well.

Against this background, AMSOJEFS started to apply the money subscribed to it by some of the richer Jewish elements in the United States. Here again the work started with some misgiving. The collectivization drive cast a shadow over the scene. Attacks by Zionists and from rightist elements abounded. "The colonization plan has not only not solved the economic problem of Russian Jewry," wrote the right-wing Zionist *Reflex* in January 1930, "but has not had the slightest effect on its economic situation. . . . The Jewish villager is not better off economically than the city dweller. They are both starving, they are both in despair, economically, physically, and socially, and they are both a prey to the Bolshevik hounds." Had the JDC's "fifteen or twenty million dollars been invested in Jewish colonization in Palestine, the Jewish position there would have been impregnable, and the Arab, instead of attacking the Jew, would have eaten out of his hand and would have considered him a savior. Woe to a people whose policies are controlled by men whose only wisdom is a big money bag."

Investment for the establishment of colonies was not interrupted. According to one set of JDC figures, in 1929, 2,276 families were settled; in 1930, 2,250; by the end of 1930, it was said that some 12,100 families had been settled by the Agro-Joint on its colonies in the Ukraine and in the Crimea. It was claimed that 289 colonies had been founded. A Jewish autonomous region was established near Krivoi Rog around the center of Kalinindorf. German and Tartar settlers in the Crimea had been moved "voluntarily" to allow for close Jewish settlement, and the situation should have satisfied the Agro-Joint. It did, too—at least in New York. But Rosen was too much of a realist not to grasp the meaning of the swift changes in Russian society that were bound to affect his entire effort.

From the beginning of its reconstructive activities in 1923, JDC had also been engaged in establishing loan *kassas,* medical aid, child care, and trade schools. This activity was called "non-Agro work" in JDC parlance. Between 1924 and 1933, $1,760,000 was spent on this kind of effort. In the 1920s, with Russian industry barely creeping up to its prewar standards, there was, and could be, no hope of industrializing the Jewish masses. Help would have to take the form of loan *kassas* and child and medical aid—the traditional standbys of JDC work in Eastern Europe. Indeed, very little else could be done—the means placed at Rosen's disposal were too small. Palliative help, such as soup kitchens, would demand much more money, degrade the recipients, and accomplish nothing in terms of the long-term improvement. Rosen did the best he could with the means at his disposal.

At first, up to July 1929, the Agro-Joint supported the loan *kassas.* These traditional institutions provided credit on easy terms to various elements; but from 1927 on, in accordance with a new Soviet law, they concentrated on loans to artisans. In 1927 there were 370 such *kassas,* and they aided some 80 percent of all Jewish artisans in White Russia and the Ukraine. In 1929 these credit *kassas* were taken over by the government, after having been helped by the state in up to 80 percent of the credits received by them in 1928. In their short existence they had tided a large number of artisans' cooperatives over difficult periods, and they were also instrumental in aiding a number of *lishentsy* to become full citizens by joining officially recognized artels (government producers' cooperatives). They did not disappear altogether. They were not all absorbed by the state, and in 1930 some sixty-seven of them, with sixty thousand members, still existed, together with twenty-one producer cooperatives not as yet recognized by the government.

However, the overall situation of the Jewish artisan was not materially eased, and new methods of working for the *lishentsy* and the artisans had to be found. This was done by means of mutual aid societies (the *dopomogs*), which were recognized by the government as legal institutions and were allowed to look after the *lishentsy* as well. Their development was very rapid. There were only

55 of them in 1927, but by 1931 there were 240 with 250,000 members. Fifty-four of these mutual aid societies were being supported by the Agro-Joint. One of their main characteristics was their gradual unification with the medical societies founded by JDC during its initial help to Russian Jewry in the early 1920s. Its clinics, hospitals, and other institutions were not aided by the government because they were serving mostly *lishentsy*. JDC supported them, and as the mutual aid societies grew these medical institutions became part of their setup, which included also productive cooperative enterprises. This meant that there was now a source of money for the medical institutions through the productive cooperatives of the aid societies. JDC, mindful of its mandate to help people to help themselves, welcomed this development. By 1931 there were 50 homes for the aged with 1,400 inmates; 40 children's homes; 100 lunchrooms, where 8,000 people were fed at nominal prices; and 4,510 welfare cases that were being handled. Most important, these mutual aid societies established cooperatives composed to a large extent of *lishentsy,* who were engaged in various kinds of artisanship and thus were working their way back into full citizens' rights.

The marketing of their products was no problem. After 1927 the Russian market absorbed anything that industry could produce, even goods of very shoddy quality. The bottleneck was the provision of raw materials, of which Russia at the time had a limited supply. That supply went to the artels, and only the leftovers, if any, were given to the cooperatives of *lishentsy*. JDC, through Agro-Joint, tried to supply the aid societies with credits, machinery, and imported raw materials, thus enabling them to establish themselves on a reasonably stable footing. By 1929 there were twenty-one producer cooperatives not connected with any society and sixty-three aid societies, whose members operated some three hundred shops of *kustar* (artisan) production. In 1929 Agro-Joint advanced about 764,000 rubles in loans to these societies—this included medical work as well—and a great deal was done with these rather small sums. In 1930, 936,000 rubles were spent on these activities, and in 1931 the aid societies operated 345 shops employing 18,680 persons, while 3,000 more persons found a living in the thirty-seven independent producers' cooperatives. The medical societies attached to the aid societies treated 1.5 million people that year.

One of the more interesting ventures in this connection, one with a wry aspect to it, was the importation of yarn. Yarn—cotton yarn mainly—was in very short supply, and this fact caused great suffering to the large number of Jewish artisans who were engaged in knitting and other allied occupations. It was simply impossible to obtain Russian yarn. Rosen, together with ORT, the vocational training organization partly subsidized by JDC, imported twenty tons of yarn in 1929. The sixty-nine cooperatives that bought the yarn had to pay high government prices for it. As a result, each of the two organizations reluctantly had to make 83,000 rubles' profit on the transaction, quite apart from providing three thousand Jewish *kustars* with raw material. This venture was repeated in 1930. In 1930 and 1931 Agro-Joint realized a profit of 309,000 and 325,000 rubles respectively on these imports; they invested part of the money in loans and advances to the societies and used the other part of the profit to cover administrative expenses.

In 1929, with the start of the five-year plan, the whole situation changed. At first Rosen did not believe that the government would succeed in its program of investment. He talked of "a tremendously overstrained investment in development of industries," and said that "the government is doing it on a much larger scale than actual conditions permit."[23] In November 1931 Rosen actually believed that Soviet economic development would be at least temporarily retarded. "With industrial development retarded," he said, "a great many of the working people will have to get out and the Jews will be the first to go, as they were the last to join the ranks." He added, "Naturally they will have to return to the farm for a while."[24]

He and his associates believed in the continued necessity to provide for the Jewish artisan and to expand his possibilities. Even if the industrialization drive succeeded in part, the artisan would still be needed, and any industrialization plan to parallel the government effort would have to organize small-scale production. This did not mean that some Jewish artisans should not be retrained and absorbed into government industries. Such training would certainly be desirable, but the mass of Jewish artisans would have to be helped to establish themselves in their present occupation.

It is of interest to note that some Soviet officials apparently encouraged Rosen in this view. On November 13, 1929, he suggested an industrialization project that was to establish the Jewish artisan in Russia on a solid, self-supporting basis, whatever the outcome of the five-year plan. The two major aims of the program were:

1. Placement of several thousand young Jewish workingmen in government factories in cooperation with the Supreme Economic Council, along the lines of their five-year plan.
2. Provision of bases for the production of raw materials for Jewish artisans—members of the Jewish Cooperative Credit societies—independent of imports and independent of government supplies.

As to point 2, which was the major issue, three trades were "Jewish" at that time: knitting, weaving, and woodworking. The idea of repeating the yarn import attempt was abandoned. Dollars would have to be spent on the import of raw materials and then changed into rubles, which could not be reconverted into dollars to provide a revolving fund. It was suggested therefore that three factories for the production of raw materials be established: an artificial silk yarn spinnery in Kiev, for which the raw material (cellulose) was available; a wool yarn spinnery at Simferopol, and a cotton yarn spinnery at Kharkov. Together these three factories would supply raw materials for an estimated 10,500 artisans out of 260,000 Jewish artisans then in Russia. The financing was to be done by JDC like the financing for AMSOJEFS: by private subscription. The first phase would have as its goal $1.5 million, spread over three years, and the subscribers would be given government bonds bearing 5 percent interest. Part of the money would still be invested in imports, such as needles and some machinery, and the ruble proceeds of these would finance the training of skilled workmen and artisans.[25]

The plan created enthusiasm among many AMSOJEFS subscribers. It was, after all, logical to supplement the agricultural settlement by a parallel industrialization plan that would help solve the Jewish problem—so they thought—by turning the Jews into an equal and integrated part of the Soviet society. Subscriptions were solicited, and Rosenwald again agreed that any sum collected would be considered to be three-eighths of the collection; he himself would supply the other five-eighths.

The five-year plan, however, surged ahead. In fact, it surged ahead faster than many Russian officials had anticipated. It created a tremendous revolution in Soviet society. At the price of a great deal of suffering during the four years of the actual operation of the plan, especially on the part of the peasantry, the Soviet Union began its transition to an industrial country. This vitally affected the Jews as well. Suddenly the notion that a large class of artisans would still be needed seemed outmoded. At an increasing rate Jewish artisans were being absorbed into industrial combines. On February 7, 1930, Rosen said that "under the present conditions in Russia, it would be undesirable to undertake to enter into a new agreement with the government for the proposed industrial project, for which subscriptions had been received from a number of subscribers to the AMSOJEFS."[26]

In fact, Baerwald seemed to sense that Rosen was not as sure of himself on the industrialization project as he had been on the agricultural one. But then there was another change. In the spring of 1930, with a setback in the collectivization drive after Stalin's *Pravda* article, the Soviets were amenable to taking another look at Rosen's program. In May and again in June Rosen pressed the New York office to give him the green light for an ambitious extension of his original program: up to $1 million was to be spent each year for three years for the projects originally proposed and a few more of the same kind.

In June, with about 50 percent of the *lishentsy* reinstated, the possibilities of such an expansion seemed to rise, but then two factors intervened that buried the project altogether. One was the economic crisis that in late 1929 began to grip the United States. Profits were sinking; businesses went under at an alarming rate; and with breadlines in the United States lengthening daily, money was not available for the reorganization of Jewish economy in Russia. Nevertheless, Hyman and Baerwald made heroic efforts to collect subscriptions. Rosen was told to scale down his demands. By August 1930 he was suggesting a subscription of a quarter of a million dollars yearly for three years. But even that was too much, and plans for JDC-Soviet cooperation on a large scale had to be abandoned.

In January 1931 Rosen suggested a budget of $100,000 for that year, but even that was unattainable. In fact, a total of $44,355 was collected, of which five-eighths came from Rosenwald. This was spent in 1931, maintaining at least partly those activities that the Agro-Joint was already engaged in. On December 23, 1931, the JDC office informed Rosenwald that they considered the matter "entirely closed."

While the economic crisis was in itself sufficient to kill any JDC participation in the industrialization program, one other major factor must be mentioned. The years 1930–32 saw the final success of the collectivization drive, with peasants entering the collectives whether they liked it or not because of government taxation pressure and discrimination against private farming, coupled with the results of the mass slaughter of livestock. At the same time, unemployment was entirely eradicated, and the surplus farm population of the Soviet Union began to be siphoned off into the new heavy industry. Jews were drawn into this maelstrom of transformation. By 1932 there were 787,000 Jewish wage earners, 350,000 of whom were employed in factories. In other words, about 1.5 million of the 2.7 million Jews in Soviet Russia were now connected with factory life.[27] This tended to eliminate not only the problem of the Jewish artisan, ex-trader, and *lishenets,* but the whole Jewish economic problem in the Soviet Union. Soviet society, by changing its basic structure, seemed to have absorbed the Jews on equal terms. In the Ukraine, 20.7 percent of the industrial workers in 1932 were Jews, although the Jewish population was only 5.4 percent. The Jews had become proletarians, which in Soviet Russia meant equality of opportunity and advancement.

Rosen, too, had changed his views. By October 1931 he was stating clearly that the development of of industries in Russia was actually proceeding apace. When Russia started out with its first five-year plan, most people were rather sceptical about it and had talked to him about it in a cynical way. By 1931 nobody could deny that Russia had made tremendous progress with its industrial development, as well as with the industrialization of farming methods.[28]

The same process deeply affected the colonization program. During collectivization, some Jewish farmers in the Crimea tended to run away because of the collectivization drive. Rosen himself stated that "400 families had run away from the colonies during the drive."[29] Zionist colonies had their Hebrew names changed, and the Communists instituted strict political control. "Great numbers of Jewish settlers who were brought during last month from shtetlach into colonies to join collectives are returning home," cabled Smolar from Moscow in April. They were saying that recent Soviet decrees opened wider possibilities for them in shtetlach than in collective colonies. This resulted in a lack of laborers on the farms and endangered the existence of many Jewish collectives, which had to go to the expense of hiring labor. Even when they arrived, new Jewish settlers didn't remain on the collectives.[30]

People began to leave the colonies not because of pressure, but because of the greater opportunities outside them. At an industrial training school in Odessa subsidized by JDC, 20 percent of the students came from Jewish colonies. The younger generation could go to the factory, back to the city life to which they had been accustomed. In time, educational opportunities opened up, and colleges and universities beckoned; Soviet Russia needed technicians and scientists. The need for ex-*lishentsy* to escape their status by settling the land diminished to an ever-increasing extent, and OZET found it more and more difficult to get candidates for the colonies.

On the other hand, the existing colonies became better established and more prosperous. Electricity was introduced into most of them. Dispensaries, schools, and even cultural institutions were opened. By 1931 Rosen and JDC sponsors in the United States were saying that the colonization experiment had proved to be a resounding success. In 1931 they still believed in "the necessity [that] still exists and will for many years" to settle Jews on land, but after 1931 this kind of sentiment was no longer voiced. However, growth of the colonies did not stop altogether or all at once. By a well-calculated stroke, Rosen obtained more land and greater compactness of settlement in return for the importation of three hundred tractors at the height of the agricultural difficulties in the latter part of the first five-year plan period. In 1931 eighteen hundred families were settled, about 50 percent of the number originally planned; the Jews had become the third largest group in the Crimea.[31]

Then in 1932/3 another famine struck the Soviet Union. The reasons for this famine were many. There was the increased expenditure for military purposes, which meant that valuable fuel resources were used by the armed forces rather than by civilians, including those engaged in agriculture. Many farmers were, of course, disaffected; the most efficient people, the kulaks, had been deported; and agriculture was, organizationally speaking, in a state of confusion. On top of all that, there was a drought. With no reserves, no resources to draw on, the result was famine.

The growth of industry, on one hand, and the repeated disasters of Soviet agriculture, on the other, made agricultural settlement considerably less attractive to Russian Jews. Settlement was much lower in 1933; after 1934 no more claims are made of families settling on land in the Crimea, the Ukraine, or White Russia. JDC claimed that altogether 14,036 families had been settled in its colonies by 1934. There are some doubts as to the accuracy of the figure, but it can serve as a general indication of the extent of the colonization effort.

One other aspect of JDC work in Russia was of great importance in the history of Russian Jewry: the development of trade schools and training courses. There were several of these, but the most interesting one was Evrabmol in Odessa. This had started as an orphans' home after World War I, under the directorship of P.M. Kaganovsky. It acquired land on the outskirts of Odessa and established a training farm. Later the home moved back into the city and became a technical school. The children, some of whom did not even know the names of their parents, were saved from life in the streets and the catacombs of Odessa and became useful citizens. Beginning in the early 1920s Evrabmol was supported by JDC and became an eminently successful school; in 1929/30 it began to pay its own way by selling the products of its shops. It then became attached to the Commissariat (Ministry) of Heavy Industry and, with the benevolent help of the Odessa town soviet (municipality), continued to develop to the satisfaction of everyone concerned.

Evrabmol, two other institutions in Odessa, and schools and courses at Dnepropetrovsk, Nikolaev, and other places had some 8,580 students in 1930. These schools and courses, originally under the Commissariat of Education, were transferred to the industrial commissariats in the course of the five-year plan. This meant that the Agro-Joint was playing a certain part in the absorption of Jewish youths into the swiftly growing industry, despite its failure to establish the industrialization program with significant American financial help. The attempt was made to direct the student toward heavy industry, mainly the metal industry, in such new trades as that of automobile mechanic. These were high-priority areas in Soviet industrialization, and had the Jews stuck to their traditional trades, their chances of partaking in the tremendous revolution that was going on would have diminished considerably.

Another factor has to be considered. In 1931 the Soviet government began a series of economic negotiations with Western governments. At the same time, foreign technicians came in in rather significant numbers, and the attitude toward technicians and experts generally was little short of adulation in Russia. Wage differentials between these experts and ordinary citizens grew swiftly, and Jewish trainees were encouraged to dream of becoming members of this favored class. The efforts of Agro-Joint to establish, maintain, and equip trade schools, apart from or in cooperation with the ORT schools, must be seen against that general background. Government encouragement and interest in these schools was very obvious, and, as industrialization proceeded, so did the hunger of Soviet industry for skilled workers. By the time the government took these schools over from the Agro-Joint in 1935, there were forty-two of them, some operating at a very high level of training.

Two of these schools should be mentioned here. One was the Vinchevsky Technical School in Odessa, and the other was a special training course instituted in the town of Kremenchug. The Vinchevsky School was actually the continuation of one of the Jewish trade schools that had been set up during the czarist regime. The Soviets had taken over this school, and the Agro-Joint developed it into one of the most important technical schools in the Ukraine.[32] Also, in their shops the mutual aid societies trained artisans who were thus enabled to escape their *lishentsy* status and eventually to enter government factories. An interesting example of this is provided by the development in Georgia, in the Caucasus. There, Georgian Jews formed a mutual aid society in 1929, with an initial capital of 16 rubles (officially, $8). The Agro-Joint stepped in, and with its help eighty-two artels were organized by 1931, employing 2,568 persons, of whom 2,053 were Jews. The chief trades were knitting and needlework, reflecting the occupational structure of Georgian—but not just Georgian—Jewry.[33]

In the course of its industrial activity, Agro-Joint made a conscious effort to direct Jews away from their traditional occupations. The production of lathes and other machinery at Evrabmol, the production of dental burrs at Kiev—these efforts were made with a clearly formulated aim of helping to change the occupational structure of Russian Jewry. Ultimately, however, the relative success of this occupational change depended on whether the Jews could be "fitted into the general structure of the economic and social life of the country."[34] This the government did, and it was the economic revolution of the five-year plan rather than any Jewish effort that enabled the Jews to be absorbed in the newly created industrial structure. The Agro-Joint helped in this process, eased the transition, and spared many Jews a great deal of privation. But it must be recognized that it was not because of any accomplishment by the Agro-Joint that some 350,000 Jews became factory workers in the course of the first five-year plan. This fact was fully recognized by Rosen, and he was to draw certain conclusions from it.

By 1934 Agro-Joint industrial work was completed. Soviet industry had become a giant, still rather unsteady on its huge feet, but a giant all the same. The help of a foreign organization dealing specifically with transitional problems could be dispensed with. The 644 shops of the aid societies were still employing 8,278 workers, and this included the 66 aided by Agro-Joint. These were taken over by the government in 1934.

At the same time, in October 1934, the Ukrainian Red Cross absorbed the medical societies under an agreement that insured equal treatment to the *lishentsy*. By that time the whole *lishentsy* problem had been solved, to all intents and purposes. Only some religious and older people (less than 5 percent of the Jewish population) were still affected, and there was no longer any justification for maintaining a large administration and special institutions for these unfortunate people. Members of their families could supply them with the bare necessities of life, and though their position was far from pleasant, JDC's help no longer seemed necessary.

In the meantime, as a result of the economic disaster that had struck America, subscribers found it harder and harder to honor their subscriptions. By 1932 the situation had become critical. It must be remembered that JDC's collections went down to a low of $385,000 in 1932, and budgets were cut most cruelly at a time when the need was overwhelming. Only the agricultural work in Russia, secured as it was by individual contractual subscriptions, continued. The society supplied its $1 million yearly and thus enabled Rosen to continue his work. This unique situation could not continue, and in 1932 AMSOJEFS found that it would have to cease payments.

The direct cause for this disaster was the death, on January 6, 1932, of Julius Rosenwald, whose wealth had been invested largely in stocks. The probate of his will was a very complicated affair, and the claims of tax collectors and creditors had to be settled before payments to AMSOJEFS could be expected. In fact, there was the real danger that with the devaluation of stocks, the estate would have difficulties in satisfying the demands of both creditors and tax people. Payments on the subscriptions to AMSOJEFS were out of the question. In this situation the leaders of JDC entrusted to Rosen the delicate task of negotiating with the Soviet government a new agreement, which would preclude the actual cash payment of any more money by American subscribers.

Rosen's trump card was the amount of ruble assets JDC had accumulated in Russia and which JDC had at least a theoretical right to take out in dollars. But by 1932 the Russians were no longer as eager to negotiate with a foreign organization as they had been before. Rumblings against foreign organizations had been heard before, and as early as December 11, 1929, Grower had declared to JTA that "some minor people agitate against foreign organizations without any hope of success in responsible circles."[35] These agitations turned out not to be so minor after all, and Diamanstein, leader of the Yevsektsia, had some very harsh things to say about the Agro-Joint at an OZET Congress in 1930. "Agro-Joint does not understand Soviet policy and does not want to understand it." He said that the Soviet people needed to utilize these organizations, especially as they had agreements with the Soviet government, but he added that the government authorities must supervise these organizations to insure that they were under the proper direction.[36]

This was too much for Rosen. At the beginning of 1931 he wrote a very strong letter to COMZET about the active campaign against the Agro-Joint. To his complaint Rosen added a threat: "The people at the head of our organization have no desire whatsoever to impose our work on anybody and it is entirely out of the question for us to be in a position of a 'tolerated' organization."[37]

The answer, signed by Smidovich, was sent after discussions with the government, and apparently the extremists were defeated. "The articles and speeches of private individuals," the COMZET letter of February 16, 1930, said, "do not in any way reflect the attitude of the government toward the work of the Agro-Joint." While this was a clear repudiation of the position of the Communist Left, undercurrents in the party against the Agro-Joint grew stronger. In April 1931 Lubarsky was arrested and spent a month in prison before Rosen managed to get him out. In 1932 the Soviets were ready to reduce the Agro-Joint work in Russia by stages.[38]

At first JDC gave some consideration to the idea of camouflaging their lack of ability to pay by suing the USSR for not having fulfilled the contract conditions, in accordance with an arbitration clause in the 1929 agreement. This clause was based on the principle of *rebus sic stantibus:* the agreement was held to have been violated by the government's having changed, by its policy of collectivization, the conditions under which the Agro-Joint conducted the work. Farm settlements in Russia would have been considerably less attractive in the eyes of Jewish subscribers in the United States had they known that their money would in fact go into the kolkhoz settlements. In the end, however, JDC refrained from any attempt to sue the Russians. The work was deemed to have succeeded after all, and the Russian government had certainly fulfilled the financial conditions; in fact, they had spent considerably more in rubles on Agro-Joint colonies than they had been bound by contract to do.

By 1933, $4,857,563 was actually paid on the subscriptions, of which the Rosenwald share amounted to about $3 million of the $5 million promised. The sum of $4,725,000 had actually been sent to Russia, and $2,475,000 was still to come under the original eight-year agreement (1928 to 1935). On April 14, 1933, Rosen signed a new agreement with the Soviet government. The Soviets had given AMSOJEFS bonds for the money they had actually received, which they would ultimately have to redeem. Interest was also to be paid up to the end of the eight-year contract. They now accepted a part of these bonds and waived payment of interest in lieu of the money the society owed them. After that, part of the bonds for the money they had received from America still remained in the hands of AMSOJEFS. They now issued bonds for the $2,475,000 they had received through the new agreement, and thus left AMSOJEFS with $5,352,000 in Soviet bonds bearing a 5 percent interest.[39]

At the same time an agreement was reached on the Agro-Joint assets in Russia. Assets worth 5.6 million rubles were handed over to the government, and the government in turn gave the Agro-Joint the equivalent in cash and credits. The Agro-Joint promised to use the money for intensive plantation programs, various kinds of training courses, administration, and other items.

The agreement was profitable to both sides. The Agro-Joint was relieved of the need to supply more cash, and the Russians obtained a firm legal hold over the Agro-Joint estates in their country, improved their financial arrangement with the society, and at the same time began the process of an orderly termination of the society's affairs in their country.

The end had clearly arrived. As we have seen, the possibilities of agricultural settlement in Russia were decreasing rapidly. Rosen claimed that in 1933 only fourteen hundred families were settled in the Crimea, but even this looked rather doubtful.[40] Jews now did not have to go to the Crimea in order to become small-scale farmers on the outskirts of villages and towns, but could do so wherever they lived. The Jewish economic position continued to improve, and the Agro-Joint and its operations seemed to be more and more superfluous. In 1931 the Ukrainian work was liquidated, the Agro-Joint having simply been told that they had nothing more to do there.[41]

In 1932–34, work was concentrated in the Crimea. Government supervision in all respects except the purely agroeconomic one was complete. Some of the assets of the Agro-Joint were not, it is true, handed over: for example, the Jankoy tractor station and repair shop, buildings in Simferopol and Moscow, supplies, and commodities. Even after the termination of its actual settlement work in 1934, the Agro-Joint still maintained a large staff of experts who, with income from the existing assets and some very small sums in dollars, continued to advise the settlements about their agricultural production. The Jankoy station was one of the prototypes of the MTS tractor stations that were to provide tractor work for the kolkhozy later on. In other respects too, such as well-drilling and horticulture, Agro-Joint help was still significant.

But Rosen's absences from Russia grew longer and longer, and the work was slowly reduced to a minimum. In 1937 the Agro-Joint still had 6 million rubles' worth of assets, but its staff (which at the peak of colonization numbered some three thousand employees) had dwindled to about one hundred. The fact that the Agro-Joint's presence was becoming undesirable in 1937/8 was made very evident. This was the time of the purges, and it was unthinkable that a foreign organization like the Agro-Joint would be allowed to carry on much longer. Smidovich died in 1935 and was succeeded by a Stalinist bureaucrat named Chuchkaieff. The end was near.

In the mid-thirties a new factor appeared, which seemed to promise a certain reversal of the trend that was pushing the Agro-Joint out of Soviet Russia. This was the question of Biro-Bidjan and the prospects of immigration into Russia.

Back in 1926 the Soviet government had put forward a proposal to set aside the territory of Biro-Bidjan, on the Amur River in the Far East, for settlement by the Jews. If enough Jews settled there, a Soviet Jewish republic would be set up; the Jewish nation would have the benefit of a territorial basis, like all the other nationalities in the Soviet Union.

Kalinin, the president of the Soviet Union, was a particularly ardent proponent of this scheme and expressed his views in a number of speeches. But acceptance of the scheme by Jewish Communist circles in Russia was rather equivocal. Some Jewish Communists thought that this was a reversion to Jewish nationalism or Zionism. Indeed, that is how the Zionists themselves saw it: as a belated recognition of the fact that the Jews were an ex-territorial nation whose national revolution could only be achieved by the settlement of a land of their own. Of course they did not accept Biro-Bidjan as the final goal, but hoped that an early failure of the experiment would open the way for Soviet recognition of Palestine-centered Zionism.

JDC was approached about—indeed, pressured into—accepting the Biro-Bidjan project and working there. Rosen, however, was wary. The Crimean venture was still in the making, conditions there were relatively good, and he was disinclined to embark on a wild project in the middle of nowhere, thousands of miles from the centers of Jewish life in Russia. Biro-Bidjan obviously needed investigation, and the fact that the government wanted to populate areas on its borders with Japanese-controlled Manchuria and to exploit its natural resources was no argument in favor of Agro-Joint's participation.

This situation changed considerably with the advent of the Hitler regime and the decided worsening of the economic conditions for Polish Jewry. Soviet Russia was now playing with the idea of providing an asylum for victims of Nazi persecution; Biro-Bidjan could develop into a national home that was not necessarily restricted to Russian Jews.

In 1931 Rosen reported that he had been officially approached by COMZET to assist in the immigration of ten thousand Jewish families, of whom half would go to agriculture, half would come from Poland, and many would go to Biro-Bidjan.[42] Rosen's reaction was cool. With the pressure mounting, early in 1932 Kahn defined his attitude to the question in a letter to Max M. Warburg in Hamburg.[43] Stating that Biro-Bidjan was one of the so-called territorialist projects (envisaging the concentration of Jews in a territory or territories outside of Palestine), he said that these so-called territorialists are now becoming stronger everywhere in the world, and especially this movement is winning support among the youth, since one can see for himself that Palestine is not in a position to relieve the needs among the Jews and that a mass immigration to Palestine is not possible. Utilizing this psychological situation, the highest Russian officialdom have now in their sessions for some time determined to make available in Biro-Bidjan a territory in which a Jewish national entity could develop.

But, added Kahn,

at the present time for the Jews of Russia the better possibility for support lies in industry and in the factories, so that the Russians have proceeded to enlist foreign Jews for Biro-Bidjan. A number of Jews from the Argentine have already emigrated there, as have also 20 young people from Germany and 200 from Lithuania and Latvia. In view of increasing unemployment, it is believed that perhaps even unemployed from America and Palestine will settle in Biro-Bidjan. At this time there are about 5,500 Jewish persons, which is approximately double the amount of a year ago. This year 12,000 new immigrants are to be sent there, and in the year 1933 they plan to settle 20,000 there. . . . I personally do not believe in the success of this settlement. What has been achieved there up to now does not justify great hopes.

This was probably an expression of Rosen's views also.

There the matter rested till about the middle of 1934. However, with the refugee problem growing worse in Western Europe and the Polish Jewish problem becoming more acute, Rosen slowly came around to the view that Biro-Bidjan should be considered. With his closest co-workers, Lubarsky, Grower, and Zaichik, he made a trip through Biro-Bidjan in October and November 1934. His observations in no way differed from previous reports, such as those of a committee of experts sent by the pro-Communist ICOR group in New York in 1929, or the observations of David A. Brown, who visited the territory in 1932. It was clear that a great deal of investment would be needed to make the territory feasible for agricultural settlement. But Rosen was now more optimistic than he had been before; the government had promised large sums to improve the land and was employing kulak prisoners and Red army men to build roads, railroads, and drainage canals. Rosen's major point was that the Soviet government had offered a place of refuge, and that could not be refused.

The JDC leadership now convened to discuss the situation. To people like James N. Rosenberg the situation was simple: "Do we wish to give hundreds of thousands of Polish Jews an opportunity to emigrate to a country ready and willing to open up their borders for immigration?"[44]

Rosen himself "conceded that years back, he had very definitely stated that no private or philanthropic organization should engage in this work until all the prerequisites had been brought about; that it would entail very large government expenditure." But now the situation was different, and so were the needs. "There are men in the government who feel very keenly the plight of the Jews in Germany and elsewhere, and whose attitude certainly can be regarded as actuated by humanitarian feelings. The importance of Biro-Bidjan lay not so much in the immediate results as in the development of potential possibilities for immigration."[45]

The Soviet proposal was that one thousand Jewish families and five hundred single people would be settled, some in Biro-Bidjan, some in the Crimea (two hundred families) and the Ukraine, in both agriculture and industry. The Agro-Joint would provide the money to transport them to the Russian border and then supervise the agricultural settlement in the Crimea and in Biro-Bidjan. The money was to come from $1.2 million of AMSOJEFS bonds that were to be handed to the Soviets. The Agro-Joint would get $200,000 in hard currency for expenditures outside Soviet Russia, and $1 million in Russian goods would be bought at gold ruble prices. The government of the USSR would add 25 million rubles as a counterpart to the American fund.

The immigrants would be chosen by the government, as the Agro-Joint refused to be responsible for that part of the scheme. The newcomers would have a right to leave Russia within a given period. But the whole question of citizenship and military service was still not agreed upon by the time Rosen brought up the proposals for discussion in June 1935. At these meetings, at one of which members of ICA participated with JDC executives, Rosen explained this scheme further. In contrast to South America and other countries outside of Palestine, Biro-Bidjan was the only undeveloped country in the world where there were vast immigration possibilities for thousands or hundreds of thousands of people, and it was the only country where the government would be willing to bear the major part of the cost, thanks to the fact that the Russian government was anxious to promote settlement in those Far Eastern regions. In his informal discussions with the Polish officials, Rosen gathered that the Polish government was alive to the problem of the Jews, knew that they could not be absorbed in Poland, and would help in any plan to send large numbers out of the country. "As I see the whole question," he said, "practically every country in Europe is trying to push the Jews out as a foreign body —some in a gross way—some in a finer way." Only Russia was prepared not only not to push Jews out but actually to take them in.

From what I know of the work of JDC, the [Reconstruction] Foundation, ICA, etc., I must say quite frankly that a good deal of this very important work—I do not want to minimize it—a good deal of the so-called reconstruction work that has been carried on is not in the real meaning of the word reconstructive. There is no use hiding your heads under your tails. . . . The people assisted there remain just petty traders with the few rubles [sic!] you give them. The younger generation is not getting the advantages of *Umschichtung* [occupational restratification] in the real meaning of the word. The *kassas* are making visible efforts, but they are all comparatively insignificant. This applies to the loan *kassas* in all countries.

The competition was great, Rosen went on, and it was highly doubtful if they could hold on very much longer. The Russians were "honest and decent and sincere" in their opposition to anti-Semitism and their support for a complete equality of opportunity.

Generally, he said, "there is no specific Jewish problem in Russia except an insignificant one—that of helping a few of the religious people out," and he was doing that. As for the rest, Russia was becoming a country of immigration, *the* country of immigration, and it would be irresponsible not to utilize that.

Rosen also suggested a scheme whereby machinery would be imported into Russia by a JDC financial operation; this would add working funds to the Agro-Joint in Russia. But it was the immigration scheme that aroused discussion and interest.[46]

Rosen, as he had made abundantly clear, was not a Communist. At a press conference held in 1931,[47] Rosen had declared that he was not a Bolshevik. But, he added, the Russian government had approached the Jewish problem better than any other government had done, and for this it should receive full recognition. There was more to it than that, however. His close working relations with Soviet officials had led him to appreciate the positive side of the Soviet regime, and he was undoubtedly impressed with the sincerity of those officials—unfortunately unknown to us—who made the offer. In 1935 it was clear to him that it was not the hope of acquiring hard currency that influenced Soviet thought, for the Soviets had developed a favorable balance of payments and they were producing gold in large quantities. It was other aspects of the project that interested them. As an experiment, they had accepted twenty-one German Jewish doctors who had been screened by JDC; for the most part these doctors came from refugee barracks in France.

The attitudes of the participants in the discussions varied. Lessing Rosenwald had doubts, but these were centered more on the climate and the fact that Biro-Bidjan was so close to the Japanese border than on the implications arising from the establishment of a Soviet Jewish state. As far as he was concerned, he said, "that would not enter his consideration. Those people who would want to seize on that as an argument would find it." Dr. Oungre of ICA and Alexander Kahn and Dr. Cyrus Adler of JDC opposed the project because they doubted the stability of Soviet conditions and were afraid of the antireligious activities of the Soviets. Warburg argued that the Russians had always honored their debts, that they were sincere, and that no one knew what would become of the three million Jews in Poland. This opportunity should not be rejected, he said. The calm reigning at the moment in Russo-Polish relations might not last, and the opportunity should be grasped now. This was the attitude that was finally adopted by a large majority of those consulted, and Rosen was given the green light.[48]

However, fate intervened. The documents themselves are meager, and we can only rely on Rosen's cables advising JDC that difficulties had arisen, that postponements were essential, and that negotiations were proceeding. This, one must remember, was the period of the first great wave of Stalinist terror, after the assassination of Kirov in December 1934. It would seem that those who had proposed the scheme to Rosen were the very persons who belonged to the forces that were destined to be purged; the Stalinist bureaucracy and ideology were hardly susceptible to the kind of argument advanced in favor of mass Jewish immigration into the Soviet Union.

On October 21, 1935, Rosen cabled that under the pressure of certain government departments, COMZET insisted that foreign organizations should not carry on direct operative work in Biro-Bidjan but should confine themselves to merely helping immigrants come to Russia; the actual development and settlement work there should be carried on by government agencies. "We prefer keeping out of Biro-Bidjan altogether until attitudes are changed or substantially modified."[49]

With Biro-Bidjan no longer on the agenda, various palliatives were considered. The negotiations dragged on throughout the spring and summer of 1936, until they finally exploded in July. In a final letter, dated July 23, 1936, Rosen attributes the failure to the changed situation, internationally and internally.

One of the German Jewish doctors whom we brought in is being accused of having been in the service of the Gestapo, and two of the Polish Jewish immigrants have been exposed as informers of the Polish Intelligence Service. These Polish Jews came in not through us, but the effect as far as the government is concerned is the same. In the case of the Jewish doctor, it is possible that he had been denounced by his father-in-law, who is an Aryan and a Nazi official. . . . It is true that one out of over 100 doctors is a small percentage but, as the Russians say, "One drop of tar spoils a barrel of honey."

Rosen still had hopes that Litvinov's influence might change the negative attitude of officialdom, but he also accused JDC of never giving favorable publicity to the Soviet help for Russian Jewry. "We have never really helped the Russians to make political capital on their Jewish policy." He proposed to remedy this by having Herbert Samuel express to the Soviet ambassador in London the thanks of Jews all over the world for the immigration opportunities already afforded to Jewish refugees;[50] this suggestion was not acted upon. Nor did Litvinov seem to be able to help very much. Russian suspicion of the foreigner and his works was transformed into a collective persecution mania under Stalin, and the immigration project was allowed to die quietly. On September 10, 1937, Rosen declared that the Russians had dropped the idea, and he added that he himself would not have the courage to suggest an immigration project at that point.[51]

The whole affair was never made public, then or later, but it shows clearly which way the collective mind of JDC was turning. The solution of the Polish problem was its major preoccupation. Only the 1936/7 wave of terror in Russia made Rosen declare that even he would not have the courage to bring additional Jews into the Soviet Union under the circumstances then prevailing.

With the failure of the Biro-Bidjan immigration scheme in 1936, Rosen realized that the time had come to get out of Russia, although Warburg was still loath to accept that conclusion. On February 15, 1938, Hyman finally accepted the idea and proposed the termination of operations.[52] The assets still in Russia had to be disposed of and a settlement reached regarding the $5,352,000 in bonds still held. Finally, an agreement was reached in July 1938. COMZET had been liquidated in June because the Soviet government "considered the Jewish problem in the Soviet Union solved." The financial settlement involved the cancellation of the bonds and their transformation into $2,430,000 in new Soviet bonds that were finally redeemed, with interest, by 1940. The remaining Agro-Joint assets were handed over to the Russians in return for the promise that they would be used largely for the benefit of Jews. And finally, "all the files, documents, and correspondence connected with the activities of the society and the Agro-Joint in the USSR and kept in the USSR are to be transferred to the government." Rosen left Russia for the last time in the summer of 1938, and the Agro-Joint Russian venture came to an end.

The final chapter of the Russian story is hidden in a dense mist of confusion and uncertainty. No documents relating to the fate of the Russian members of the Agro-Joint board have survived. Not a single central figure in Agro-Joint work seems to have reappeared after the war and Stalin's death. We know that Lubarsky, Grower, and Zaichik were arrested, were shipped to camps or prisons, and disappeared without a trace. Their fate was shared by hundreds of agronomists and Agro-Joint officials. As to the reasons, we can but guess. Millions of Russians suffered for crimes they did not commit; one of the recurrent accusations was that of contacts with capitalist countries. Members of the Agro-Joint had quite eagerly and openly participated in the activities of a foreign capitalist organization in Russia, and apparently they paid the price.

In a personal letter to Rosenberg and Baerwald dated December 11, 1937, Rosen provided an insight of sorts into this process. Three members of the Agro-Joint bureau in Moscow—among them Dr. Grower—had just been arrested. Rosen connected their arrest with the earlier arrest of his brother-in-law, the former health minister (commissar) Kaminsky ("not a Jew but a very decent man"), who had been responsible for bringing the German doctors into Russia. "A plot is being developed to accuse Kaminsky, in cooperation with the Agro-Joint or perhaps with myself personally as his foreign relative, of bringing German spies into Russia under the cover of helping the doctors." Fourteen of the doctors had been arrested, though some of these were simply deported from the country. "It would not be impossible," said Rosen, "for Kaminsky to 'confess' and for some of the doctors who have been arrested also to 'confess'; and the results may be rather unpleasant." The arrest of Agro-Joint officials followed these developments.

From Paris Rosen wrote to the Soviet security organs (he knew very well who to write to) and assumed responsibility for anything that had been done by the Agro-Joint. He asked for a visa into Russia and stated "that as far as I am personally concerned, I am ready to waive diplomatic protection as a foreigner. This I consider my duty to do in relation with my friends and colleagues, with whom we have been working together for years. I would feel like a dog should I let them go down under Stalin's tyranny and myself escape because I happen to be an American citizen."

He himself was allowed to enter Russia once more, to wind up the affairs of the Agro-Joint. But apparently he could do nothing to help his friends and relatives who were caught up in the Stalinist purges.

As to the colonies, they seemed to have suffered a great deal under the impact of the terror. Equally important in their lack of success was the pull of the towns and their growing industries. Baerwald stated in 1940 that "Weizmann says [that] Russian colonization has not proved a success. Most people have left [the] colonies as he always said they would. Have you any definite news or views on numbers still remaining in [the] colonies?"[53] There was no answer. Weizmann apparently had been right. Then the flood came, and the Jewish colonies were wiped off the face of the earth by Hitler's hordes.

Evaluation of the Agro-Joint work presents a very complicated problem. Rosen's dictum was that if JDC had not turned to colonization work, great numbers of Russian Jews "would undoubtedly have literally perished. While at present the government would undoubtedly continue the work, should the Agro-Joint terminate, it would not have started it without our initiative and our actually originating it."[54]

The first part of the statement is probably true as regards those ten or twelve thousand families settled by the Agro-Joint before the relative improvement of conditions in the early 1930s. The second part is more doubtful. But there is no doubt that tens of thousands of Jews were saved from economic disaster by being settled on the land. This itself enabled the Agro-Joint to do its so-called "non-Agro" work, and that alleviated conditions all over the former Pale of Settlement.

The medical institutions, the trade schools, the various *kassas* and aid societies—they were all by-products of the colonies, and they were a blessing to hundreds of thousands of human beings in a very difficult situation. The very presence of an American Jewish organization was of great value and should not be underestimated. The reinstatement of the Jewish *lishentsy* in June 1930, the change in attitude toward the mutual aid societies, the opportunities for help to the Zionist pioneers, on one hand, and Orthodox rabbis and some of their followers on the other, the hundreds that were enabled to leave Russia because of Rosen's intervention—all these must be taken into account.

What were the motivations of the people who supported this work—apart from their having been influenced by the truly great personality of Rosen? They were mostly men of rather limited social and political vision, but of great sincerity and considerable wealth. They were rarely in the mood for philosophizing, but William Rosenwald's account of his father's motivation contains a most interesting philosophy:

He believed that Jews, given an opportunity to become productive, self-supporting citizens in their native lands, would succeed. He wanted to show that Jews can earn their livelihood by the sweat of their brows. He believed that emigration could not solve the mass problem of Jews in Eastern and Central Europe. So he welcomed the opportunity afforded in Soviet Russia for Jews to prove that they could be self-supporting farmers and industrial workers on a large scale.

These achievements, under Rosen's guidance, were thought of as permanent improvements, not palliative measures.[55]

Several attitudes were inextricably interwoven in this statement by Rosenwald: the feeling of inferiority of the Western Jew toward his surroundings, contained in the hope that the Jews could be just as good as others, given the opportunity (not that they were as good, but that they would have to prove they were, because prima facie they were not); the belief that Eastern and Central European Jews should stay where they were, especially since there was no practical possibility for them to go anywhere else; and the inherent romanticism of a wealthy American Jew cooperating with the Soviet authorities in turning the Jew into a farmer and peasant. Nineteenth-century liberalism and Jewish Reform and a great deal of goodwill cooperated to produce this attitude.

Of course, anti-Zionism entered the field as well. Lessing Rosenwald, as we have seen, was not opposed to a Jewish state in Biro-Bidjan—that would be a Bolshevik creation owing allegiance to the Soviet Union, and would not embarrass a Western Jew politically. But Zionism was different, and "should a national homeland be established in Palestine, I believe it would be one of the greatest catastrophes that could possibly happen."[56]

Dr. Maurice B. Hexter, a moderate supporter of JDC who was a non-Zionist and worked with the Jewish Agency in the upbuilding of Palestine in the 1930s, expressed the opinion that "it would be an inhuman blunder to arouse hopes in the breasts of our unfortunate brethren, to imply and to state that Palestine can solve their entire problems, even if one has faith (I for one do not have it) in the astronomic predictions of the absorptive capacity of either Palestine as a whole, or of the portion proposed for the Jewish state under the partition. There would still remain hundreds of thousands who would not be taken care of and for whom other outlets must be sought."[57]

Warburg and Baerwald did not share the extreme anti-Zionism of Lessing Rosenwald; they cooperated with Weizmann of the Jewish Agency, whom they admired and in a way feared. But they were equally opposed to the radical nationalism of the majority of the Zionist movement. Besides, they too could not see how little Palestine could solve the problem of East European Jewry. Agro-Joint work at least helped solve the Russian Jews' economic problem. It might be a beacon to follow, and Polish Jews might perhaps go the same route.

They were all subject to the limitation that Rosen himself labored under, when he declared that "there is no specific Jewish problem in Russia anymore."[58] They all saw Russian Jewry in purely economic terms. Even in those terms they only saw the present, and failed to consider the implications inherent in Soviet economic development. With the pull of the cities and the lack of an ideological counterpull, the town-bound tradition of the Jews would induce them to abandon agricultural areas as long as there was no compelling economic reason to remain. Only an insignificant proportion at best would remain on the land surrounded by farmers of other nationalities. This would probably have been true even had there been no German invasion. But the point is that Jewish existence did not consist solely of economic factors, important as these were.

When Warburg was asked to comment on the persecution of rabbis in the Soviet Union, he answered that while he deeply deplored this situation, one must not forget that the Soviet government was helping the Jews get back on their feet economically. The philanthropist saw the problem almost solely in terms of bread and butter. The faith of the nation, its cultural and political freedom, its past values and future hopes—whether Orthodox or secular, liberal or Zionist—were of marginal concern. The Reform Jew wanted to break down the barriers between the Jew and his neighbor, whereas the Russian Jews by and large clung to certain vestiges of separateness.

In the end, the breakdown of barriers did not succeed. Jews left not only agriculture but also, to an ever-increasing extent, factory work as well. They concentrated in the Commissariats of Trade and Commerce, in the professions, in the bureaucracies of the industrial establishment and their accounting departments.

In the long run the Agro-Joint work in Russia brought few results. What of the short run? Was it worth spending $16 million between 1924 and 1938 for that purpose?[59] A very good case can be made that this was not only good, but essential. Others have pointed out that this money could have been used in Palestine to better purpose, but what better purpose was there than saving Jews from hunger? Was it, after all, possible to take the Jews out of Russia and send them to Palestine in the 1920s and 1930s? If not, what should Jewish philanthropists have done with them? There was certainly a case to be made, then and later, for concentrating all efforts solely on Palestine. But not very many, even in the Zionist camp, dared to put a Palestine-centered demand quite as exclusively as that. Rosen settled sixty thousand Jews on the land. This was considerably more than the agricultural settlement in Palestine had achieved in the comparable period, working without government help and with less expertise than Rosen's team could command.

The final results of the colonization work were themselves rather unclear. How many families did the Agro-Joint settle in Russia? The figure is apparently close to 60,000 persons. The estimates vary between 14,000 to 20,000 families, but it is reasonably certain that not more than 14,000 families remained on the land by 1938, probably considerably less than that. Kahn's estimate was that the total Jewish farming population in 1941 amounted to some 160,000 persons and that some 70,000 more were connected to the land by having vegetable plots on the outskirts of towns and villages. It seems to us that of these, some 50,000 to 60,000 had been settled by the Agro-Joint.[60]

In about 1934 a consolidation of the tracts settled by the Jewish settlers in the Crimea took place. Villages were united under a common administration, and five autonomous Jewish districts were founded (Freidorf in February 1931, Stalindorf in June 1930, Kalinindorf in March 1937, New Zlatopol in 1929, and Larindorf in January 1935). This was the sum total of the work that ended in the eviction of the Agro-Joint and in the arrest and death of most, possibly all, of its Russian Jewish officials. There were achievements and there were disasters. The full story will have to wait until the Agro-Joint files in Russia are opened to scholarly inspection at some future date.

3

Germany: *1933–1938*

As we have seen, the crisis in Germany did not find JDC entirely unprepared. The warnings of Dr. Kahn and the rumblings of the rising Nazi tide in Germany had focused the attention of the organization upon the German scene even before the advent of Hitler. Once the Nazis came to power, it was only natural that JDC should try to come to the aid of German Jewry. However, the attitude of JDC was contested within the inner circle of its own leadership—this despite the fact that most of its lay leaders were descendants of German Jewish immigrants to the U. S. or had themselves been born in Germany.

During the first months of 1933, discussions of whether JDC should enter the German picture at all were held in New York. Arthur Hays Sulzberger of the *New York Times* thought that JDC was

making a fundamental and woeful blunder in this connection. It seems to me impossible to conceive that 600,000 persons in Germany can be supported from now on from any outside community. Since this obligation cannot be carried out, it should not be assumed. To do so, in my judgment, merely relieved the German Government of its responsibility that now rests upon it to permit its citizens an equality to earn their own livelihood.[1]

At a Board of Directors meeting in July, James N. Rosenberg argued that there was no point in providing relief for the Jews in

Germany, because JDC simply did not have the means to do so. The aim of the organization should be to get the German government to agree to a program of reconstruction. In this, JDC might be of some help.[2]

The majority of the organization's leaders, however, adopted Dr. Bernhard Kahn's attitude that "the liberal principle in business had met its end in Germany," and that JDC must help German Jews enter into those economic fields in which they were still allowed. He was certainly in favor of constructive efforts in Germany: "Even if a district attorney can only open a stenographic office, that is surely better than if these people leave the country and go completely to wrack and ruin." But Kahn was very much against limiting JDC help to reconstruction only. He foresaw the necessity of providing funds to create new schools for Jewish children. At the same time, he thought that Palestine was at least a partial answer to those who could no longer stay in Germany: "Jewish youth and the younger adult must have a permanent land to which to go and, under the circumstances, this can only be Palestine. Of course, exceptionally large amounts are required for the preparation of Palestine and the work for this preparation. For this purpose special means must be provided."[3]

The first immediate problem as far as Germany was concerned was political. Zionists and others demanded protests in the form of Jewish mass meetings. Kahn's opinion was expressed after meeting Morris D. Waldman, the secretary of the American Jewish Committee. He thought that Jewish mass meetings would be useless and might even be harmful. However, he foresaw a time when such meetings, particularly with the participation of prominent non-Jews, might become necessary.[4] In the ensuing months he was to stick to this opinion. On March 21, 1933, Paul Baerwald cabled to the State Department in Washington, asking that American protection be given to the JDC offices in Berlin. That same day, the American Jewish Committee and the B'nai B'rith of America published a protest against Hitler that was published in the *New York Times*. This apparently was considered to be a moderate form of public intervention; friends of JDC in Germany (for example, Edward Baerwald, brother of Paul Baerwald) were opposed to more militant protests.[5]

It was soon clear to Kahn that his position as the European director of JDC was untenable as long as he remained in Berlin. During the last days of March, Kahn prepared his departure. On April 1 he cabled from Paris that the removal of his offices had become unavoidable. He had been personally warned, semiofficially, that because of his connection with the widely hated American Jewish community, his departure from Germany would be desirable. He added: "Future passing of German border not possible without special visa which I very likely would not get; nevertheless prepared return by end week." He never stood on German soil again.[6]

The next day, April 2, Kahn asked for protest meetings along nonsectarian lines, emphasizing the humanitarian interest in what was happening in Germany. However, such protests were to take place only if negotiations then in progress between influential Jews in London and the Nazis were fruitless. Joseph C. Hyman went to Washington to see William Phillips and Pierrepont Moffat at the State Department with this message on April 4. On April 6 a meeting was held at the home of Paul Baerwald, where the leadership of the German Jewish aristocracy in the United States convened. Participants included Henry Morgenthau, Jr., Ludwig Fogelstein, Irving Lehman, Arthur Hays Sulzberger, Judge Rosenman, Solomon Lowenstein, James Marshall, Frederick M. Warburg, Judge Proskauer, Jonah B. Wise, and others. The suggestion was made that the whole situation be turned over to the International Red Cross, but the argument was advanced that IRC could not act except through the local societies of the Red Cross, which would mean that in practice the German Red Cross would have to intervene more or less against the wishes of the German government.

Proskauer, Lehman, and others were very much against what they called "separatist Jewish protests," and wanted whatever protests were made to remain on a purely humanitarian and nonsectarian level.[7] Kahn was asked by cable whether funds could be sent into Germany. His first reply on April 12 was that funds could indeed be sent and that the best people to handle such funds would be the Hilfsverein or CV (Central-Verein deutscher Staatsbürger jüdischen Glaubens), the political organization of liberal Jewry in Germany.

As a nonpolitical organization, JDC could not be involved in any demonstrations against German persecution of the Jews. Such protests, if made, had to be left to the American Jewish Committee, whose leadership, as we have seen, was to a certain extent identical with that of JDC. Influential British Jews tried to convince Felix M. Warburg to put pressure on the American government to try to influence the British government to intervene in behalf of German Jewry. The British prime minister, Ramsay MacDonald, was in the United States during the latter part of April, but Warburg did not place much hope on any direct contact that Jewish leaders might have with the British premier.[8]

The immediate problem confronting JDC was what to do about the new situation that had arisen in Germany. The first reaction was well summed up by Dr. Kahn, who wrote in the memorandum from which we have already quoted that he was of the opinion that JDC could not give up German Jewry as completely lost. JDC had to defend to the last every position that the Jews still held in Germany.[9] This did not mean that JDC was opposed to the emigration of large numbers of German Jews. The panic exodus that followed the Nazis' assumption of power would have made any such position hopeless in any case. The policy of JDC was enunciated clearly by Hyman when he said that, in line with the wishes of the German Jewish body, "there is no hope for the younger generation; that it is therefore necessary to make this group capable of productive activity by being trained to vocations of agriculture, handicraft, and the like," in order to settle outside of Germany.[10] Kahn added that emigration was a necessary part of any future action in Germany. His own opinion was that the tragedy was of such dimensions that one feared to consider its issue. He was convinced that the conditions would not improve. "On the contrary, they must become worse."[11]

One of the immediate steps that JDC took was to send its chief fund raiser, Rabbi Jonah B. Wise, into Germany to try to arrange for a German counterpart to JDC, which would be capable of receiving funds from America and distributing them in line with JDC policy. A leader in this endeavor was Max M. Warburg, Felix M. Warburg's brother, the head of the family banking house in Hamburg. Also involved were Karl Melchior, a high German official and a partner of Warburg in the Hamburg firm, Dr. Cora Berliner, Ludwig Tietz, a physician and a well-known public figure, and others.

Largely because of the work of Max Warburg and Ludwig Tietz, on April 13, 1933, the so-called Zentral-Ausschuss für Hilfe und Aufbau (Central Committee for Help and Reconstruction) was formed. In this, Jonah B. Wise played a significant role. ZA was an umbrella organization that included welfare, educational, emigration, and vocational training organizations that had existed in Germany prior to the events of 1933. Officially, ZA was founded by the provincial organization of the Jewish communities (Landesverbände), which had in their turn created a Reichsvertretung Jüdischer Landesverbände (All-German Association of Jewish Provincial Community Organizations), headed by Judge Wolff and Rabbi Leo Baeck. This first Reichsvertretung (RV) did not last very long, however, German Jewry being influenced more by its major political division into liberal and Zionist wings than it was by the organization of Jewish communities.

In Berlin the head of the community was a very forceful individual by the name of Heinrich Stahl. Stahl wanted RV to be under his own influence, but this proved to be impossible because the major political organizations opposed such a solution. Tietz and Warburg, who had founded ZA, were themselves nonpolitical and, being in sympathy with both the liberal and Zionist wings, thought of themselves as the natural mediators between the two. Tietz went to see Dr. Weizmann in London, and Warburg's connections with JDC through his brother had helped to forge a link with the American Jewish organization. ZA became a success, with Karl Melchior and Tietz at its head, but the first attempts to set up an RV failed almost immediately.

During the summer of 1933 new attempts were made to create an overall political organization of German Jewry. These attempts centered in the community of Essen in western Germany. The initiators were local leaders like Dr. Georg Hirschland and Rabbi Dr. Hugo Hahn. They organized a meeting attended by the leading non-Zionist personalities in Germany and convinced them to set up a countrywide organization which also would be called the Reichsvertretung. It was Max Warburg who persuaded Dr. Baeck to assume leadership of the proposed organization, and it was he who convinced Direktor Stahl to desist from his attempts to create a separatist organization led by the Berlin community, and instead to accept a leading position in the new RV. At last, on September 17, 1933, the new Reichsvertretung came into being, with Dr. Baeck as president, Dr. Otto Hirsch as vice-chairman, and with liberal and Zionist representatives taking a share in the work of the executive committee (Präsidialausschuss).

An immediate connection was established between the new RV and ZA. Baeck was both the president of RV and chairman of ZA. The intelligent and popular Dr. Hirsch, whose experience as a high government official in the south German state of Württemberg helped him to master the difficult work of ZA, was the administrative chairman of RV. Other individuals occupying central positions in RV also occupied parallel positions in ZA. In this way, RV could appear vis-à-vis the Jewish communities as the dispenser of foreign funds and as the organization to which the individual and the community had to turn for practical purposes.[12]

One of the central figures in German Jewry, Dr. Werner Senator, a representative of the non-Zionist groups on the Jewish Agency who had emigrated to Palestine, returned to Germany in order to participate in the work of ZA. In a memorandum submitted to

JDC in August, Senator demanded that German Jewry try to establish a dialogue with the new Nazi authorities. This should lead to a kind of concordat, like the arrangements between the Roman curia and European states, an idea which was by no means new in German Jewry, and which had almost come to fruition before the rise of Hitler to power. Such a concordat should provide for the right of the Jews to leave Germany, as well as for the rights of those who would remain in the country. Such a dialogue, Senator thought, was still possible, though the results might be painful for the Jews. In general, however, Senator agreed to the policy that was by then evolving on the part of the foreign organization toward the German Jewish problem. He emphasized the central position of Palestine in the creation of a new Jewish society where the truly constructive forces of German Jewish youth would go, but he also stressed the necessity for providing havens for such youths in other countries. At the same time, he demanded the defense of German Jewish economic and social positions in the new state to the very last. The negotiations that he proposed with the German authorities should take place on an honorable basis. The implication was that the Jews should reorganize as a national group and that only on that basis would the Nazis deal with them.

While Senator's proposals were not accepted in toto, his way of thinking was by no means unique, both among German Jews and their supporters outside.[13] JDC was inclined to support such an action. Rosen, who visited Germany in June 1933, wrote to Kahn that the aimlessness of German Jewry's endeavors frightened him. Outside pressure might produce some results, he said, but there was no possibility of a real improvement "unless some understanding is arrived at with the government from within."[14]

It was in this atmosphere of hope and illusion that JDC started its great rescue work for German Jewry. Its aim, after the first few months of confusion, seemed to be fairly clear: it had to help in emigration, and it had to provide training facilities for those German youths who left Germany and also for those who would have to stay in the country and adjust to the new anti-Semitic laws that the Nazis were in the process of enacting. Aside from that, there loomed the problem of providing schooling for Jewish children if they were forced out of the general schools. Also, it was essential to support cultural and religious institutions in the hope that these might fortify the sinking morale of German Jewry.

In the meantime, economic disaster had befallen the Jews of Germany. On April 1, 1933, just two months after Hitler's accession to power, the Nazis instituted a boycott of all Jewish stores and Jewish professionals. An official prolongation of that boycott beyond one day was prevented by a vociferous protest movement abroad. However, the elimination of Jews from the German economy proceeded at a very quick pace. On April 4 a decree was published practically revoking the right of Jewish lawyers to practice in Prussia. On April 7 a law ("for the reestablishment of the professional civil service") provided for the forcible retirement of all civil servants who had one Jewish grandparent or more, with a few exceptions. On April 22 Jewish doctors were dropped from panels of sick funds, which until that time had provided most of them with the bulk of their income. A similar law was enacted on June 2 for dentists. After September 29 authors, actors, and musicians (and after October 4, journalists as well) had to belong to Nazi organizations, which of course excluded Jews. On June 30 officials and professors of the "Jewish race" were, to all intents and purposes, banned from exercising their functions in government and universities. By the end of June, Kahn estimated that 20 percent, or about 33,700 of the gainfully employed Jews, had lost their jobs.[15]

The worst, however, was not the legal situation, but the permanent insecurity that now had entered German Jewish life and was to remain until the final destruction. Nazi officials used to deny that the boycott against the Jews was still in existence after April 1, 1933, but in practice the boycott not only did not stop—it increased in ferocity as time went on. German Jewry, with its peculiar occupational stratification, was particularly vulnerable to this kind of economic warfare. Over 60 percent of gainfully occupied

Jews engaged in trade.[16] In the beginning the Nazis made what seemed to be certain exceptions in their anti-Jewish measures. This was done in deference to pressure by President Hindenburg. They declared that 1 percent of the persons in official positions could be Jews; pre-1914 public servants and people who had been frontline soldiers in World War I were also to remain. However, in practice, these exceptions were quite insignificant. Among the people regarded as Jewish, the Nazis included persons with one Jewish grandfather. Also, only those who were politically reliable could keep their positions. Of the six thousand Jewish public servants in Germany, at least five thousand lost their jobs during the first months of the Nazi regime. Of twenty-eight hundred Jewish lawyers, at least fifteen hundred lost their jobs in April 1933. Of seven thousand Jewish doctors, four to five thousand were to lose their livelihood during those spring months; a similar fate was in store for dentists, druggists and chemists, municipal officials, and public welfare workers, who together numbered another twenty-five hundred gainfully employed people. The actors, musicians, journalists, and others accounted for some thirteen to fifteen thousand Jews who were now out of work. Although their numbers were not very significant, Jewish workers were deprived of the possibility of maintaining their jobs as the Nazi regime tightened its hold over Germany. A law was passed forbidding Jewish membership in the official Nazi worker's organization, the Arbeitsfront. All workers who wished to take advantage of insurance, sick benefits, and other essentials had to belong to the Arbeitsfront. Soon there were no German workers who did not belong to that organization—except Jews.

The importance of all these factors for an organization like JDC which wished to help German Jewry was all too clear. "All that has been done during the past fifty years by world Jewry for their oppressed and needy brethren all over the world will now have to be repeated within three to five years for German Jewry alone."[17]

On the education front the picture was no better. No German school could have Jewish students in excess of 5 percent of the total enrollment. Up to that time the percentage of Jews in German high schools had exceeded 10 percent. Only 1.5 percent of new pupils in the universities could be Jews, and among the older students only 5 percent could be Jews. No East European Jew who had arrived in Germany after 1914 could be a student at a German university. All these factors presented JDC with an emergency situation.

The total number of Jews in Germany in 1933 was officially listed as 499,682. However, this included only people who had declared themselves as Jews by religion. Additional tens of thousands of people were Jewish by Nazi definition. There were 50,000 individuals who were sons and daughters of Jewish parents but did not belong to the Jewish community living in Germany at that time, an estimated 35,000 of whom were partners in mixed marriages. So-called three-quarter Jews (that is, people who had only one non-Jewish grandparent but did not belong to the Jewish community) numbered about 2,000. Half Jews (that is, people who had two non-Jewish grandparents) were estimated at 210,000 people, and quarter Jews were estimated at 80,000 individuals. This meant that what the Nazis considered to be the non-Aryan population of Germany—that is, Jews, three-quarter Jews, and half Jews—numbered together about 760,000 people.[18]

ZA had to deal not only with the members of the Jewish community, but also with fairly large numbers of those who, although of Jewish parentage, had severed their link with the Jewish community prior to the Nazi rise to power. The various components of ZA dealt with different aspects of the German Jewish situation. The Hilfsverein was the emigration agency for countries other than Palestine or Eastern Europe; the Palästinaamt dealt with emigration to Palestine; the Hauptstelle for Jewish wanderers dealt with repatriation of East European Jews to their countries of origin. In addition, CV was also a part of ZA, as were the welfare organization of German Jews (Zentralwohlfahrtsstelle), the committee for education of RV, the center for economic aid, the center for Jewish loan *kassas,* the united center for Jewish labor exchanges, and the organization of Jewish women.

The immediate major problem as far as Germany was concerned was that of emigration. With the rise of the Nazis to power, large numbers of terrorized Jews crowded the offices of the Hilfsverein and the Palestine office in search of an opportunity—any opportunity—to leave Germany. Quite a number of people who had crossed the frontiers into some of the West European countries had to return to Germany soon afterward because they could not find a place to live or an occupation that would provide them with a livelihood.

The exodus of 1933, which was brought on by panic, soon subsided. At first, exaggerated figures were given as to the number of those who had left Germany. At the end of 1933 fifty-two thousand Jews were said to have fled Germany. However, it appears that a considerably smaller number left the country. Apparently not more than thirty-seven to forty thousand Jews actually left Germany during that year and stayed away.[19]

Yet the problem of whether to support emigration from Germany, and to what extent, was to be an ongoing one for the Jewish organizations outside the country. JDC, as well as other organizations, had to come to grips with the emigration problem. The official position of JDC was to support an organized and orderly emigration and oppose a panicky and disorderly flow. Yet its emigration work was not universally accepted by its lay leaders in America. These voices were echoing their German counterparts. Thus the Reform group in Berlin stated on May 1, 1933: "We have absolutely no intention of cutting ourselves off from our German national community and our national ties and of changing over to a Jewish national or folk community."[20] The liberal paper *CV-Zeitung* in Germany echoed this sentiment as late as May 9, 1935, when it asked why the Jews should help the German government to liquidate the Jewish problem by organizing their own exodus while more than half of the German Jews still looked upon Germany as their home and would remain there.[21]

Many Jews in Great Britain and America held a similar view. On October 11, 1935, the *Jewish Chronicle* in London asked whether we are to confess ourselves, as well as the cause of tolerance, beaten, and evacuate the German Jews, nearly half a million of them, to God knows what other country. . . . Repulsive? Yes, indeed it is scuttling! . . . Jews will fight on. There is no other cause. Better help them than beckon them to a surrender which would disgrace them in the eyes of history and be denounced by all lovers of progress—even, perhaps, by a future regenerate Germany—as a betrayal of humanity.[22]

The chief proponents of such opinions in JDC councils were James Marshall and James N. Rosenberg. Marshall thought that emigration was "a concession to the Hitler theory that the Jews must get out." Emigration "helped only a few people, whereas the bulk of the problem has to be handled in Germany itself."[23] In light of the economic difficulties that prevailed in other countries, JDC was only aggravating the Jewish situation there by encouraging emigration, without substantially alleviating the situation in Germany.

Moreover, there were other groups in Germany that have seriously suffered. Mr. Marshall felt that in trying to emigrate, German Jews tended to set themselves off from other groups who in the long run would be helpful to them. These were issues of fundamental importance, and it was not worth the price of losing out on them to get a few thousand Jews out of Germany; neither was it helpful to bring large numbers of Jews into Palestine at this time.

Rosenberg added that "he was not willing to accept the Nationalist Separatist philosophy of Zionism, for he valued his American citizenship too much for that."

To voices like these, Warburg had a simple answer: "The German Jews want to leave and have come to JDC with their problems. JDC contributors wish to help reeducate and retrain German Jews and get them out."[24] The general line of JDC on the emigration issue was that there had to be as much emigration as there were places that could be found for immigrants.[25] Warburg, Baerwald, Hyman, and the majority of the lay leaders accepted Kahn's view that German anti-Semitism was not "a passing violent action, that comes with all revolutionary movements, or temporary legal discrimination that may be abolished again, or may quiet down."[26] Anti-Semitism was the fundamental basis of the new German state. There was no place there for German Jews. German policy was to get rid of the Jews. When this would be achieved was hard to say. It could take a generation or more if the present government stayed that long, or it could come about sooner.

There was no contradiction between that and the JDC view that "by the hundreds of thousands they must remain there, and we must lend them our sympathetic help," as Rosen stated. He added that it was very tragic to be a German Jewish refugee in Paris in 1934, a place where he was equally unwanted as in his German home and where he was not allowed to earn a living. In these circumstances it was sometimes even better to stay in Germany and to work out some salvation there.[27] Rosen's opinion was based on some harsh facts: because of the difficulty of obtaining entry visas to various countries, not more than fifteen to twenty thousand Jews could hope to leave Germany yearly; over half the German Jews would have to remain there, at least for ten more years, whatever the conditions.[28]

The consequences of this stand by JDC were sometimes rather confusing. Jonah B. Wise stated early in 1934[29] that (a) there was no decent future for the Jews in Germany; (b) some would have to remain and adjust there; and (c) Germany had been and would continue to be a center of Jewish and world culture. Palestine, and emigration generally, were not the only answer.

But slowly, inexorably, it became apparent that all other aspects of German work, while necessary and important in themselves, were secondary to the necessity of removing as many Jews as possible from Hitler's grasp. This was not altogether evident in 1934, when many saw a certain stabilization in the Nazi regime's attitude to the Jews; but by 1935, and especially after the promulgation of the Nuremberg laws in that year, the situation had become clear.

In May 1935 Max Kreutzberger, secretary of ZA, declared to

the members of the JDC's Executive Committee that while in the beginning there might have been divergent views and opinions, by now all elements of German Jewry regarded their condition as hopeless. The younger generation had to be prepared for an exodus, and the only course for those who remained was to let them live out their old age and die in peace.[30] JDC's leaders had always taken a clear stand in opposition to a program like that. They had opposed mass emigration from countries where anti-Semitism was rampant. Their argument had been that any such emigration was a surrender to antiliberalism, and that Jews should fight and strive to become equal and loyal citizens of their countries of adoption, as they had in America. This theoretical position was bravely defended as late as 1937 by Joseph C. Hyman, when he said, in a letter to Prof. Oscar I. Janowsky, that anti-Semitism was but a temporary setback to democracy and liberalism. "We still believe that a way can be found to integrate the Jew with his environment under a liberal and tolerant system of society. . . . I am not so sure that it is impossible, in this vale of tears, to count on strengthening goodwill between the Jew and his neighbors."[31]

All this was theory; from a practical point of view, JDC had to take realities into account—and the realities were unfortunately quite different from the liberal theories of Hyman and his friends. The practical efforts of JDC were directed toward vocational readjustment, the establishment of loan *kassas,* help in education, relief, aid to cultural institutions, and emigration—to Palestine, to other countries—and also repatriation of East European Jews. However, contrary to its mode of operation in Poland, JDC wished to have nothing to do with the actual administration of the funds. ZA submitted reports and suggested allocations for a variety of purposes, to which JDC usually agreed, because in Germany, unlike Poland, JDC found men and institutions who could be relied upon to administer the funds in a satisfactory manner. The men and women in Germany, after all, were people with the same kind of background as the leadership of JDC itself; and with the establishment of ZA, in which JDC had been involved, a responsible central Jewish body was created of the type that JDC had wanted to see everywhere, which could now take over tasks of a practical nature. In this way JDC actually contributed to the first centralized institution German Jewry had known in modern times.

For Kahn, who was administering the funds in Europe, it was obvious that vocational retraining was essential on two counts— first, because the elimination of Jews from trade and the professions left open only manual labor as a possibility for Jews in Germany; and second, because only manual workers of various kinds might hope to be accepted as immigrants to other countries. To make matters worse, unemployment among Jews had been serious even before the Nazi repressions. In Berlin alone Jewish unemployment in October 1932 was put at 7,372. If one added the unregistered, this would have reached 10,000–11,000, or about 25 percent of all Jewish wage earners.[32] Under the circumstances, the various autonomous organizations affiliated with ZA started a large-scale program of vocational training directed largely toward agriculture, gardening, domestic science (for girls), and crafts, mainly carpentry and metal work.

Part of these courses were organized by Hechalutz, the Zionist organization training pioneers for Palestine, which increased its membership from about five hundred prior to Hitler's rise to some ten thousand after he came to power. In 1933 approximately twenty-three hundred youngsters, just slightly below half the total, were receiving training (largely agricultural) at Hechalutz centers; but some of the others made it to Palestine too, even though their training was not directed specifically toward any country of immi-

T A B L E   3
Vocational Training in Germany[33]

Year	1933	Jan. 1934	July 1934	Dec. 1934	1935	1936	1938
No. of Trainees	5,169	6,069	6,771	4,005	7,346	7,676	3,068

gration. A number were directed specifically to South America. For instance, a farm at Neuendorf had been founded as early as 1931 by non-Zionist groups such as Jüdische Wanderfürsorge (Care of Jewish Migrants)—which was later to engage in the repatriation of East Europeans—to train farmers for the ICA project at Avigdor in Argentina, where many of the trainees eventually went.

In early 1936 RV established another large farm, Gross-Breesen, under Dr. Kurt Bondy, for 125 trainees. While the Zionists opposed the principle of its establishment, some Zionists (for example, Dr. Georg Lubinski) acted as special advisers. Gross-Breesen was a Jewish estate in Silesia, and after it opened in May 1936 it trained people for agricultural and carpentry work. The leaders of RV, men like Otto Hirsch and Julius Seligsohn and other liberal leaders, saw Gross-Breesen as a ray of hope for liberal Jewry in Germany. The inspired leadership of a great educator like Bondy gave a measure of excellence to character training at the farm, besides its real technical achievements. By the spring of 1938 Gross-Breesen was actually self-supporting. But emigration plans lagged, and in 1938 plans for group settlement had to be abandoned, despite JDC attempts to settle the groups in Virginia with the help of a generous Jewish citizen of Richmond, William B. Thalheimer. (Ultimately, a small settlement was founded there at Hyde Farmlands, which lasted until 1941.) After the November 1938 pogrom most of the trainees, including Bondy, went to Holland and England.[34]

The Zionists, on the other hand, concentrated a great deal of their efforts on taking German Jewish youngsters out of Germany and training them for Palestine in other European countries, away from the Nazi atmosphere. There was one such center in existence prior to 1933, namely, the one at Deventer, Holland, which had been established in 1918. By 1936 there were 1,248 youngsters who were being trained in twenty-six centers. These also included some that were not exclusively Palestine-oriented, such as Wieringen in Holland. Holland took 378 of these young people, Czechoslovakia

141, France 124, Denmark 213, Fascist Italy 137, and little Luxemburg 88; the rest were sent to various other countries. Among the problems that were never solved was the lack of girls and of professions to train them in.

Most of the training was agricultural, which accounted for over 80 percent of the work done abroad. Hechalutz usually tried to lease farms where the people could live communally; but sometimes this did not work out, as in Denmark and Czechoslovakia, and the trainees were forced to live with individual peasants— which of course limited the possibilities for cultural and religious activities. There were certain places, as in Luxemburg, where only the fittest were sent, because work was especially hard in the vineyards of that country. Nevertheless, the vast majority withstood these trials, and many of them did go to Palestine and other countries in the end. In the towns, communal centers were set up for those who were learning a trade or a craft, some of them with aid of ORT (as in Lithuania).[35] All this activity, known as Auslandshachsharah (Foreign Training), was largely organized by Shalom Adler-Rudel, a Zionist expert in the training field, and by the German Hechalutz, with some JDC supervision and financial support. After 1936 the Foreign Training program declined, because it became more and more difficult to place German Jewish youngsters in training abroad. By 1937 only 774 were in training.[36] Nevertheless, many hundreds of youngsters had found their emigration prospects enhanced by participation in these programs.

Connected with problems of training was the larger question of the future of German Jewish children generally. Owing to the great emphasis Jewish tradition placed on children and their education, stress was laid on programs that dealt with solutions for the younger generation. As early as 1932 Recha Freier, wife of a Berlin rabbi, a wonderful and immensely strong-willed woman, foresaw the need to save the Jewish children. She set up an umbrella organization composed of the following groups: representatives of the Ahavah home, a famous children's institution in Germany, which was then in the process of moving to Palestine; representatives of the Palestine children's village, Ben Shemen, which was under the direction of a great German Jewish teacher, Ernst Lehman; and a unified body representing all the Zionist youth movements in Germany. On July 14, 1933, the umbrella organization, the Working Body for Children and Youth Aliyah, submitted a plan to ZA for settling six hundred children in Palestine by 1934, at a cost of 293,300 German marks.[37] It would accept children between the ages of thirteen and sixteen, who would be sent to institutions like Ahavah or Ben Shemen or to kibbutzim, or placed with individual families. The program was adopted, and in Palestine a central organization known as Youth Aliyah (immigration to Palestine) was set up, headed by the veteran American Zionist Henrietta Szold. After a six-month training course in Germany, the children, who had been very carefully screened, were sent to Palestine. It was only in 1936, however, when 640 Youth Aliyah children had reached in Palestine, that the original 1933 goal was finally met. But the adjustment made by the children was very successful, and the JDC funds were well used through this program to pay for part of the cost both of training and of transportation.

From the inner circle of the JDC leadership in America, too, there was a response to the need to save children. In October 1933 Dr. Solomon Lowenstein and Jacob Billikopf, head of the National Conference of Jewish Social Workers, were instrumental in setting up a committee known as the German Jewish Children's Aid to deal with the transfer of children from Germany to the United States. It was difficult for the liberal Jews of America to accept the need for the emigration of German Jewry, especially that of unaccompanied children. It was doubted that German Jewish parents would consent to the procedure. Hyman told Billikopf that it was preferable to send the children to German-speaking countries on the Continent rather than overseas, and that it would be even better to keep them in Germany altogether.[38] There were great legal and financial difficulties. A guarantee of $500 per year for each child had to be given and the placement of children with families "had encountered a great many difficulties." Nevertheless, a first group of fifty-three children arrived in America in November 1934. But Dr. Lowenstein declared in May 1935 that "the expenditure would seem out of proportion to the amount actually required for general relief in Germany for tremendously large numbers of persons and projects. We have, therefore, regretfully, come to the conclusion that we could not bring over any other children."[39] By that time about 150 had been brought here.

After the fall of 1935 the immigration of children became feasible again, and by early 1937 the committee had filled its original quota of 250 children (actually 235) and continued to accept them at a rate of 10 to 12 a month. The total number of children who came to the United States under this program until the outbreak of the war in 1939 was 433.[40]

A beginning was also made in children's emigration to England and Switzerland, where 18 children were placed in 1933 and 1934. All these efforts made very little difference statistically to the estimated 101,000 children under fifteen who lived in Germany in 1934. Psychologically, however, parental consent to the emigration of about 1,000 unaccompanied youngsters by 1938 made a significant difference to the climate of exodus that was swiftly engulfing German Jewry. People began to be willing, especially after 1935, to send away their most precious possession—their children—to more hospitable lands.

No matter how large the special emigration programs for children might be, a large majority of them had to remain in Germany. As these children were slowly forced out of the general school system, the need arose to give them a Jewish and humanist education in special Jewish schools. Because of the small funds JDC had at its disposal at the beginning of what was inappropriately called "the German emergency," Kahn was at first against founding new institutions, for which large capital investments would have to be made.[41] He was in favor of increasing the number of children in the existing schools by enlarging them, and he vigorously defended the need to provide funds for Jewish education. The British Jews, mostly Zionists, argued that no money should be given for schools

in Germany, as the children would soon be brought out in any case.
However, reality soon made this discussion academic.

In early 1933 only six thousand out of some fifty thousand
Jewish children went to Jewish schools, but the numbers grew by
leaps and bounds each year.[42] This tremendous effort to absorb
children who were driven out of schools by the attitude of class-
mates and teachers and the general hate-filled atmosphere[43] was
made possible by the resolution on the part of the German Jewish
educational and spiritual leadership, men like Leo Baeck, Martin
Buber, Ernst Simon, and others, to build a better spiritual world
for Jewry by returning to Jewish and humanist values and tradi-
tions. There probably were few eras in German Jewish history
when there was such a flowering of Jewish education and thought
as in those short years prior to the catastrophe. JDC, unlike the
British organizations, insisted on aiding and supporting these activities. Kahn especially was a convinced believer in the value of
spiritual resistance, and he encouraged the German leaders to use
the funds they had for purposes such as these.

An area of activity that had to be included in ZA work, which
JDC strived to avoid as much as possible in Eastern Europe, was
relief. In Germany there was little choice: JDC understood the
need and supported large expenditures for relief. The number of
welfare recipients prior to 1938 usually averaged about 20 percent
of the Jewish population. For example, in 1935/6 the number was
83,761; this increased somewhat in 1937. In addition, funds were

T A B L E 4
Jewish Schools in Germany

Year	No. of schools	No. of pupils	Total Jewish children of school age
1933	70	14,300	50,000
1935	130	20,000	
1937	167	23,670	39,000

given to the Jewish Winter Help, though during the first years of the German regime some aid was still received from the German government. (Indeed, the Germanic mind operated so efficiently that until the outbreak of war, even those Jewish recipients of government pensions who lived abroad received them punctually.)

However, the continual decline of the Jewish population expressed itself in the impoverishment of the local communities, where most people in need had been receiving help without recourse to the central organizations, and in the parallel population movement from small towns to large urban centers. In 1937, of the 1,400 or so communities *(Gemeinden)*, 309 were classified by ZA as being in need and 303 as partly in need; 120 more asked to be placed in that category. Berlin itself had fifteen soup kitchens, where large numbers of free meals were given out, and about one-third of the total public Jewish funds in Germany were spent on welfare in 1935.[44] German Jewish welfare was efficient and followed modern practice—a whole generation of Jewish welfare workers had, after all, been trained in Germany prior to Hitler, although with quite different prospects in view.

JDC reacted to the German situation with great speed. The sum of $40,000 was sent to Germany immediately after Hitler's assumption of power; and after Jonah B. Wise's trip, $254,000 was sent.[45] The JDC offices in Berlin were searched by the Nazis in May 1933, whereupon Hyman spoke to the U.S. State Department, and the American consul in Berlin intervened "energetically and effectively," as did the British consul.[46] After that, the JDC office in Berlin was maintained only formally, under Prof. Eugen Mittwoch, who was responsible for it until 1939.

Very soon the problem arose of whether to send dollars into Germany. In 1933 and 1934, and to some extent even in 1935, dollars were sent in; but JDC was looking for a way to prevent foreign currency from accruing to the Nazi regime through JDC's support of German Jewry. As early as July 24, 1933, James N. Rosenberg penned a memo to Paul Baerwald and Felix M. Warburg saying he was against sending dollars to Germany,[47] and by the end of the year a way was found to avoid this. In a letter dated December 16, 1933, Eric Warburg, son of Max M. Warburg, wrote to James N. Rosenberg that the German Jewish financial expert and friend of the Warburg house, Hans Schaeffer, had worked out the so-called educational transfer plan, which had the approval of the German authorities.[48] Under this scheme well-to-do parents would send their children abroad to study; they would pay for this in German marks at a somewhat higher rate than usual, the money to be given to ZA or RV. JDC would then pay all the children's fees and expenses in hard currency abroad. It took some time until all the needs of ZA could be covered in this way, but generally speaking no dollars were sent into Germany by JDC after 1935. ZA's budget was for the central organizations only. The communities had their own budgets and raised taxes to meet them. ZA's central budget was met by local collections, contributions by the communities, and the grants of foreign organizations. But in actual fact, German Jews were covering the larger part of their needs themselves, and JDC contributed only to a part of the German Jewish community's effort, namely, to the budget of ZA.

The money thus received was then spent on the various ZA activities in different proportions. For example, in 1935 emigration accounted for some 20 percent of the expenditure, whereas in 1936 this rose to about 40 percent. Economic aid and vocational training remained fairly stable at around 25 percent of the budget. All the other items—schools, welfare, organizations, and the like—took less by percentage, but with the overall increase in the budget this did not mean a reduction in absolute figures. On the whole, these were the proportions that prevailed in subsequent years as well.

Some small sums of money allocated by JDC to Germany did not go through ZA. Late in 1933 the American Friends Service Committee (AFSC) offered their help in dealing with individual cases in Germany, where operations through recognized German agencies were impossible or inconvenient. Much of this work was actually only half legal, and the Quakers did the job very efficiently. The relationship between the two agencies, based on a common

T A B L E 5
JDC Expenditures in Germany[49]
(In German marks—about 2.5 marks per $)

Year	JDC expenditure*	Total ZA budget	Total raised in Germany†	JDC percentage of ZA budget‡
1934	855,427	2,418,146	13,000,000	35.0%
1935	933,000	2,863,000	21,000,000	32.5%
1936	1,188,884	4,123,125		28.7%
1937	1,610,000	4,400,000	20,000,000	36.3%

*JDC in New York had the following figures (this included small allocations that did not go through the ZA budget): 1933: $197,000; 1934: $440,000; 1935: $290,000; 1936: $546,000; 1937: $686,000.[50]

†That is, the total sums raised for public purposes by all Jewish groups, communities, and organizations, including RV and ZA.

‡Local fund raising brought forth 42.8 percent of the funds for the 1935 budget of ZA, 41 percent in 1936, and 35.8 percent in 1937. The difference between that and the JDC contribution, on one hand, and the total required, on the other, was provided largely by ICA and the Central British Fund for German Jewry (CBF).

idea of service without political strings, had been very close ever since World War I; in the German emergency this relationship prompted Kahn to say, "I should like to do something for the Quakers, who have behaved very well, as always."[51]

Reports by W. R. Hughes, the Quaker representative in Germany in 1934/5, gave JDC some insight into the type of work the Quakers did. Apart from the Quakers, JDC also gave money to other nonsectarian efforts, the total for the period up to 1936 being $116,557.[52]

The problem of Jews being able to take out enough capital to start a new life outside of Germany occupied JDC's attention to a large degree. The Germans had no interest in this, of course, because one of their aims in pressing for Jewish emigration was to spread anti-Semitism abroad by dumping poor Jews on unwilling countries; another aim was to use the money of rich Jews to get rid

of the poor ones; and a third was to squeeze the Jews dry before
they were allowed out of the country. The fact that all this stood
in contradiction to the Nazi aim of ridding Germany of as many
Jews as possible did not bother the Germans. But whenever it was
possible to gain a commercial or political advantage, or whenever
foreign pressure made it a desirable thing to yield on the question
of allowing the emigration of Jewish capital, the Nazis might re-
lent.

In August 1933 the Haavarah agreement was arrived at between
Palestinian Jewish interests supported by the Jewish Agency and
the Germans; under this agreement Jews could transfer capital to
Palestine—by promoting German exports to that country. The
procedure was as follows: a Jewish immigrant deposited his money
(usually the equivalent of the 1,000 pounds that entitled him to a
"capitalist" immigration certificate to Palestine) in a German
bank; then a German exporter shipped goods to Palestine for which
he was paid with the immigrant's money; in Palestine the goods
were sold to customers who paid the price to an authorized bank,
which in turn paid it out to the immigrant. The Jewish Agency
justified this arrangement by saying that it was essential to save
Jews and their money, and that importing capital into Palestine
enabled that country to absorb many others who came there without means. According to one calculation, the total transferred by
Haavarah between 1933 and the end of 1937 amounted to about
4,400,000 pounds.[53] JDC had no part in this particular transfer
scheme, but the program aroused its interest because it shared the
view of the Jewish Agency that no stone should be left unturned
in the effort to bring Jewish capital out of Germany, and thereby
improve the prospects of emigration for those who had to leave.

In Germany it was mainly Max M. Warburg who displayed
great interest in that sort of plan. The Germans at first allowed
Jewish men of means to buy free foreign currency at tremendously
inflated prices through a special office (Golddiskontstelle); then in
1936 another office, the Reichsstelle für Devisenbeschaffung, allowed the transfers of sums up to 4,000 gold marks, for which 8,000

marks were paid in Germany—although people actually had to pay in considerably more than that under various pretenses. In early 1937 a Jewish bank called Altreu was established to receive these payments, which then went partly to finance ZA. Whereas the Haavarah bank—the Paltreu—dealt with transfers to Palestine or to the Middle East only, Altreu transferred monies to other countries.

Warburg was connected with all these ventures. He was also behind the establishment, in March 1936, of a bank in London called the International Trade and Investment Agency (INTRIA), whose managing director was Siegfried Moses, a German Zionist. This bank placed orders for German goods in Germany; Altreu then paid for them out of the funds paid into it by emigrants. The goods were then sold outside Germany, and the emigrant received his money back in foreign currency from INTRIA when he arrived in his country of destination. The principle was the same as with Haavarah, and really amounted to saving Jewish capital at the price of promoting German exports, albeit with no foreign currency accruing to the Germans.[54]

In the summer of 1936 the Germans suggested to JDC a somewhat different arrangement for the transfer of funds: the emigrants would pay the German marks into a JDC account in Germany; the Germans would give to JDC Polish zloty for their marks (Germany had a superabundance of zloty at the time), and this would finance JDC programs in Poland; JDC would then pay the emigrant back in foreign currency once he had left Germany. Kahn's answer was negative, because the Polish program was too small to satisfy the capital transfer needs of German Jewish emigrants; in any case, Zionist funds in Poland were used to effect a similar arrangement between JDC and the Jewish Agency (the Jewish Agency getting pounds in Palestine from JDC in return for its Polish zloty, which were used by JDC in Poland). Obviously, the Jewish Agency arrangement was preferred.[55]

By 1937 another plan for the transfer of funds was arranged—the "benevolent" marks. A benefactor outside Germany who wished to help an individual in Germany would pay a sum of money into a bank in his own country. The bank would transfer the money to INTRIA. The equivalent of that sum in marks would then be paid by Altreu to the recipient in Germany out of funds deposited by an emigrant. When that emigrant left Germany, the money would be repaid to him by INTRIA. There was no export involved in this kind of transaction, and JDC, which was of two minds about the various export arrangements, had no hesitation in supporting this scheme. It was estimated that in 1937 some $400,-000 was transferred to Germany in this way.[56] The Germans, for reasons of their own, liberalized these arrangements in late 1937 and early 1938; people could pay up to 50,000 marks to Altreu, and sometimes received up to 50 percent of this sum in foreign currency. RV received a certain percentage of these monies for its operations. However, on the whole JDC tried to avoid any direct connection with these banks and agencies, children of Max M. Warburg's resourceful brain—many Jews were opposed to any kind of transaction with Nazi Germany, and JDC was intent on remaining as independent as possible, and not exposing itself to attack by any side.

Reconstruction was, of course, another sphere of activity in which JDC took a very special interest. Much was said about the need for reconstruction in the German situation, though the emphasis on this decreased as the Nazi intent to evict the Jews became obvious. In the early 1930s, however, this was not quite so clear,

---

T A B L E 6
Loan Kassas *of the Reconstruction Foundation in Germany*

Year	No. of kassas	Capital (in marks)	No. of loans	Amount loaned (in marks)
1933	42	934,000	1417	465,000
1935	60	848,000		880,000
1937	45		3500	1,070,000

and JDC tried, through the Reconstruction Foundation, to create loan *kassas* in Germany on the well-tried East European model.

After 1937 a swift decline set in as the German government made the *kassas* operations practically impossible, and at the end of 1938 they were terminated. JDC also tried to create Free Loan *kassas* outside the Reconstruction Foundation system, as in Poland, and invested over 400,000 marks in them between 1933 and 1937. But before they could take root, the Nazis made their operations impossible too, and they were liquidated along with the rest of the *kassas* in December 1938.[57]

The situation in Germany itself fluctuated from year to year. It cannot even be said that there was always a distinct trend for the worse. For instance, in 1934—the year of the great purge in the Nazi party (June 30)—it seemed that the anti-Semitic wave had abated slightly, and there was no new wave of terror or boycott directed against the Jews. "Superficially regarded," said Kahn, "it would appear that a certain halt has been called in Germany to the measures adopted against the Jewish population."[58] Hitler himself had reportedly said as much at a meeting with the German *Statthälter* (state governors). In other words, there was still room for a certain measure of self-delusion.

Against that background a great controversy between the nationalist and liberal wings of Jewry continued in Germany. Zionists demanded the recognition of Jewish separateness on the basis of Jewish national identification. The liberal CV rejected this point of view with "determined unanimity," because they saw in Germany the center of their endeavors "now, just as in the past."[59] The liberal Jews of Germany obviously thought that they would outlast the Hitler regime, and in 1934 and early 1935 it was still possible to believe that. In early 1935 Dr. Jonah B. Wise, one of the leaders of JDC, who had just come back from Europe, agreed with this position mainly from a pragmatic point of view. The question was "to meet the onslaught of Hitler and survive it. They [the German Jews] feel they have possibilities of surviving for some years. If conditions do not radically change, many affluent persons will remain in Germany. Most of them will remain because there is no place for them to go and no country wants people over forty unless they have the highest specialization for some work." However, Wise added a remark that reflected a growing conviction among German Jews in the spring of 1935: "That the young people will leave is almost certain. It is said that Germany will be an old folks' home and a graveyard."[60]

RV was largely under the control of liberals like Hirsch, Seligsohn, and Brodnitz. At the end of 1933 it came out with a declaration supporting Hitler's foreign policy; this was done not because of Nazi pressure but because of the German-centered convictions of its leading members. In January 1935 it "heartily welcomed home" the forty-eight hundred "Jewish Saar Germans" after the Saar plebiscite had resulted in the annexation of that area by Germany. (Saarlander Jews even came from abroad to vote for the inclusion of the region in Germany![61])

There was an even more extremist Germanic section of Jewry, led by Dr. Max Naumann, whose organization tried to create a category called the National German Jews (Nationaldeutsche Juden). "We would regard it as a national calamity for Germany and for us National Jews, who are among the best Germans, if Hitler did not take the fate of the German people in his hands. The members of our league, more than five thousand people, voted as one man for Hitler as Reich president. Hitler is our future. No one but he can solve the Jewish question."[62] This, of course, was the opinion of but a small lunatic fringe, but it is significant that these opinions should have been stated as late as the end of 1934 and early 1935.

RV, however, was far from a supine servant of the Nazi dictatorship. Throughout 1935 Baeck and Hirsch and their friends tried to fight back, supported by the foreign organizations, and took their case to the still-legal Jewish press in Germany. For instance, on February 8, 1935, the *CV-Zeitung* published a frontal attack by Rabbi Eschelbacher on *Der Stürmer,* Julius Streicher's obscenely anti-Semitic paper.[63] In the same issue there was a direct attack against Streicher himself, for "accusing" an opposition leader—

wrongly—of being Jewish. One argument used by RV was that since the Nazi rule was totalitarian, the Nazis could have done more against the Jews than they actually did. Since "only" certain restrictions were in force, the conclusion was that German Jewry had the right to fight back on the basis of the actual laws on the books, that they could prevent a worsening of the situation by appealing to the law.[64] In the January 31, 1935, issue there was even a public protest by RV, signed by Baeck and Hirsch, against Streicher. Entitled "The Honor of German Jews," it culminated in the statement that "for the guarding of our honor nothing remains to us but a solemn public protest."[65] A possibility of appealing to the courts under the laws of libel was hinted at.

This point was made in even more explicit terms on February 14, when a direct attack was printed on the Nazi minister Schemm, the "leader" of the Nazi Teachers' Association, who had abused the Jewish religion. Schemm was told that he had thereby maligned the Christian God and had "harshly insulted, not only the religious feelings of German Jews, but those of Jews all over the world as well."[66] The Zionist *Jüdische Rundschau* published an article demanding that the government cease to defame Jews, that it guarantee decent material conditions under prevailing legislation, and that it establish orderly emigration procedures and autonomous cultural institutions.[67] It must be remembered that this took place in Nazi Germany almost two years after the abolition of all parties and the independent press. The courage displayed by RV was wholly admirable, but of course no results were achieved.

All these attempts at maintaining a foothold in Germany collapsed with the publication of the Nuremberg racial laws on September 15, and the first of twelve detailed provisions *(Verordnungen)* on November 14, 1935. Immediately following the publication, RV came out with a four-point program demanding that, on the basis of the new laws, the government stop the defamation and the boycott, grant cultural and religious autonomy to the Jews, and recognize RV as the central Jewish organization. Under these conditions, the Jews would accept the new laws.[68]

This stand produced a bitter argument between the Zionists,

who demanded nonrecognition of the Nuremberg laws, and the RV leadership. The Zionists had been in the peculiar position of opposing the Nazis more vigorously than the liberals and yet being supported, in a way, by the government because of their advocacy of emigration to Palestine. The Nazis argued that Zionists helped Germany solve the Jewish problem and that Palestine could absorb a million Jews. If only half of these were German Jews, then the whole Jewish problem might be solved.[69] This did not mean, of course, that the Nazis did not attack the Zionists as well; Goebbels's *Angriff* did so frequently.

Inside the Jewish community, the Zionists pressed for a policy of national definition and speedy emigration, and demanded a greater say in the affairs of RV. A spokesman of the Zionist Right in the Berlin community (the so-called Jewish Volkspartei), Georg Kareski, took a different position in an interview published in the *Angriff* (quoted in the *Jewish Chronicle,* January 3, 1936), where he defended the new laws as offering an answer to the problem of an alien nationality, provided they were executed on a basis of mutual respect. The Zionists now turned against Kareski as well, and he was practically ostracized at a conference held at Berlin in early February 1936. However, during the following year Kareski tried repeatedly to oppose a reconstructed RV, in which the Zionists now had a greater say.

This situation came to a head in the spring of 1937 when the leaders of RV appealed to the foreign organizations to prevent the takeover of RV by Kareski, who, they insinuated, was cooperating with the Gestapo. After consultation between JDC and the British Jews, on June 11, 1937, a letter was written over the signature of Sir Herbert Samuel to Leo Baeck, in which confidence was reiterated in "the present personnel and management" of RV. Serious misgivings were expressed in the event of any change in the composition of RV.[70] It is not clear whether it was this intervention that changed the situation, but it is probable that it had at least some influence. At any rate, RV maintained its independence of internal Gestapo pressure for some time longer, and Kareski's attempt was repulsed.

The problem of Zionism exercised JDC, too, to a considerable extent, though from a different angle. In the United States the Palestine appeals were the direct competitors of JDC in its fund-raising efforts. From a practical as well as an ideological point of view, JDC emphasized that Palestine, whatever its undoubted contribution to the solution of the German Jewish problem, could not be the only solution. Hyman, a man inclined to search for the deeper meaning of things and processes, termed Zionism in this context a millennial movement. He scoffed at the idea that nothing should be done until a millennium was reached by the aid of one program or another, because indeed "all other things are merely palliative."[71] The Zionists thought in terms of a national future and an overall solution, whereas JDC tended to see the immediate practical problems involved in helping persecuted Jews. The Zionists therefore were inclined to minimize avenues of rescue other than Palestine, at least until 1937/8, and often would not seriously consider the possibilities of rescuing Jews by sending them to other countries; while JDC did not see beyond the immediate present and could not tear itself from its cosmopolitan concepts, which perhaps had been valid in the liberal pre-Hitler era but had little validity in the growing catastrophe of European Jewry. Even practically speaking, from 1933 through 1937, 38,043 out of 174,803 emigrants from Germany had found refuge in Palestine. This is even more significant when one remembers that those who entered Palestine were settled and absorbed there, whereas the majority of those who remained in Europe were neither settled nor absorbed.

Hyman was very much concerned about the pro-Palestine statements that many of the liberal Jewish leaders in Germany made to the effect that "everything is hopeless in Germany; . . . practically all want to go to Palestine." The logical conclusion from this attitude, he said, was that Palestine work and the Palestine program were the only kind of program that the American Jews should support. This was most unfortunate, Hyman stated; surely JDC was entitled to be reinforced by the Jewish leaders in Germany with a plea for aid and support of the institutions that must be maintained inside Germany. This despite the "full acknowledgment of what Palestine has meant to these Jews of Germany."

Hyman thought that a statement should be made by the German Jews that Palestine was not the sole outlet—which of course, factually speaking, it was not.[72] Kahn agreed, but explained that the Nazis supported Zionism because it promised the largest emigration of Jews from Germany; hence German Jewish leaders could not make any public statement about other outlets. Still less could they mention the desire to maintain Jewish institutions in Germany. The Nazis had dissolved one meeting in Germany simply because the speaker had said, "We have to provide for the people who go away and for the Jews who must stay in Germany."[73]

The sharp reduction of emigration into Palestine in 1936—only 12,929 emigrated there from Germany that year—somewhat changed the Zionist policy. Weizmann, for his part, had never taken a completely exclusive point of view, and many individual Zionists shared his stand: now, the Zionists began to cooperate in the search for outlets other than Palestine. Despite the insistence of Zionists on Palestine for national and historic reasons, the difference between them and the other became smaller. JDC abandoned its doubts about supporting emigration and began to see that maintaining institutions in Germany was only a holding operation. The Zionists outside of Germany in turn began to perceive the importance of maintaining those institutions as long as there were Jews in Germany who needed them. The two main wings in Jewish life drew slowly closer on purely practical grounds as the 1930s progressed and the situation in Germany became more and more difficult.

After the Nuremberg laws were promulgated, the economic situation of German Jewry deteriorated swiftly. Kahn reported in November 1935 that Jewish businesses were being sold at ridiculously low prices and that Jewish unemployment had risen. Of 150,000 self-employed persons, 37,000 were now unemployed, including 20,000 who were on relief. Of the 120,000 employees and workers, 48,000 were unemployed, and of these 32,000 were on relief. In 1936 forty-one soup kitchens distributed 2,357,000 meals, and three thousand places in old age homes were reserved for people whose families could no longer take care of them: the numbers were increasing.[74] Jonah B. Wise's forecast, made a year previously, that Germany would become an old age home and a graveyard to its Jews, was obviously in the process of realization.

After early January 1937 all Jewish labor exchanges were closed, and the Arbeitsfront pressed for the discharge of Jewish employees in non-Jewish stores. A short respite was granted to German Jewry because of the 1936 Olympic Games, which took place in Germany, but persecution never really stopped. Jews were eliminated from newspaper staffs and from the arts, and they ceased to function as public notaries, apothecaries, veterinarians, and similar professions. The exemptions that had been granted earlier for frontline soldiers in World War I were now revoked. In early 1937 there were no longer any illusions anywhere. JDC, which had moved from a position of qualified support for emigration to one of unqualified support, was quite certain that "the German problem is bound to solve itself before long. Certainly, it will not solve itself in an agreeable way. . . . More people will leave in much larger numbers than statistics show; a great many have left and are here and elsewhere on visitor's passes and will never go back."[75] By early 1938 only 380,000 Jews were left in Germany; of these, 82,000 were receiving winter relief and an additional 20,000 were getting special Jewish relief.[76]

German Jewry was approaching its end.

4

Refugees: 1933–1938

The initial exodus of Jews from Germany in 1933 caught the Jewish philanthropic organizations with little money at their disposal. JDC had spent only $340,815 in 1932, and with the economic crisis in the United States reaching its height, the prospect for additional funds was bleak.

As we have seen, estimates of the numbers of Jewish refugees were overstated at first: about thirty-seven thousand Jews left Germany in 1933, the discrepancy arising largely from the fact that a considerable number of German Jews returned to Germany before long.[1] The reason for that was the inhospitable reception they got in the refugee countries, where unprepared and ill-financed ad hoc Jewish committees were incapable of coping with the flow of refugees. The refugees themselves were often taken aback by the hardships that freedom had in store for them, and for which their mostly middle-class backgrounds had not prepared them.

This was especially true in France, to which the bulk of the refugees (some 21,250) turned in 1933. It should be remembered that in that first year a high proportion of refugees (72–74 percent) stayed in Europe because they had not prepared for emigration overseas.[2] This picture was to change materially in subsequent years.

The Jewish organizations tried to come to the aid of the refugees. In the early spring of 1933 a conference of the leading Jewish

T A B L E   7
Jewish Emigration from Germany, 1933–1937*

Year	1933	1934	1935	1936	1937	Total
No. of emigrants	37,000	23,000	21,000	25,000	23,000	129,000†

*Based on Werner Rosenstock; see note 2.

†Of these, 85,490 were assisted through the Zentralausschuss (about 66 percent of the total). Of those assisted, 44,311 were "repatriated," mostly to Poland and other East European countries; 17,130 went to Palestine, 10,196 to European countries, and 13,853 to overseas countries. The large proportion of repatriates among those assisted is due to the poverty of many East European Jews who had settled in Germany after 1918. The percentage of the total number of emigrants who went to overseas countries other than Palestine grew from 7–9 percent in 1933 to 41–46 percent in 1936, and 60 percent in 1937 (see also JDC *Primer* [New York, 1945]).

philanthropic groups was held in Paris, convened to all intents and purposes by Kahn. Three million francs ($160,000) was allocated on the spot—one million each by JDC, the Alliance Israélite Universelle, and ICA. A small steering committee, composed of Neville Laski of the British Board of (Jewish) Deputies, Dr. Louis Oungre for ICA, and Kahn, was to distribute the money. With these funds it was hoped to establish loan *kassas* in Germany, supply refugees in France and other countries with essential relief, and work for emigration and resettlement. The sums were soon found to be insufficient, especially the 250,000 francs that went to support refugees in France.

Apart from such well-established organizations as JDC, ICA, and the Alliance, British Jewry now organized itself for effective aid to refugees. In March 1933 an old aid committee to help Russian Jewish immigrants to Britain, the Jews' Temporary Shelter, was transformed into the Jewish Refugees Committee, headed by Otto M. Schiff, a cousin of Felix M. Warburg's wife. Quite contrary to the American practice, a delegation that included Schiff, Neville Laski of the Board of Deputies, and Leonard Montefiore of the more conservative Anglo-Jewish Association went to see the officials of the Home Office in London and assured the British government that Jewish refugees arriving in Britain would not be allowed to become public charges. An Academic Assistance Council headed by Sir William Beveridge tried to help refugee intellectuals, and managed to support over two hundred such persons during the first two years of the Nazi persecutions. A separate Jewish Academic Committee helped professionals. All these and other efforts were unified in April 1933, when a committee was formed at the Rothschilds' residence in the New Court in London, which soon became the Central British Fund for German Jewry (CBF). There was parity in the new body between Zionists and non-Zionists, and the first chairman of its Allocations Committee was Sir Osmond d'Avigdor Goldsmid, president of ICA. Separate collections of Zionist funds ceased, but in fact a large proportion of the funds collected went to Palestine.[3]

JDC was not very happy about the new body, its composition or its policies. JDC thought that CBF was too much under Weizmann's influence—and indeed, despite the parity principle, Weizmann and Nahum Sokolow (then president of the World Zionist Organization) were the main forces behind CBF. By February 1934 CBF had collected 203,823 pounds, which was proportionately more than JDC and the United Palestine Appeal (UPA) had managed to raise in the United States in the same period.[4] Of this sum, 132,519 pounds were allocated; 32 percent went to support Palestine programs, 23 percent was used for the twenty-five hundred refugees who came to Britain in 1933, and 25 percent went to support vocational training of refugees outside of Germany, most of which was directed toward Palestine. The allocation for French refugee committees, who were bearing the brunt of the German refugee problem in 1933, amounted to 10,479 pounds (or about $50,000). JDC had no choice but to assume the main burden of the effort in the refugee countries generally and in France in particular; in 1933 it spent $125,000 in France.

French Jewry itself set up a number of bodies to deal with the situation. An older aid committee, the Comité d'Aide et d'Accueil, was absorbed into a national committee[5] under Senator Henri Berenger, with Baron de Rothschild as the active chairman. The committee's budget for 1933 amounted to $477,000, of which JDC covered 20 percent.[6] Another committee, called Agriculture et Artisanat, engaged in vocational training, mainly but not exclusively for Palestine. HICEM (an emigration association), Hechalutz, and OSE were also active in France from the start, OSE specializing in aiding children.

The very fact that thousands of refugees returned to Germany during 1933 shows quite clearly that all these efforts to help were of little avail. JDC, together with other interested agencies, was desperately looking to governments and the League of Nations to find solutions that a private agency could not possibly undertake. On September 29, during the seventy-third League of Nations session in Geneva, the Dutch foreign minister, de Graaf, made a plea to the second committee of the League Assembly to help German refugees. Money, he thought, would probably come from Jewish organizations, but organized international help was essential. At that stage, however, Germany was still a League of Nations member and threatened to vote against any proposal to set up a League commission for refugees from Germany. Unanimity was a condition for League decisions, and therefore the Germans were able to block action effectively. Several of the smaller nations proposed that a commission be set up that would technically be outside the League machinery. On October 11 a resolution to this effect was passed by the League.

It was obvious from the start that any international commission of this kind would have to include representatives of the United States if it was to be at all effective. As a matter of fact, the Dutch had approached the American representative in Switzerland on September 28, the day before their abortive effort in the League, and asked his help in setting up a commission.[7] The American Jewish organizations were very much interested in such a commission, which would lend international support to refugee aid. They were also aware that the success of such a commission might well hinge on the personality who would head it. For that reason, on October 18 Henry Morgenthau, Sr., wrote to Secretary of State Cordell Hull suggesting that James G. McDonald, a respected member of the *New York Times* staff and president of the Foreign Policy Association since 1918, be nominated. Significantly, he added that this proposal had the support of both the American Jewish Committee and JDC.[8]

Support by the two closely allied agencies was not surprising at all. The *Times* was owned by Jewish liberals of the old school, and McDonald, a devout Christian and humanist, had gained the respect of Jew and gentile alike. On top of that, he was a personal friend of Felix M. Warburg's, and Warburg had apparently supported his candidacy with Morgenthau. In his letter to Roosevelt on October 19, Hull said that he thought an American might indeed be suggested for the post, but he himself was by no means enthusiastic about American involvement in this essentially European affair. In case the president thought differently, Hull suggested a number of prominent Americans who might be considered for the post; McDonald's name was not among them—apparently, Morgenthau's letter had either not reached Hull or had been ignored. However, Roosevelt did indeed think differently, and McDonald was nominated for the post of "high commissioner for refugees (Jewish and other) coming from Germany," and on October 26 was appointed by the League of Nations.

Twelve member states composed the governing body of the High Commission, chaired by Viscount Cecil of Chetwood. The United States was represented by Prof. Joseph P. Chamberlain of Columbia University, an expert on refugee matters. An advisory council of voluntary organizations was to include twenty bodies, ten of them Jewish.

Immediately after this commission was set up it became clear that at least some of the governments saw its existence as a convenient way of shelving the whole problem and handing it over to the Jewish organizations to deal with as best they could. Here, as in so many other instances throughout the 1930s, JDC central leadership proved that its understanding of international politics as they applied to the Jewish refugee problems was characterized by a naiveté that was sometimes quite unbelievable.

The situation of the refugees in Western Europe on the eve of the establishment of the High Commission was extremely precarious. On October 11, 1933, Kahn cabled to New York that the French National Committee was without funds and that therefore the French government would immediately close the border. At the same time, the Belgian committee was in the process of being liquidated, and five to six hundred refugees would have to leave Belgium; they would probably try to enter France. A similar situation was developing in Holland. These and other countries were now closed to refugees. What was worse, Kahn said, the Geneva decision to set up a High Commission meant, in fact, that the private agencies were expected to foot the bill and that the governments would not spend a penny on the refugees.

Baerwald answered in a rather hurt tone that Kahn's cable seemed "surprising to me"; why did handing over the refugees' problems to the government in France mean the closing of the borders? As to Geneva, although the new commission would not be part of the League of Nations machinery, the very fact that it had been proposed by a number of governments made it "seem to us that governments cannot refuse [to] provide part of funds."[9] It seems that Baerwald, the liberal Jew and humanitarian, could not bring himself to believe that the governments would actually wash their hands of the Jewish refugee problem. More than that, the self-interest that motivated governments was something that he and his friends categorically refused to see.

JDC involvement in the McDonald Commission was considerable. JDC not only had to pay for a significant part of the High Commission's expenses[10] and support McDonald personally, but also had to enter the lists with other groups to get their proportionate contributions to keep the commission going. McDonald's secretary was Nathan Katz, secretary of JDC's Paris office. McDonald asked for and obtained the advice of Kahn or Warburg for most of the projects and negotiations in which he was engaged.

At its first meeting in London, the government representatives to the High Commission announced that their respective governments were under no obligation to pay any part of the commission's expenses. Two of the invited states (Argentina and Brazil) did not bother to send their representatives. Expenses were in fact covered by the Jewish organizations, which meant that JDC, CBF, and ICA footed the bill. The governing body was therefore more of a hindrance than a help. On top of that, rivalries, both among the governments and the voluntary organizations, made things difficult. The British, a JDC report from London said,[11] had resented McDonald's appointment in the first place, having hoped that Lord Cecil would get the post. Among the voluntary agencies, ICA insisted on the exclusion of "democratic and mass organizations," whereas Weizmann and Goldman, representatives of essentially just such groups, wanted the commission to have the widest popular appeal.[12]

Under the circumstances it was surprising that McDonald achieved anything at all. He had visited the Dachau concentration camp in September 1933, before his nomination, and had easily seen through the propaganda effort of the Germans. Hence he was, to a large degree, persona non grata in Germany. Schacht, the Nazi minister of finance, with whom McDonald had hoped to conduct negotiations concerning the easing of emigration procedures for Jews, refused to see the new high commissioner or to arrange for an interview between him and Hitler. After protracted preparations McDonald finally managed to visit Berlin in late 1934.[13] There he negotiated with a vice-president of the Reichsbank (German State Bank), and finally arranged for the educational transfer.[14] In fact, the mission and the negotiations ended in failure.

McDonald was not much more successful in his other endeavors. He did intercede with governments and persuade them to accept refugee academics, and thereby helped voluntary organizations (most of them supported by JDC and CBF) to take out some seventy-five hundred such persons from Germany by the middle of 1934.[15] McDonald also thought that the Jews should set up a corporation that would deal with settlement and exploration. This was accepted by Warburg, who set up two organizations to implement McDonald's suggestion. One was the Émigré Charitable Fund, which was to advance emigration by supporting vocational training, resettlement loans, and transportation. By 1936 ECF had called upon $275,000 of the subscriptions to its fund, but had managed to spend no more than $66,186, most of it for retraining emigrants in Latin America. Another body set up by Warburg was the Refugee Economic Corporation (originally called Refugee Rehabilitation Committee), which was incorporated in 1934. The success of this venture, in which Charles J. Liebman was the moving spirit, was not much greater. By the end of 1936 REC had appropriated $550,000, over half of it to the Huleh and other development projects in Palestine.[16]

The distinct impression is gained that these were cases of dissipation of efforts at a time when it was extremely difficult to find essential funds to support the emigration of refugees. JDC was involved in all this, although not formally: the boards of the two bodies mentioned above were manned by JDC and American Jewish Committee stalwarts, friends of the Warburgs. The same circle of persons was again called upon to help, and the results were mediocre, to say the least.

McDonald tried very hard to obtain entrance for Jewish refugees into Latin America. His quiet negotiations with the respective governments met with some, but by no means spectacular, success. Brazil closed her gates to immigrants in June 1934, except for those who had a minimum of $200 in cash. In Argentina at that time 25 pounds were needed, and the immigrant had to arrive as a first-class passenger. Later in the year Argentina became closed to all but agricultural laborers, and of the major countries of immigration in South America only Paraguay and Uruguay remained relatively easy of access to refugees.[17]

Immigration to Latin American countries was very expensive.

Except in cases where refugees had relatives there who could pay
for their passage and produce the "landing money," and except for
a relatively few families of means, HICEM and other emigration
and resettlement agencies had to pay the bill. JDC participated in
HICEM's efforts to the tune of over one-third of HICEM's budget.[18] All these efforts brought four thousand German Jews to Latin
America between April 1933 and October 1935, of whom over
one-third were assisted by HICEM and ICA.[19]

In the meantime, negotiations were being conducted between
Joseph A. Rosen and the Soviet government. In a memorandum
of February 3, 1934, Rosen reported to Warburg that the Russians
might allocate five thousand acres in the Crimea for the settlement
of Jewish families, three thousand of whom would be Russian
refugees and five to six hundred German Jewish refugees.[20] After
one year of acclimatization, the refugees would be given the choice
of either Soviet citizenship or exit from Russia. Negotiations in this
vein continued throughout 1934 and 1935, but the only Jewish
refugees accepted by the Soviets were a number of doctors. (Their
fate was briefly dealt with in chapter 2.)

As time went on, McDonald became more and more pessimistic
regarding the efficacy of quiet diplomacy in convincing the governments to act in favor of refugees. Yet the problem generally did not
seem to him to be insoluble. True, German Jews had to leave their
country of origin, but only half a million people were involved.
JDC saw the problem in a similar light. In 1935 there were no more
than forty thousand Jewish refugees in European countries awaiting settlement. "Considering their number, the problem of these
refugees would not ordinarily have been insoluble. But severe economic depression forced nations to limit the number of immigrants
and to debar foreigners from employment because many of their
nationals were without work."[21] McDonald had a simple solution
for the problem: one-half of German Jewry should be absorbed in
Palestine, one-quarter in the United States, and the rest dispersed
throughout the rest of the world. And yet it seemed that there was
no way to implement this simple formula. Economic crisis, politi-

cal obstacles, prejudices—all these vitiated a perfectly sensible and straightforward approach.

McDonald had always been a friend of Zionism. Now, with the doors of the West increasingly closed to Jewish refugees, he was led to state that the more he heard of "vague and always indefinite talks about possibilities of immigration to other parts of the world, the more I appreciate the value of Palestine."[22] This attitude differed materially from that of JDC; even Warburg, whose connections with the Jewish Agency were quite close, expressed his essentially non-Zionist views fairly strongly. As early as October 1933 he had written to Goldsmid, chairman of ICA, that "we cannot trumpet Palestine too loudly without raising false hopes in the people who cannot get in."[23] Indeed, JDC's main objection to the policies of CBF was that it was under Zionist influence and that a large proportion of its funds—too large, JDC thought—were destined for Palestine.

But in 1934 JDC slowly began veering around to McDonald's point of view. Warburg himself was arranging for money to be paid to McDonald, who was by no means a rich man, in order that McDonald could remain independent of his small salary as a high commissioner. But McDonald was in no sense a blind follower of anyone, certainly not of Warburg. Relations were cordial, opinions were allowed to differ, and in the end Warburg tended to see McDonald's point. Hyman seems to have expressed his chief's views when he states that "no other single place has been able to receive thus far as many refugees as has Palestine. To that extent, without indulging in questions of Zionist or non-Zionist philosophy, we must all recognize the great utility of Palestine as a place of refuge."[24]

In the course of his attempts to open up the doors of America to refugees, McDonald tried to break the administrative blocking of Jewish emigration from Germany to the United States by the so-called Hoover executive order of September 8, 1930. That order had instructed consular officers to refuse visas to applicants who could not prove that at no time in the future would they become public charges.[25] The result had been a drastic reduction in visas to the United States. Consequently, in October 1935 McDonald approached Warburg and asked him to use his influence with the Roosevelt administration to ease these regulations.[26] Warburg turned to Herbert H. Lehman, and on November 1, 1935, Lehman wrote to Roosevelt. Only 10 percent of the yearly immigration quota from Germany—about twenty-six thousand persons—was being utilized, he argued. The people who wanted to come were of the same ilk as "my father, Carl Schurz, and other Germans who came over here in the days of 1848."[27] An increase up to five thousand visas for refugees was asked for.

On November 13 Roosevelt sent his answer.[28] In fact, the administration argued, while the German quota was 16.9 percent of the total allowed immigration, Germans comprised 26.9 percent of all those actually coming in, because the total number of immigrants allowed into the United States was small. In 1933, 1,798 Germans were allowed in; in 1934, 4,715; and in 1935, 5,117. This, of course, included non-Jews as well, but about 80 percent were estimated to be Jews. However, the letter went on, the State Department had issued instructions, "now in effect," that refugees should receive "the most considerate attention and the most generous and favorable treatment possible under the laws of this country." It appeared that McDonald's initiative had brought positive results but the facts were different. It has been proven quite conclusively that both at the State Department and at lower levels, obstruction continued and even intensified as far as the issue of visas to Jewish refugees was concerned.[29]

McDonald was no more successful in his attempts to have the great Western powers intervene diplomatically. Late in 1935 he tried to obtain British support for an intervention with the Germans, but failed. In October 1935 and again in February 1936 he failed similarly to get the United States government to intervene on behalf of German Jewry.[30]

Besides trying to find places of refuge for Germany's Jews, McDonald saw that his main task was to ease the fate of those German

Jewish refugees who were now in European countries. There he encountered governmental indifference—sometimes even hostility —that nullified much of his work. He was perfectly aware that the governments saw in him a means of getting rid of the refugees.[31] At a meeting of the governing body of the High Commission in early November 1934 he chided the governments for harrying the refugees, making them pay exorbitant sums for official papers, and especially for refusing them the right to work. He tried to prove to them that they would only gain by allowing refugees to enter their countries and work there. However, German anti-Jewish and antirefugee propaganda had obviously been successful, and had "made the position of the refugees more uncertain in some countries and their admission more difficult in others."[32]

McDonald's main problem was France. There, in early 1935, French Jewish committees defending French government policy explained why no work permits could be given without increasing anti-Semitism in an economic crisis situation. JDC, McDonald's main ally, was represented by Kahn, who stated his strong disapproval of the French Jews and argued that many people, including twelve hundred children, were literally starving in Paris—a situation that was completely unjustifiable.[33]

The partial or complete failure of his efforts finally led McDonald to consider resigning his post. By the autumn of 1935 the French were treating McDonald "like a small office boy whose services are no longer needed and who should be dismissed on the spot," as Kahn put it.[34] McDonald was too independent, too demanding, and too energetic. He was moving to radical positions. In a letter to Eleanor Roosevelt he prophesied a further great exodus of German Jews and asked how long these matters were to be regarded as purely of German domestic concern.[35] Finally in September he decided to resign, and suggested Norman Bentwich as his successor.[36]

His resignation was a political act. It took the form of a letter to the secretary-general of the League of Nations and was published in the world press either verbatim or in fairly extensive form.[37] Norman Bentwich, James N. Rosenberg, and Felix M. Warburg had been fully consulted, and the letter was really something of a collective effort. Specifically, McDonald condemned Nazi policy toward Jews and called for "collective action" by the League of Nations, denying that this was an internal German problem. Practically speaking, his demand for "friendly but firm intercession with the German Government, by all pacific means, on the part of the League of Nations, of its Member States and other members of the community of nations" was hardly likely to move the Germans, even had it been accepted. But the value of the document lay mainly in the unequivocal condemnation of German policies emanating from the international official charged with dealing with the refugee problem.

McDonald's resignation had no immediate positive effect. Some papers in Britain that published extracts from the letter showed in their comments how far removed they were from a realistic appreciation of the situation. On December 10, 1935, for example, the London *Times* wrote that Germany would not be able to withstand the pressure of public opinion, and the *News Chronicle* added that Mr. Hitler would ignore world opinion at his peril.

On February 14, 1936, the League of Nations designated a retired British general, Sir Neil Malcolm, as the new high commissioner. When asked what his policy would be, he replied clearly and succinctly: "I have no policy, but the policy of the League is to deal with the political and legal status of the refugees. It has nothing to do with the domestic policy of Germany."[38] The attempt to deal with the Jewish refugee problem on an international and humanitarian level had met with its first failure; it constituted a severe check to JDC's efforts of rescue and aid to German Jewry.

These efforts centered mainly in France and other West European countries, where the bulk of the remaining refugees were languishing. The attitude of French Jewry to German Jewish refugees was a source of constant and occasionally bitter criticism by Kahn in his letters to JDC in New York. French Jews were inclined to criticize American Jewry for not helping enough—this was in 1934, at the height of the economic crisis in the United States. The solution advocated by French Jews was to get the German Jews to emigrate as quickly as possible. They even repeated these demands in official bodies where they were represented such as the Advisory Council of the McDonald Commission, and Kahn thought he had to threaten with a negative reaction on the part of American Jews if it became known that French Jews wanted to get rid of the refugees.[39]

The National Committee that had been set up in 1933 dissolved in June 1934. A liquidating commission, which was to have taken over support for deserving refugees, refused help to certain categories of emigrants. These included people who had not applied for aid previously but had now used up their resources and could not continue without aid. Having sold all their effects, including clothing, people had to find money for hotel bills. Many were faced with the "alternatives of stealing or begging. Thefts, and what is more frequent, cases of petty larceny"[40] were reported. Well-to-do German Jewish refugees managed to collect 200,000 francs in early 1934, but this was not enough. A similar effort in Britain had to cease when CBF demanded that all money be channeled through its own organization. Facilities in Paris were bad: the only shelter in Paris was crowded and vermin-infested. Groups that tried to train refugees for emigration, such as Agriculture et Artisanat, could show only very modest results: by 1935, the latter group had trained 350 men, of whom 200 had left France. HICEM helped 2,343 people to emigrate in 1934.[41]

There seemed little possibility of solving the problem with the means then at the disposal of Jewish organizations. Kahn summed it all up by saying that the economic crisis and the many unemployed in the very cities where the refugees were trying to settle "had led humanity back to those savage days of human history when every stranger who came to a foreign land was considered an enemy who had to be destroyed."[42]

There was really no successor organization to the National Committee, and JDC simply did not have the means to feed and clothe

the refugees. There were about ten to twelve thousand Jewish refugees in France in 1934, of whom probably not more than thirty-five hundred were completely dependent on aid. Yet JDC had to spend $170,000 directly on refugees in France, because local support withered. JDC tried to obtain work permits by direct intervention with the French premier, Flandin. "The French Jews did everything possible to frustrate our efforts at constructive work there. . . . We might have been able to settle several hundred families on the land in France, and it would have done a great deal of good for the Jews there. We may still be able to do so, but we have already met with insurmountable opposition there. The reason is that the French Jews are afraid of anti-Semitism."[43]

The truth of the matter was that French Jewry was frightened by the rise of French Fascist movements, which caused serious disturbances in Paris in February 1934. After the assassination in Marseille of King Alexander of Yugoslavia and the French foreign minister, Louis Barthou, on October 9, 1934, the head of the French Jewish Consistoire, the highest religious institution of French Jewry, declared that nothing should be done to settle the refugees permanently in Paris.[44] JDC had little alternative but to aid, to the best of its very limited resources, as many refugees as possible to emigrate from France. During 1934 many refugees had no other choice but to return to Germany. Twelve to fifteen hundred did so from Holland and twice that number from France. In 1935 the refugee committees ceased this practice because they learned that the Germans had been sending Jewish returnees to concentration camps from late January on. A JDC bulletin quoted a German government circular to the effect that "these repatriates should be brought into a concentration camp to learn there the National-Socialist tenets, which they had no opportunity to learn while they were abroad."[45]

In 1935 the situation worsened. Welfare for German Jewish refugees came to a virtual stop. JDC efforts to have French Jewry inaugurate a new campaign to raise funds met with no success. The French government was issuing deportation orders by the thousands, though few were actually carried out against Jews. In the early part of the year there probably were not more than nine thousand refugees in France, of whom about two thousand were estimated to be in hiding from deportation.[46]

By the end of 1935 and in early 1936 the refugee aid committees that had mushroomed in France in 1933/4 began to disappear. Agriculture et Artisanat dissolved in 1936;[47] others followed suit. With the advent of the left-wing Popular Front government in 1936, the Rothschilds and their supporters tended to withdraw from the scene. Kahn, usually so conservative in his opinions, was moved to say that apart from JDC "nobody cares about the German refugees in France, neither ICA, the Jewish community, the British [Jews], nor any other organization."[48]

The steady worsening of the situation was punctuated by the passage of the September 1935 Nuremberg laws in Germany, which openly made Jews into second-class citizens. After the fall of 1935, it became clear to many that German Jewry had no choice but to emigrate. The problem was how long this would take and what the financial and political tools would be necessary to effect such emigration.

McDonald's last, and this time at least partially successful, effort was to bring together the British and American Jewish bodies for common action in face of the threat to German Jews. The irony of a non-Jewish humanitarian's being the essential factor in achieving cooperation between Jews should not be overlooked: McDonald reported to a rather reluctant Warburg in November 1935 that he was trying to persuade Lord Bearsted and Simon Marks, two leading British Jews, to come to the United States to meet with American Jewish leaders.[49] Among British Jews he found, he said, a unanimous appreciation of the dangers and of the necessity for speedy action. Soon the moving spirit in the British camp became Sir Herbert Samuel, the noted liberal leader and moderate Zionist (he had been the first British high commissioner to Palestine after World War I).

Events then moved at unaccustomed speed. In December 1935

Lord Bearsted and Marks announced the forthcoming visit of a "leading Jewish statesman"—obviously Samuel was meant—and asked for the postponement of separate fund-raising campaigns in America until consultations regarding a concerted emigration plan from Germany could be agreed upon. They were thinking of a plan to take twenty-three thousand Jews out of Germany yearly. Warburg's reaction was guarded. The visit would be welcome, but JDC was quite clear about preserving its independence.

In Britain, meanwhile, ICA took a similar stand: Goldsmid promised cooperation and coordination, but declared that ICA would retain its independence. The reluctance with which the more conservative groups regarded the proposals stemmed at least partly from the fear of being swamped by Zionist influence. Their caution was strengthened by the fact that early in January items appeared in the *New York Times* playing up the emigration plan and the forthcoming British Jewish visit to the United States—Warburg was quite certain that any publicity at that early stage was most unhelpful. Also, Warburg was not quite clear what the plan actually consisted of. According to one version it would cost $16 million; another version said $12 million for four years.

On January 21, 1936, three representatives of British Jewry arrived in New York: Sir Herbert Samuel, Simon Marks, an ardent Zionist, and Lord Bearsted, a non-Zionist. To JDC the delegation seemed obviously weighted on the Zionist side. For about two weeks the delegation held talks with JDC, the Refugee Economic Committee (REC), and the Zionists. The plan now became clearer: there were, the guests said, some 94,000 young Jews between the ages of seventeen and thirty-five still in Germany. It was proposed to help 8,000 of these to emigrate yearly to Palestine, 4,000 to the United States, and 4,000 to other countries. Altogether, 64,000 young adults would emigrate in four years. On top of that, an annual emigration of 5,000 children, and 500 Youth Aliyah to Palestine, would mean another 22,000 in four years. Older people who would leave with their younger relatives would swell the total number to 42,000 yearly, or a total of 168,000 in four years.[50] The cost of all this would be about $15 million, of which two-thirds would be borne by United States Jewry and one-third by British Jewry. A central coordinating committee, to be called the Council for German Jewry, was to be set up in London.

The American Jewish bodies agreed to these proposals in broad terms after some rather heated discussions. JDC leaders declared that they understood the council to have coordinating functions, because JDC's contributors would hardly agree to having the distribution of their funds determined by people in another country. Also, what JDC undertook to do was essentially to devote their funds (other than their commitments to Eastern Europe and other places) to the saving of German Jewry in coordination with the others. This, of course, was what JDC had been doing in any case, so that behind the façade of declarations of goodwill the situation had not changed materially when the British delegation left on February 5, 1936. On January 1 Samuel had been received by Roosevelt, who had promised him "a sympathetic attitude on the part of the [U. S.] German consulates in the case of all suitable applications for emigration visas to this country."[51] Yet at the final meeting of the delegations, Marks was more realistic than the enthusiastic newspaper reports when he said that in fact the British delegation had accomplished very little.

Some JDC leaders saw even the small measure of agreement as a mistake. Vladeck, Marshall, and Rosenberg argued that the Zionists would simply use the agreement for getting Jews into Palestine. Zionists, Vladeck said, agreed with Fascists that Jews should get out of Europe. That was the reason why the Zionist flag was protected in Germany. Repercussions in Eastern Europe to such large-scale emigration might increase anti-Semitism there because governments would think that they could evict Jews with Jewish financial support. If this meant, said another participant in the discussion, "that when Jews are hurt, they shall immediately be taken out of the country through a grand exodus, and . . . that money is paid to bring people out of places merely because conditions are bad there, we would only succeed in muddling up the situation for other Jews all over the world." On the other hand, William Rosenwald argued, the Zionists got their funds on the strength of the German crisis and yet only about 13 percent (actually about 20 percent) of the admissions into Palestine were from Germany. If, as a result of the new plan, the Zionists would devote a larger proportion of their funds to help German Jewry, he said, the plan would commend itself "to many of us."[52]

Warburg's influence neutralized the opposition, and the overwhelming majority of the leading JDC laymen supported the new plan. However, events in London soon made it seem that at least some of the criticism had been justified.

The council was to be set up in London and consist of six men —three each from Britain and the United States. The three Americans were to be Warburg, Baerwald, and Rabbi Stephen Wise, the Zionist leader. With Samuel and Marks considered as Zionists, there would thus be an equal representation of Zionists and non-Zionists on the council. However, after the British delegation had returned to London, Marks invited Weizmann to join and, probably in order not to appear partial, Goldsmid of ICA as well. This was done without prior consultation with the Americans. On top of that, the British now interpreted the agreement in New York to mean that JDC would raise funds over and above what it was spending for all its other purposes. In the early April session in London of the council's Preparatory Committee, Kahn emphatically denied this interpretation. On April 6 Warburg wrote a very outspoken, though humorous, letter to Bentwich, who had been appointed director of the council, together with Sir Wyndham Deedes, a non-Jew and a pro-Zionist. The council was, Warburg said, clearly top-heavy on the Palestine end. His enthusiasm, he added, was somewhat dampened. The English had allocated their money to Palestine "in its entirety"; the consultations were therefore somewhat futile and, he added, "some of us feel that we had better stay at home and saw wood and satisfy the givers, as we have in the past, by spending their contributions as the givers would want and as the recipients desire."[53] In the end only about half of the British funds went to Palestine.

In the spring of 1936 the Zionists were demanding that 250,000 pounds be allocated to aid the immigration to Palestine of thirty-five hundred young trainees. This would have meant that a very large sum of money would go to settle a relatively small number of people, and JDC felt that it could not agree to that—although there seems to have been no protest on JDC's part when HICEM and ICA spent very large sums to effect the settlement of equally small numbers of people in Latin American countries.

One of the paradoxes of the situation was that the Zionists, especially in America, had not been at all enthusiastic about the establishment of the Council for German Jewry. Under the influence of Stephen S. Wise, American Zionism had come to support the boycott of German goods that had been started by Abraham Coralnik and Samuel Untermeyer in 1933, to which JDC was very much opposed. American Zionists thought that the council's plan was similar to the Jewish Agency's German transfer scheme, to which American Zionism was largely opposed. This, as we have mentioned, consisted of an agreement to take out Jewish capital to Palestine in return for the promotion of the export of German goods. The boycott trend in the United States was so strong that JDC, itself eager not to clash with the Zionists on this issue, decided that no plan should be implemented that would facilitate the export of German goods.[54] Now, after the delegation had returned to London and the Zionist influence had gained weight, the situation was reversed: the Zionists had been enthusiastic supporters of the council's plans, whereas JDC's ardor had cooled considerably.

The marriage then had hardly taken place when a separation occurred, though both sides took great care not to announce a divorce. On paper there were soon five American Jewish members of the council, of whom three were JDC representatives (Warburg, Baerwald, and Liebman; Liebman represented REC, which was a JDC affiliate). The two others were Zionists. In reality, there usually was an American delegate representing the JDC members in London who partook in the council's deliberations. Practically speaking, the money the council spent came from England only and was allocated by the British members of the council. As to the rest, there was much exchange of information and consultation and some common action in Europe, especially in the refugee countries, but no pooling of resources. The grandiose plan to evacuate young German Jews remained on paper.

To be sure, the reason for the inaction did not lie mainly with interorganizational differences of opinion. Money alone, even had there been much of it (which there was not), would not have solved everything. There had to be places to which emigrants could be directed, and on this major point the council did not advance beyond what McDonald had done. Max Warburg and Otto Hirsch from Germany "begged and pleaded for action, meaning that monies be made available to start sending [refugees] at the rate of 500 a month out of Germany to various parts of the world, in addition to immigration to Palestine."[55]

In the spring of 1937, during the last months of his life, Warburg was working on an idea to create an umbrella organization of Jewish leaders of major organizations, to be weighted very definitely on the non-Zionist side.[56] Such a committee was in fact set up and met in July in Paris for the first and only time. But one may doubt whether a mere reshuffling or organizational change would have made much of a difference in a situation that was determined by the non-Jewish world rather than by Jewish leadership. Warburg himself had been to Europe in early 1937, and his report was not encouraging.[57] Small numbers of people could emigrate to a few places with the help of large sums of money, provided this was done quietly; the same was true of the United States, where fear of anti-Semitism caused Jews to keep very quiet regarding the numbers of Jews entering the country. Palestine was, in 1937, awaiting the verdict of the Peel Commission, and immigration was becoming restricted. The outlook was bleak.

Until 1936 Palestine was, as we have seen, a main focus of emigration for German Jews. This fact and the emotions aroused in the Jewish world by the controversy about Palestine, as well as the bearing it had on the relations in the United States between

JDC and the Zionists, caused JDC to devote a fairly significant part of its thinking to the Palestine problem.

JDC's involvement in Palestine had begun with the founding of the organization, for JDC had come into being in the wake of efforts to aid suffering Jews in Palestine in 1914. In the 1920s Warburg's and Baerwald's non-Zionism did not preclude a deep interest in what they considered to be constructive work in that country. They took a businesslike approach to the growth of Palestine's economy by investments that would produce profits, loans to sound enterprises, and the development of natural resources.

The Zionist-inspired funds had a different policy. What was important to them was the development of the country's capacity to absorb immigrants—and if money had to be "wasted" in order to build enterprises or to develop social experiments whose results would take many years to prove themselves, they were not averse to that. The desire for economic profit to them was secondary to national interests.

To a number of JDC leaders, Palestine was essentially an Arab country into which Jews had a right to immigrate and in which they should settle and develop their institutions, in much the same way that they had done in North America. "The picture of British guns," one of them said, "forcing a foreign rule upon a majority population so that a minority can obtain political, economic and cultural privileges does not accord with the conscience of peoples bred to the principles of free self-government."[58] Warburg, with his penchant for neat organizational structures, was trying in 1929 to set up tripartite committees of Moslems, Christians, and Jews. This was to be crowned with a committee for cooperation, chaired by his friend, Judah L. Magnes, chancellor of the Hebrew University.[59] All this came in the wake of the August 1929 disturbances during which Arab rioters brutally murdered large numbers of defenseless Jews at Hebron and other places. Basic to the approach of JDC leaders was a misunderstanding of the tremendous drive of a desperate Jewish nationalism, now swiftly spreading to the North American continent as well, with which they were utterly out of sympathy. They thought they could channel what they considered to be the more moderate Zionist ideas into investment companies and business expansion and ultimately arrive at some political compromise guaranteeing civil rights to Jews. But they, too, felt that they had to participate somehow, that in some way Palestine was their concern as well; and in the process they helped to build solid foundations for a Jewish national movement in Palestine—a result that they had not foreseen and certainly would have deprecated.

In line with JDC principles generally, work in Palestine in the 1920s was slowly transferred to responsible groups that carried on under indirect JDC supervision. JDC supported the Hebrew University and some yeshivoth directly. But in June 1925 it joined the Brandeis wing of the Zionists in setting up the Palestine Economic Corporation (PEC). To this body it transferred all its economic work in Palestine and promised additional funds. All this came to a total of $1.5 million, which was to be paid within three years. Most important among the assets transferred was the majority share of JDC in the Central Bank of Cooperative Institutions (founded 1922), of which the other main partner was ICA. That bank, run (starting in May 1925) by Harry Viteles, an American who had settled in Palestine, had become a central banking institution for Palestine's budding cooperatives. Between 1922 and 1929 it loaned $3 million to a variety of local bodies and individuals. Other assets transferred included the Loan Bank (Kupath Milveh), reorganized in 1924, which provided small loans mainly to small businessmen and artisans on the same lines as the JDC *kassas* did in Eastern Europe. All these activities were vital in enabling the young Jewish settlement in Palestine to weather the crisis of 1926/7, which resulted from an ill-advised building boom and rash investments in trade.

JDC could not fulfill its obligations to PEC because of the economic crisis in America. Had PEC not been, practically speaking, a JDC affiliate, JDC would have run into considerable difficulties because of its inability to pay the full amount promised. But with

Warburg as honorary president, and Bernard Flexner, another JDC stalwart, as chairman, work continued despite the fact that JDC had only paid in $1,164,000 by early 1930 and was paying PEC only small amounts of the rest of the sum throughout the 1930s.

PEC invested its funds in Palestine not only through the institutions already mentioned but also by supporting the Mortgage and Credit Bank, which helped finance the building of much of modern Jerusalem and northern Tel Aviv. In 1932, with PEC help, the bank participated in setting up the Kiriat Hayim suburb in Haifa and a number of smaller urban settlements elsewhere. PEC joined PICA (ICA in Palestine) in supporting the Palestine Water Company and helped equip them with modern American drilling machinery. The Haifa Bay Land Company, in which PEC also invested handsomely, bought land in Haifa Bay and provided settlers with easy access to land. Flexner, Warburg, and Robert Szold also represented PEC on the board of the Palestine Potash Company, which was developing the Dead Sea resources, after PEC had acquired $262,631 worth of the company's shares. In March 1929 PEC provided 20,000 pounds of the 165,000 pounds subscribed to the Palestine Hotels Company, organized by private investors in Egypt and England. As a result, the King David Hotel in Jerusalem was completed in January 1931.[60]

Another JDC involvement in Palestine affairs resulted from the August 1929 disturbances. Moslem crowds, incited by the mufti of Jerusalem, Amin El Husseini, killed and pillaged in Jewish settlements wherever they could. On August 23 the news regarding the slaughter of Jews at Hebron had reached the United States, and within four days an Emergency Fund for the Relief of Palestine Sufferers had been set up under David A. Brown of JDC, with the full participation of the Zionists. Julius Rosenwald, Nathan Straus, and Felix M. Warburg were honorary chairmen. The participation of Rosenwald marked the effort as essentially humanitarian and nonpolitical. Twenty-five thousand dollars was donated by each of the three chairmen and $50,000 by JDC. In the end total contributions amounted to $2,210,474. Together with contributions collected in Palestine itself, the total amount was 589,768 pounds.

The next problem was how to spend the money. In September 1929 Warburg nominated Judge Jonah J. Goldstein and his wife, Mrs. Harriet B. Lowenstein-Goldstein, comptroller of JDC, to go to Palestine and distribute the funds there. On their way the Goldsteins stopped over in London and arranged for the coordination of British and American efforts.

In Palestine, local and British Jews soon took charge, and the Goldsteins became but partners in the effort. They left in December 1929, and the expenditure of funds was supervised by a committee composed of Brig. Frederick Kisch, a British Zionist leader who lived in Palestine; Pinhas Rutenberg, founder of the Palestine Electric Company; and Maurice B. Hexter, who represented JDC interests. The practical work was done at first largely by Mrs. Bentwich, later by the Palestinian Zionist Elijah Berlin and Charles Passman (Passman, an American, represented ICA in Palestine).

The funds collected were much larger than the situation actually required. The families who had had to leave Hebron and a few other places were quickly settled, and their needs seen to. In fact, local funds had satisfied most of these needs before the American fund became effective. In December a reorganization of the fund led to a change from relief to reconstructive activities. As a result, quite unexpectedly the Emergency Fund, originally intended as a pure humanitarian gesture, became an investment fund that supported such things as land buying (together with ICA), the development of the Huleh Valley concession, lands in the north of Palestine, the settlement of Hartuv near Jerusalem, Ein Zeitim near Safed, and the resettlement of Be'er Tuvia, which had been destroyed in the disturbances. Apartment houses near Haifa, security buildings (which, in fact, meant subsidies for the Haganah), telephones, access roads, and so on were financed by the Emergency Fund. In Jerusalem the agricultural school at Talpiot and the fortress–dining hall at Ramat Rachel, which in 1948 broke the Egyptian attack on the southern approaches to the city, now stand as monuments to the Emergency Fund.[61] A total of 332,748 pounds was spent on this kind of reconstruction, as distinct from relief.

In the early 1930s, until Hitler's takeover, JDC did not spend large sums of money in Palestine; it limited itself to partial support of some yeshivoth and the Hebrew University (the latter, one suspects, largely because of Judah L. Magnes's personality). However, after the advent of the Nazis in Germany, the situation changed completely. German immigration to Palestine increased sharply.

During the first three years, 1933–1935, the figures were most impressive. Of a total of about 81,000 Jews who left Germany, 22,700 (28 percent) left for Palestine. In 1935, when 62,000 Jews entered that country, it seemed as though this was the most practical solution to the problem of the refugees, politics and ideology aside. Yet even in that heyday of optimism as regards the future of the Jewish settlement in Palestine, two problems arose to plague JDC. The first was the obvious fact that while the German emergency was getting grimmer year by year, the Jewish Agency allocated to German Jews well under a third of the entry permits into Palestine. JDC exerted considerable pressure on the Agency to change this policy and to give German Jews an absolute priority.

T A B L E   8[62]
Immigration (Legal) to Palestine of Jews from Germany and Austria

Year	From Germany	From Austria	Total	% of total (legal) immigration
1933	6,803	328	7,131	22.3
1934	8,497	928	9,425	21.4
1935	7,447	1,376	8,823	14.5
1936	7,896	581	8,477	26.8
1937	3,280	214	3,494	28.1
1938	4,223	2,964	7,187	40.5
Total	38,146	6,391	44,537	22.3

However, the Central Bureau for the Settlement of German Jews in Palestine, an Agency office run by Dr. Weizmann, could not accede to the request. The Agency had to consider the claims of Jews in Poland, Lithuania, and Romania, because those were the main constituents of the Zionist organization and also because the situation of the Jews in Eastern Europe was, from the economic point of view certainly, even worse than that of the Jews in Germany. In desperation, the Zionists even looked to Syria and other Middle Eastern countries as temporary havens. Weizmann stated that "there was plenty of room in Syria for Jewish immigrants and that he understood that Jews would be welcomed to that country."[63]

JDC's second problem was that the Zionists attempted to make it use its funds for transporting emigrants to Palestine. In this they succeeded in a large measure. JDC put the cost of transport to Palestine, including its expenditures for vocational training for Palestine, at about $993,000 between 1933 and the end of 1938.[64] Even if the computation was exaggerated, as it seems to have been, there is no doubt at all that JDC did in fact support immigration to Palestine to a marked degree. This was at a time when there was considerable competition for funds in the United States between JDC and the United Palestine Appeal. According to one JDC compilation, various Palestine-oriented appeals collected a total of $2,848,000 in the United States in 1933/4, whereas the JDC collections amounted to $2,553,000[65] at the same time. Weizmann's Central Bureau in London received 936,000 pounds[66] between October 1933 and December 1938, or about $5 million. JDC income between 1934 and 1938 came to about $12.8 million; but JDC had to give aid to East European Jewry, apart from looking after refugees everywhere and supporting German Jewry as well. Why then should JDC also support Palestine ventures? In April 1934 JDC issued a statement of policy, which said: "Were the CBF, the ICA, the Jewish Agency for Palestine to agree to a sharing of these responsibilities [for everything outside of Palestine], which no other agency in large measure has attempted to meet, the JDC could see its way clear to an understanding whereby important parts of its resources can be applied toward the settlement of German Jews in Palestine."[67]

Despite the declaration, in practice JDC had no choice but to support the Palestine immigration office in Berlin, because it was part of the Zentral-Ausschuss, and JDC could not help supporting ZA in all its activities. Even apart from that, Kahn found it necessary to support Hechalutz in France and Poland, in Holland and Austria, because it was one of the agencies that made the most effective use of the money given them. On Palestine, JDC suffered from a split personality; while heated arguments might take place in its Executive Committee on how to avoid spending too much money there, Warburg would declare at the National Council that "the money spent there, which at one time might have worried us, is well founded and well spent."[68]

After 1935 the situation changed. Growing Arab unrest finally flared up in early 1936 into a rebellion that was to last, with interruptions, until 1939. The British sent a royal commission under Lord Peel to investigate the causes of the unrest. The Peel Commission reported in July 1937 and suggested that the country be partitioned into an Arab and a Jewish state.

JDC was not a political organization, but its leadership consisted of men who, as members of the Jewish Agency's non-Zionist wing, were deeply involved in Palestinian affairs. Warburg and his friends were very definitely against partition, because that would create a Jewish state, and they thought that such a state would be a calamity for the Jewish people. The whole concept of Jewish nationhood, as we have seen, ran counter to their brand of Judaism, and they became very active in trying to combat partition with all the strength they could command. JDC was not only informed of Warburg's opposition to the plan, but also at JDC Executive Committee meetings he took the occasion to explain his views and to get the unanimous support of the members. The Jewish state would be a declaration of war against the Arabs, Warburg argued. Besides, the Jewish state itself would be so small that it would soon have to restrict immigration. The goal of American Jews was to "open Palestine as wide as possible for the immigration of Jews from countries of the Diaspora, at the same time safeguarding the English interests in Palestine and assuring the Arabs that they will not be outnumbered."[69]

Despite the stand taken by JDC leaders on partition, the argument with Zionism receded somewhat into the background after 1936. The British began restricting immigration into Palestine, and Palestine could no longer be the immediate answer to the pressing problems of European refugees. In 1937 and 1938 the proportion of refugees that were absorbed in Palestine dwindled to a half and then a third of what it had been in the first few years of the Nazi crisis. This and the failure of the partition scheme—despite its acceptance in principle by a majority of the Zionist movement— caused JDC and UPA to draw progressively nearer to one another. Both were now interested in opening the doors of Palestine, and the Zionists could not but accept the idea that other countries too would have to be persuaded to accept a share of the refugees coming from Nazi Germany.

Another aspect of the relationships between JDC and the American Zionists was the eternal problem of competitive fund raising. Two problems arose: what proportion of funds raised by the American Jewish communities for all purposes should be diverted to what was known as overseas relief; and how these overseas funds would be divided between Palestine and other areas. As far as the first problem was concerned, the interests of both Zionists and non-Zionists obviously coincided. They both wanted a growing proportion of the funds raised to go to help Jews abroad, including those in Palestine. After the worst of the depression was over, that is, from 1935 on, the proportion of overseas relief as compared to local expenditures began growing.[70] During the depression an attempt was made to set up a combined fund-raising agency, the United Jewish Appeal. This body was set up in March 1934 by JDC and the United Palestine Appeal under Louis Lipsky and Morris Rothenberg; their aim was to raise $3 million, of which

JDC was to get 55 percent. However, no more than $1,246,000 came to JDC, and the 1935 results were even less impressive: total JDC income went down to $917,000. Disagreement on what the money should be spent for also troubled the relationship between the two agencies. A case in point was the question of who should pay for the transportation for immigrants to Palestine, discussed above. This was a major reason for JDC's terminating the agreement with UPA. The attitude of the Zionists, so JDC thought, was to get money from American Jews on the strength of the German emergency and force JDC to use it for transportation to Palestine, while themselves refusing to contribute to expenses in Germany or the refugee countries. Behind this argument[71] lay the feeling of Warburg and his friends that the Jewish Agency, in which they were supposed to be equal partners, had in fact become a Zionist front organization. The breakup of UJA by JDC in October 1935 was probably intended also as a warning to Weizmann to take the non-Zionists more seriously.

In 1936 and 1937 relations with American Zionism remained strained organizationally, despite a growing recognition of a similarity in aims and objectives. Ideologically, the case for JDC was put very clearly by Hyman in 1937. Stating that non-Zionists supported a "great Jewish settlement of refuge and of cultural development in Palestine," he said that they "decline to regard themselves as actually or potentially elements of a Jewish nation, with its center in Palestine." Zionism, he thought, was giving anti-Semites the pretext for evicting Jews from their countries. To him and his friends, "America, France, Holland, England is home and homeland." Hyman was against a "fusion" (that is, a combination for fund-raising purposes) of Zionists and non-Zionists. He wanted the proponents for each program to appear before the public separately: "The one that seeks to make Palestine the Jewish homeland, the core and kernel of Jewish conscious objective; the other that deems the primary goal the integration of Jews with the life of their lands of birth or of adoption."[72]

In actual fact JDC probably was bound to lose by an alliance with the Zionists, simply because alone it could get more funds out of the richer elements in Jewry, who generally were more inclined toward Hyman's ideology than toward that of the Zionists. This situation was to change considerably in the last year before the war, but even before that, JDC was having more difficulties because local welfare funds tended to refuse to raise funds separately for UPA and JDC. In a growing measure they and the professional associations in the large Jewish communities insisted on united campaigns, the proceeds of which would be handed over to the overseas relief agencies according to prearranged percentages. Slowly but surely this grass-roots attitude left the JDC leadership isolated in its desire to continue independent fund raising. As the situation in Europe deteriorated, JDC reluctantly began to come around to the idea of a more permanent alliance with UPA. This development itself reflected the shift in emphasis in Jewish leadership: the welfare funds were increasingly controlled by professionals—social workers, fund raisers, and the like. The lay leadership was slowly losing ground.

The other main center of immigration for Europe's Jewish refugees was, of course, the North American continent itself. Much has been written to show how restrictive United States practices were, and how occasional attempts by groups and individuals to break through the wall of hostility were foiled by the great latitude that was given to local consuls in their application of visa-granting procedures, and by the support these consuls were given in their restrictive attitudes by State Department officials.[73] The actual statistics of immigration from Germany to the United States in the 1930s certainly bear witness to these strictures, at least as far as the first years of Nazi rule in Germany are concerned.

The total up to 1938, according to this source, was 63,485 persons from Germany (including Austria, after March 1938). If 85 percent of these immigrants were Jews, then the Jewish immigration from Germany would have been about 54,000. The quota for Germany was 26,000 (together with the quota for Austria it came

T A B L E 9[74]
Immigration from Germany to the United States

Year	1933/4	1934/5	1935/6	1936/7	1937/8	July–December 1938
No. of immigrants	4,392	5,201	6,346	10,895	17,199	19,452

to 27,370); it is therefore clear that up to 1936, U. S. immigration practices even under the existing quota arrangements were very restrictive.

But this is no longer quite so clear after 1936. The quota was utilized in 1936 to the extent of 40 percent, rising to 63 percent in 1937 and to 71 percent in slightly over half of fiscal 1938/9. The quota itself was very small, and the fact that even that was not fully utilized is a grim reflection of American practices. The increase in immigration into the United States came just as the British were restricting entrance to Palestine, and by the end of 1938, 38 percent of the Jews emigrating from Germany had come to the United States.

JDC's attitude toward Jewish immigration into the United States was ambivalent. The main desire of the organization was to avoid publicity about the numbers of Jews entering the country, for fear of an outcry from the many restrictionist elements in and out of Congress. JDC allocated money to groups and organizations engaged in absorbing these immigrants in the United States, but efforts were made to avoid publicity. These expenditures came to $237,180 in 1936 and climbed to $342,000 and $500,313 in the two succeeding years.[75]

The great advantage in bringing so many refugees to countries outside of Europe was that for the majority, their wanderings were thereby ended. Overseas settlement meant final absorption within a reasonable period of time. By contrast, refugees in European countries could not expect to remain there indefinitely. Most of them had to plan another move, and their stay in Europe was fraught with economic difficulties and endless frustrations.

One of the major havens for refugees in Europe was Holland, with Belgium not far behind in importance. Holland had no visa requirements for entrants from Germany, and it was therefore quite easy to escape to the friendly republic to the west. In March 1933 an ad hoc refugee committee was first created there under the auspices of David Cohen, a professor at the University of Amsterdam, who was active in Jewish causes. After the April 1 boycott in Germany, the stream of refugees increased considerably, and Professor Cohen and his collaborators asked Mrs. Gertrude van Tijn, a social worker of independent means who was herself of German Jewish birth, to take over the refugee work. A Committee for Jewish Refugees was set up, and fund-raising machinery was created. In 1933 some 3,682 refugees arrived in Holland,[76] and they were helped to either integrate into the Dutch economy or emigrate. For this latter undertaking another committee was set up, in which Mrs. van Tijn also occupied a central role. As in France, there was never enough money, and when there was little chance of either emigration or absorption into the Dutch economy—there were 451,000 unemployed in Holland in 1936 out of a population of 8,000,000—the committee could only advise the refugees to return to Germany. In 1933, 615 are said to have returned; by 1934 the total number of returnees was between 1,200 and 1,500. This was about a fourth of the total number. The rest were either absorbed in Holland or emigrated (5,500 in 1933 and 1934).

With the relative abatement of anti-Semitic persecution in Germany in 1934, it seemed that the emergency might soon be over. Mrs. van Tijn, in a memorandum entitled "Liquidation of Dutch Jewish Relief Committees," wrote that soon the whole problem would be solved. She was not expecting much more help from JDC, and consequently did not know what to do with the refugees that still remained. "As we have from the beginning always repatriated as many people as possible (in all nearly 900), it will not be an easy matter to send back many people now. In some cases the alternative of stopping relief money is being adopted."[77] The Dutch government was also anxious to remove these refugees from the Dutch cities, and Kahn reported in August 1934 that even non-German Jewish refugees who had come to Holland and Belgium prior to 1933 were being repatriated. Two thousand such "old" immigrants were being threatened with expulsion by the Dutch.[78]

The relations between the Dutch committee and Kahn in Paris were excellent; in retrospect it appears that Mrs. van Tijn thought they were more rosy than they actually were.[79] The committee repeatedly threatened to close its doors because the means put at its disposal by local Dutch Jewry and by JDC and other bodies simply were not in proportion to the needs. At the last moment it was always JDC that provided the needed sums; Kahn was very partial to Mrs. van Tijn's powerful personality, accurate bookkeeping, and German Jewish background, and in New York these sentiments were echoed as well.[80]

By the end of 1934 some 9,000 Jewish refugees had arrived in Holland. There seems to have been a marked decrease in 1935, but after the Nuremberg laws in the autumn the movement increased again. In 1936, especially toward the end of the year, an estimated 600 people were coming in monthly. Of these, many found a solution to their problems by themselves; but over 1,000 people were dependent on the committee, and 361 had to be supported by it. In 1937 another decrease in the flow of refugees made the local committee believe that its task might soon be over. But 1938, with its multiple disasters in Austria and Czechoslovakia, caused the flow of refugees to increase again. Dutch restrictions on the entry of Jews from Germany grew, and border-crossing became very

T A B L E   10[81]
JDC Expenditures in Holland

Year	1933	1934	1935	1936	1937	1938	1939
$ spent	41,269	88,160	49,690	120,037	118,905	128,248	439,000

difficult. All told, probably at least 30,000 Jewish refugees entered Holland from Germany between 1933 and 1940.[82]

A similar situation developed in Belgium. Two committees functioned there: one in Brussels under Dr. Max Gottschalk, and a second, less effective one, in Antwerp. JDC allocations to Belgium also grew, approximating the expenditure in Holland,[83] and about the same number of refugees arrived there. By 1940 thirty thousand refugees were estimated to have entered the country since 1933. Of these, about one-half arrived before 1938 and the rest after March 1938.[84] The Belgian government, which had been very liberal during the early 1930s, became more and more restrictive toward the end of the decade. Gottschalk's committee was in serious trouble by the autumn of 1938.

Probably the most impressive piece of work done by the refugee committees in the Benelux countries was a retraining farm at Wieringen in Holland, established on March 13, 1934, by Mrs. van Tijn's group. On the lands of a typical Dutch *polder*—land reclaimed from the sea—an attempt was made to prepare young German Jews to emigrate and become farmers in various countries. After social difficulties encountered during the first couple of years of Wieringen's existence, owing to the presence there of Communist youth, the farm became a great success. The Communists disappeared from the farm during the Spanish Civil War, and the majority of the young people who remained and those who joined later from Germany leaned toward Palestine. Wieringen was in fact run by a Palestinian couple, Moshe and Lea Katznelson. By April 1936, out of 60 youngsters, 33 had gone to Palestine. In late 1938, after the November pogroms in Germany, a noted German Jewish educator, Dr. Kurt Bondy, brought over 20 pupils from the training farm at Gross-Breesen in Germany. Up to 1939, it appears, 245 pupils had left Wieringen, of whom 111 went to Palestine.[85]

The position in Switzerland was in many ways unique. There was no need to possess a visa to enter the country, though identification papers were, of course, demanded. Switzerland was interested in maintaining her tourist industry, and she also had a strong tradition of granting asylum to political refugees. At the same time, however, there was a strong anti-Jewish feeling in many of the more conservative parts of the confederacy (Switzerland did not allow the general entry of Jews into the country at large until 1866), and in early 1933 the National Front, supported by the ex-chief of staff of the Swiss army, revealed itself as a Nazi group, its propaganda based largely on anti-Semitic themes. In the autumn of 1933 the Swiss Nazis achieved significant gains in cantonal and municipal elections. Their propaganda provided the background for an action brought in a Swiss court against the libelous *Protocols of the Elders of Zion;* ultimately the *Protocols* were proved to be a forgery.

Swiss Jewry numbered about eighteen thousand persons in 1933.[86] It was organized under the Schweizerischer Israelitischer Gemeindebund (SIG), founded in 1904, and in the early 1930s its president was a member of one of the old Swiss Jewish families, Jules Dreyfus-Brodsky. As in Holland, but unlike the situation in France, the existence of a united Jewish representation made work for refugees from Germany considerably easier. An existing organization affiliated with SIG, the Verein Schweizerischer Israelitischer Armenpflegen (VSIA) undertook to care for the refugees. Among the leaders of VSIA, a manufacturer from Saint-Gall, Saly Mayer, soon stood out as a prominent personality in the field of aid and rescue.

At the beginning a mass flight into Switzerland occurred, largely of fairly well-to-do persons. It appears that from April until September 1933 some ten thousand people, presumably mostly Jewish, arrived in Switzerland via Basel alone.[87] As in other countries, however, a high proportion of the refugees returned to Germany before long. It seems that the number of Jews who remained in Switzerland exceeded five thousand in 1933, and the Swiss Jewish community collected over 150,000 Swiss francs to support about a half of these who were without means. Thus in 1933 no JDC help was needed.[88]

The attitude of the Swiss government toward these refugees was ambiguous. A police circular of April 20, 1933, based on a government (Bundesrat) decision of April 7, declared that Jews could be considered political refugees only if they had actually been politically prominent personalities in Germany; the general anti-Semitic actions of the Nazi government did not entitle Jews to the status of political refugees.[89] A circular of March 31 defined what became standard Swiss policy in the years thereafter: Jews could come to Switzerland on a purely temporary basis, that is, provided they undertook to leave the country again at the earliest possible opportunity.

Two arguments were advanced against the settlement of Jews in Switzerland: unemployment and the danger that the country would be swamped by strangers *(Überfremdung)*. The problem of unemployment was serious indeed, for in a population of less than four million there were sixty-eight thousand unemployed in 1933 and ninety-three thousand in 1936; the trade unions objected strongly to the entry of additional workers into labor's ranks, especially in the professions. Yet the number of Jews trying to find work in Switzerland was very small; the total Jewish population in Switzerland amounted to less than 0.5 percent of the Swiss people. The *Überfremdung* argument was therefore based not so much on facts as on prejudice. This was directed especially against Jews from Eastern Europe, who were declared to be alien to the Swiss way of life *(Wesensfremd)*. It was true that the proportion of foreigners in Switzerland was higher than in any other European country (14.7 percent in 1910 and 8.7 percent in 1930), but the percentage of Jews among these was infinitesimal.[90]

SIG, faced with an extremely careful if not actually hostile attitude on the part of the Swiss Ministry of Justice and Police, therefore undertook to support any refugees who might be without means, and tried its best to keep the problem of Jewish refugees out of the public view. It seems that Dreyfus-Brodsky took pains to make clear to the Swiss authorities that while SIG was interested in the entry of as many refugees as possible, it was in agreement with the policy of trying to get them to emigrate as quickly as was feasible.[91] It is not clear whether this was said because it was politically wise to say it, or whether fear of anti-Semitism or other motives were at work. At any rate, whereas SIG waged a public battle against Swiss anti-Semitism and in 1936 became a member organization of the World Jewish Congress, it made no attempt to try to change the restrictive practices of the government by political pressure or by direct or indirect intervention.

The federal government continued to waver between restrictionism and a tendency to maintain the liberal tradition of aid to refugees. When Germany began to deny citizenship to an everlarger number of refugees, thus making them into stateless persons, the Alien Police Department issued another circular (on September 14, 1934), asking cantonal authorities not to deny refuge to people simply because they had become stateless; yet when the Swiss Emigrant Children's Aid Organization (SHEK) asked the government to allow emigrant children into the country, the reply was a harsh negative.

In the meantime, international organizations as well as governments were becoming concerned over the problem of identity papers for refugees. MacDonald had failed in his attempts to persuade the governments to provide the refugees with special identity documents. After his resignation in July 1936, a conference took place under League of Nations auspices in Geneva, where there was proposed for ratification by the governments concerned an agreement that would provide the refugees with appropriate papers, similar to the Nansen passports of an earlier decade. Under the new convention, the governments undertook not to deport refugees to Germany unless the person concerned willfully refused to prepare for his emigration to another country. Although the Swiss did not want to be the first to sign, they began to implement the convention's terms. Finally Switzerland signed the convention, after a number of other states had done so, in August 1937. Following this act, the Alien Police declared (also August 1937) that deportations of refugees to Germany should be undertaken only in exceptional cases.[92]

JDC help was not forthcoming for VSIA until 1938, when it

became clear that the local community could not possibly pay for the large number of Jews escaping from Germany and Austria. From April 1933 to the end of 1937, over 700,000 Swiss francs were spent by Swiss Jewry, or about 8 Swiss francs ($2) per person yearly, which was considerably more than any other Jewish community gave at that time. Yet while JDC did little more than watch the situation, the relationship between Kahn and his successor, Morris C. Troper, on one hand, and the heads of SIG, on the other, grew progressively closer. This was especially so after 1936, when Saly Mayer became the president of SIG. The importance of this connection was to make itself felt later on. Until the great rush into Switzerland in 1938, the number of refugees there was not high. In 1935 Kahn estimated them to be two thousand, of whom only a few hundred needed help.[93]

Jewish refugees went to other European countries as well. In Italy there were one thousand refugees in 1935; and varying numbers of people were temporarily stranded in other countries. But most of these small groups of Jews found their way sooner or later to countries overseas where they could hope to establish a new life. During the first two years of Nazi rule those who could find no way to emigrate usually had to return to Germany. Thousands returned not only from Western Europe, but also from Poland, because they "preferred the bitterness in Germany to the misery in Poland."[94] Apart from the repatriates from Germany, one report puts the German Jewish refugees in Poland between 1933 and 1938 at six thousand. These were either German citizens, some of them of Polish origin, who had lost all contact with Poland, its language, and its Jewish population, or else actually German Jews proper. Most of them either returned to Germany or left Poland for other havens. The total number of Jews who returned to Germany in 1934 was put at eleven thousand.[95] It was not until early 1935, when the Nazis began sending returning Jews to concentration camps, that the stream of returnees dwindled to a trickle; most of these were people who had been deported from countries of refuge to Germany by the police in those countries.

One country that served as a transit point for thousands of Jews in the 1930s was Czechoslovakia. In 1933, with the first wave of refugees, some four thousand Jews arrived there. At first there were separate refugee committees in the main towns, and of course most of the refugees (twenty-five hundred) were cared for in Prague. By 1933 a Comité National Tchécoslovaque pour les Réfugiés Provenant d'Allemagne had been founded to represent Jewish and non-Jewish political refugees to the government. The chairman of this committee was Mrs. Marie Schmolka, head of the HICEM office at Prague. Up to 1936 a total of some sixty-five hundred refugees passed through Czechoslovakia, but most of them left the country. In 1935, when only eight hundred Jewish refugees remained, Mrs. Schmolka became the head of a central Jewish refugee committee, the Jewish Social Institute (Sociální Ústav), which in effect became the equivalent of the Dutch and Swiss type of centralized community efforts.[96] Indeed, there was much in common between the energetic and resourceful individuals at the head of each of these committees: Gertrude van Tijn, Saly Mayer, Marie Schmolka; and JDC trusted them fully. In Czechoslovakia, JDC contributions were very small, and until 1938 the Czech Jewish community itself paid for the help it gave to German Jews under the fairly benevolent protection of a government, whose intense dislike of the Germans contributed to its humanitarian attitude toward the refugee problem.

A special problem arose in Danzig, which was a free city under the protection of the League of Nations. Danzig's population, which was almost wholly German, became more and more influenced by Nazi ideology. The local Nazi leader, Artur Greiser, had declared in August 1933 that no "Aryan" legislation would be introduced in the city; another declaration on July 2, 1934, even went so far as to say that the constitution of the city "makes it impossible for inhabitants to have their rights restricted in any way on account of their race or creed."[97] Yet despite these fine words —representing probably not only a tactical move of the Nazis but also the more moderate policies of the first Nazi ruler in Danzig,

Hermann Rauschning (who later changed sides and turned against Nazism)—the actual situation deteriorated steadily. Newspaper attacks sparked a boycott, and Jewish lawyers and doctors soon found their jobs threatened by an unofficial but effective line of action. There were about three thousand native Jews in Danzig; in addition, about five thousand Polish Jews, who had been attracted by the favorable economic conditions there, had entered the city.

In late 1937, a time when there was relatively little overt anti-Jewish activity in Germany, disaster struck the Danzig community. Two days of violent outrages (October 21 and 23) were followed by the arrest of Jews and the seizure of the property of prominent Jewish merchants. JDC had not supported Danzig Jews prior to these events, save for $1,000 it had once donated for the creation of a Free Loan *kassa*. Now it sent the head of its Warsaw office, Isaac Giterman, to investigate and to send back a recommendation for action. Giterman reported that the situation was disastrous and that emigration from Danzig should receive the same kind of priority as emigration from Germany.[98] Some money was sent to support relief cases, but the problem was how to handle the larger issue. It was clear that a significant proportion of the newer Polish immigrants would have to leave the city and return to the misery of Polish Jewish existence. Kahn was quite reluctant to support Danzig openly for fear that other governments would draw the conclusion that Jewish organizations would always rescue the Jews if they were threatened with expulsion.[99] In the end a small sum ($12,500) was appropriated for the support of Polish Jewish returnees from Danzig, on the condition that the recipients prove they could make themselves self-supporting with the help of the money they received. There was to be no relief and also no support for large-scale emigration.

Giterman's opinion was different: he thought that the situation in Danzig paralleled that in Germany; he felt that there was no escaping the conclusion that the Jews had to leave Danzig. At the end of November 1937 Giterman sent another report to Kahn, in which he repeated his previous statements and added that Jewish capital in the city was no longer transferable because Jews were forbidden to sell their property, and therefore they had to be supported.

Despite the reluctance of JDC, Jewish organizations in Danzig saw no other alternative but to help as many Jews emigrate as possible. Between October 1937 and the end of 1938 forty-nine hundred Jews left Danzig; thirty-three hundred went back to Poland, and the rest went abroad. These were the official figures. But Giterman thought that in actual fact fewer people had emigrated and that fifty-five hundred Jews were still in Danzig. Giterman was in favor of a well-organized emigration plan, whereas the Danzig community, under the influence of the Zionist-Revisionists (whose leader Giterman rather rashly suspected of being in the service of the Gestapo), was trying to find the means for mass illegal emigration to Palestine.[100] JDC, Giterman warned, should not give its support to these plans. In the end, of course, the people who did go on illegal ships to Palestine were saved from what followed in their native city.[101] JDC, on the other hand, increased its support for Danzig. It spent $24,885 there in 1938, and $54,000 in 1939.

In early 1938 the situation as far as Jewish emigration was concerned began to change for the worse. In March 1938 Hitler conquered Austria by a *Blumenkrieg,* that is, the only things that were thrown at the German soldiers upon their entry into Austria were flowers. Austrian Jews, 185,246 of them, and an unknown number of persons considered Jewish by Nazi criteria found themselves trapped.

5

Prelude to the Holocaust

After the Nazis came to power in Germany in the 1930s there was a tendency for the attention of well-meaning Jews and non-Jews to concentrate on the plight of the half million German Jews. Poland and East European countries generally seemed, by comparison, to be havens of safety and prosperity.

Nothing could have been further from the truth.

Politically, the Jews of Poland were caught between the Polish government and the opposition, and they became a totally helpless minority. In 1926 a military coup brought down parliamentary government, and a military dictatorship was set up under Marshal Józef Pilsudski. Originally, the left wing—composed of the United Peasant party and the socialists (the Polish initials were PPS)—maintained a benevolent neutrality toward the new regime. Soon, however, they turned against it. The right-wing National Democrats (or Endeks, as they were called), representative of the Polish middle classes, had been the party in power before 1926; now they were in bitter opposition. In the rigged parliamentary election in 1930, government-sponsored deputies had gained a majority. With the destruction of democratic parliamentarism, the minorities—and the Jews among them—could no longer hope for adequate and free representation in the Sejm (Polish parliament).

The government tried to gain popularity with the opposition by leaning to the right. In the Endek party itself, a younger, semi-Fascist, and virulently anti-Semitic clique gained ascendancy. Even that was not enough, however, and an extreme pro-Fascist and anti-Semitic group split off from the Endeks to found a party called ONR. The government did not wish to relinquish power, and it institutionalized its dictatorship by a new constitution, which the Sejm passed in April 1935, a few weeks before Pilsudski's death. In order to maintain power, however, the government adopted many of the policies advocated by its right-wing critics, including the anti-Semitic measures.

After May 1935 the leadership of the government was in the hands of a clique of army officers and aristocratic politicians concentrated around the weak and vain Marshal Edward Smigly-Rydz. Pilsudski himself had been opposed to active anti-Semitism, and the feeling among the Jews was that he had protected them against the right-wing tendencies of the regime. After his death these tendencies had a much freer reign. In early 1937 government supporters themselves founded a new party, known as OZN, which represented the views of semi-Fascist elements in the army, the bureaucracy, and the middle classes. OZN was intended to catch the votes of the government's right-wing opponents, and it engaged in anti-Semitic propaganda. The Jews could not support the rightist opposition; and the government, originally considered a protector, had become an enemy.

There remained the left-wing opposition. The peasants, under their radical leader, Stanislaw Mikolajczyk, tended to the left after early 1937. Together with PPS, they probably represented well over half the population. The peasants, despite anti-Semitic tendencies, saw through the government policies and refused to let Jew-baiting sidetrack them from their basic demand for the division of land. Nor was PPS free from anti-Semitism; its Jewish ally, the Bund, was never able to conclude an open political alliance with PPS. Nevertheless, on a local plane and on a number of issues there was cooperation between these two socialist parties.

The actual strength of the political parties in Poland can be gleaned from the events of late 1938. In November of that year the government's OZN group received an absolute majority in general elections held under conditions of virtual terror. Yet in the communal elections of December 1938 PPS and the Bund, working in unison, received 43 percent of the votes in Warsaw, 35 percent in Cracow, and 55 percent in Lodz. Undoubtedly, this victory of the Left eased the Jewish position somewhat in the late 1930s.

The internal political structure of the Jewish community was characterized by the large number of political organizations. Their relative strengths have never been satisfactorily established, for all elections in the 1930s were rigged and could not mirror the true state of affairs. In 1930 there were ten Jewish representatives in the parliament, of whom three were elected as a result of government pressure. Of the rest, six were Zionist; the Bund had not participated in the elections. In 1935 Jewish representation dwindled to four, of whom three were Zionists and one a government supporter, an Agudist. In 1938 there were three Zionists and two Agudists. In late 1938 and early 1939, on the other hand, it was obvious that a large majority of Jewish voters in the cities had voted for the Bund in the municipal elections. This meant that the Jewish population had become more radical and preferred the Bund, but it did not mean that Jews had weakened in their interest in Zionism and Palestine.[1] One could vote for the Bund in municipal elections and support Zionism at the same time. The vote for the Bund was really the expression of despair. The overall picture, then, was one of political decline, of a government pandering to anti-Semitic prejudices, and of progressive radicalization among the Jewish population.

Back of this situation lay, of course, the economic crisis, which persisted in Poland until late 1938. Official unemployment statistics in Poland were traditionally suspect, but even these showed that while in 1927 there were 165,300 unemployed, by 1935 this number had increased to 402,000. One historian put the real number of unemployed in Poland in the second half of the decade at 1.5 million.[2] Government bureaucracy was omnipresent, large, and costly.

The economic problems, which will be discussed below, were accompanied by a growing crescendo of physical attacks by anti-Semitic elements on the Jewish population. At times these attacks tended to overshadow the dismal poverty into which the Jewish masses were sinking. The physical attacks were accompanied by acts of deliberate discrimination that equaled, and often exceeded, the steps taken by Germany's Nazis at that time.

In early March 1935 the Endeks ruling in the municipality of Lodz (a town with a Jewish population of two hundred thousand) abolished all subsidies to Jewish institutions.[3] Late in 1935 the long-standing Endek demand to separate Jewish university students from their non-Jewish colleagues was put into operation in Lwów; the Warsaw Polytechnic followed suit in October 1937, as did the universities of Vilna, Cracow, and Poznań.[4] Starting in early 1935, boycotts of Jews spread all through the Polish countryside. These were followed by pogroms: window-smashing, the overturning of Jewish market stalls, beatings, arson, and finally murder. The details of these brutalities are repetitive and terrible. In 1935 pogroms took place at Radomsko in April, at Radosc (near Warsaw) and Grochow in May, at Grodno in May. In December these isolated occurrences began to harden into a campaign: disturbances in Klwow, Lodz, Katowice, Kielce, and Hrubieszow were followed in January 1936 by attacks on Jews in Cracow and Warsaw, among other places. On March 9, 1936, a terrible pogrom occurred at Przytyk, where two Jews were killed and many houses burned: Bombs were thrown in those same months in thirteen more towns, including Mińsk Mazowiecki; there, a second pogrom occurred in early June and, after four Jews had been killed, most of the Jewish population left for Warsaw. During 1936 and early 1937 the pogroms became a daily occurrence in Poland, and clearly indicated increasingly better organization. In Czestochowa riots started in June 1937 with a fight between two porters; a well-organized boycott movement against the Jews prolonged the unrest there for months.

Kahn discerned "carefully planned activities of anti-Semitic elements, in which high government officials participated." In the course of the Czestochowa pogrom, the Endek paper *Ganiec Czestochowski* gave lists of streets on which Jews had not as yet been robbed.[5] Seventy-five Jews were wounded in this particular outbreak.

In May 1937 another outbreak occurred at Brest Litovsk, where a number of Jews were killed and some 200 wounded.[6] Between May 1935 and January 1937, 118 Jews were killed and 1,350 wounded; 137 Jewish stores were destroyed. A total of 348 separate violent mass assaults on Jews were counted during the period, and the compilation was termed both "unofficial" and "incomplete." Another compilation showed that between the end of 1935 and March 1939, 350 Jews had been killed and 500 wounded.[7]

The wave of pogroms did not abate throughout 1937 and 1938. In August 1937 five severe outbreaks occurred in central Poland, and anti-Jewish demonstrations occurred in seven towns, including the capital.[8] One result of these events was an increased movement of the Jews from smaller places, where they felt themselves exposed, to the larger towns, where they thought they would be safer.

But in early 1938 the riots spread to Warsaw, and from then on attacks on Jews in the larger cities became a normal occurrence. Several times the Jews reacted by demonstrations and general strikes (March 1936, May and June 1937). In Warsaw and Lodz the Bund tried to create Jewish self-defense units. These were supported by PPS as well, but police intervention in favor of the pogromists[9] neutralized Jewish opposition.[10]

In 1938 and 1939 the anti-Jewish boycott movement became more and more effective. Again, it was mainly the small Jewish communities that were hit, and in this a parallel to the experience in Germany can clearly be discerned. These boycott actions were usually organized by the Endeks, but by early 1939 the government OZN group also supported them. In February 1939 an OZN-inspired boycott in the Lublin area caused Jewish economic life to be "practically ruined".[11] The number of Jewish stores in town after town decreased, while the Polish stores grew in number, despite the continued economic crisis.[12]

In early 1939 Jews were forced to leave certain frontier towns because they were considered to be unreliable elements—as though Jews were less interested in resistance to the Germans than were the Poles. In this connection "almost one-quarter of the Jewish population of Gdynia was deported." At Katowice it was "feared that half the local Jewish population may be forced to emigrate elsewhere."[13] Riots, pogroms, and boycotts now spread to areas in western and northwestern Poland, where the number of Jews was very small; up till then these areas had been spared from excesses.[14]

Jews, especially observant Jews, who formed the majority of Polish Jewry, were hard hit by Polish laws against ritual slaughter (shehita) enacted in April 1936 and, in a final and drastic form, in March 1939. Not only was religious freedom sharply diminished, but a large number of Jewish butchers and supervisors of ritual slaughter were threatened with economic ruin.

The general and extreme anti-Jewish movement, both political and economic, continued until the spring of 1939. Only with the increased Polish-German tension after Hitler's conquest of Czechoslovakia in March did Polish anti-Semitism show signs of weakening, as the attention of the Polish nationalists became directed outward. Yet the long campaign against the Jews was even then by no means over; on the contrary, it was the clear intention of the middle-class parties to enact openly anti-Jewish legislation. Laws modeled on Nazi legislation were to include "the revision of citizenship and the elimination of the Jews from the economic and cultural life of Poland."[15]

Polish anti-Semitism in the 1930s drew its inspiration from three sources: the traditional, historic enmity of a Catholic people to the Jewish minority; economic competition exacerbated by crisis conditions; and a virulent form of nationalism that was influenced by Fascist models.

The historic element was most clearly expressed by the church, which exercised a tremendous influence and used it to agitate in fairly extreme terms against the Jews. Although paying lip service to its abhorrence of "the eruption of human passions" generally, a statement by the Catholic Press Agency in early 1936 declared the Catholic belief in "the cultural separation of Poles and Jews." It thought that Jewish youth was generally "badly brought up, which sets a bad example for Christian youth." Jews were accused of having Communist leanings. "As to other negative traits of the Jewish character," the statement continued, "even writers of Jewish origin do not fail to emphasize them. In the forefront of the fight against Christianity in Poland, there too Israel's sons are being found." Anti-Jewish boycotts were justified because it was no sin to defend the laborer against exploitation.[16] "The Jews are ulcers on the Polish body," declared a Polish paper, and another Catholic writer thought that while "no power will be able to stop" the hatred between the Jews and Poles, "this hatred is highly beneficial to our Polish trade and to our country."[17] Traditional anti-Semitism could also be discerned in aristocratic circles, as in the newspaper *Czas*, which was under the influence of Prince Radziwill and Prince Lubomirski. The peasant leaders declared that they opposed anti-Semitism radically, "but they could not ignore the importance of polonizing industry and relieving the peasant from exploitation by the Jewish traders."[18]

One can see in these opinions the overlapping of the economic and nationalistic aspects of anti-Semitism with the more traditional element. The peasants were hard hit by the crisis, which caused agricultural prices to fall from an index of 100 in 1928 to an index of 34 in 1934, whereas government and private monopolies in industries contrived to prevent a similar decline in prices of manufactured goods, which only fell to 82.[19]

These fluctuations in prices affected the small Jewish trader no less than they did the peasant, for indeed the economic decline of the peasant was the root cause of Jewish rural poverty. Of course, the peasant leaders failed to see this. On the other hand, the crisis increased cutthroat commercial and industrial competition. In this area the Polish middle class was supported by the government in its violent attack on Jewish competitors. Essentially, therefore, it was the task of JDC as the major Jewish aid organization to fight a rearguard action to protect the helpless Jewish trader and artisan as far as possible against the combined onslaught of government, mob, and economic competition.

Economic and nationalistic anti-Semitism was clearly Nazi-influenced. Revocation of Jewish equality in Poland became a declared Endek policy in April 1937. Boycott measures and pressure on Jews to emigrate referred constantly to the German example.

The number of Jews in Poland in 1921 was 2,845,364;[20] by late 1938 it was approximately 3,310,000. The annual rate of growth was about 30,000.[21] The Polish census of 1931 gave the number of gainfully occupied Jews as 1,123,025.[22] Of these, 277,555 were classified as workers, about 200,000 were artisans,[23] and 428,965 were traders. In 1931 the number of registered unemployed workers was 78,256, or 28.2 percent of the total. In 1935 Kahn reported that no less than 60 percent of the workers and employees were unemployed; of these, only workers employed in enterprises employing more than twenty people were entitled to unemployment insurance. Those who did work received an average of 30–40 zloty ($6–$8) a week. Of the artisans, one-third were estimated to be "in distress." In 1931 the traders and their families had numbered 1,140,532. In 1935 Kahn estimated that there were 1,150,000 and that 400,000 were living in "dire poverty." Of the 120,000 whom he classified as "intellectuals" and their families, 60,000 had no steady income. Kahn estimated the total number of Jews who were without any income, unemployed, or distressed to be over 1,000,000, or one-third of Polish Jewry.[24]

This estimate was given credence by a number of other authorities.[25] Two years later the London *Jewish Chronicle* could describe the Jews in Poland as "a helpless minority sunk in squalid poverty and misery such as can surely be paralleled nowhere on the face of the earth. Today it is generally agreed that one-third of the Jewish population is on the brink of starvation, one-third contrives to obtain a mere existence, and the rest are fortunate in securing a minimum of comfort."[26]

A fair indicator of the economic condition of the Jews was the number of people asking for charity at Passover. In 1933, 100,000 of the 350,000 Jews of Warsaw applied for such assistance,[27] or less than a third. In 1935, 60 percent of Warsaw Jews applied.[28] In the spring of 1939 a JDC memorandum estimated the number of Jews wholly dependent on charity at 600,000, or close to 20 percent of Polish Jewry, while a total of 38 percent (1,250,000) were wholly or partially dependent.[29] In August 1934 Neville Laski, president of the British Board of (Jewish) Deputies, reported from Poland that he had "never seen such poverty, squalor, and filth. It made one despair of civilization." What was more important, he discerned a downward trend and foresaw that "even this year will be looked back upon as a happy year."[30]

This prediction was fully borne out by Alexander Kahn, chairman of JDC's Polish Committee, who reported in 1937 that "in Poland the Jew is in the midst of his ruthless enemies, bound hand and foot, and without a chance." He described how the "bands of savage youths, wild-eyed and bloodthirsty, with every human instinct obliterated, jump upon old men, women, and young children in the streets and in the public parks of Warsaw." The Nazis, Kahn thought, were "more honest"; the Jews in Poland were faced with "extermination or expulsion."

Polish competition was, with government help, fairly effective.

T A B L E 11
Jewish versus Non-Jewish Enterprise in Kalisz[31]

Type of Enterprise	1934	1936	Increase or Decrease
Jewish businesses	1,292	1,163	− 129
Non-Jewish businesses	789	907	+ 118
Jewish artisans	328	311	− 17
Non-Jewish artisans	497	536	+ 39

Some detailed researches affirmed this. Table 11 illustrates the situation in the town of Kalisz.

In early 1939 a JDC memorandum estimated that between 1933 and 1938, some thirty thousand non-Jewish shops had opened and that about the same number of Jewish shops had closed.[32]

The deterioration of Jewish economic life led to serious social and medical consequences. Sholem Asch, the famous Jewish writer, claimed that "people made the impression as if they were buried alive. Every second person was undernourished, skeletons of skin and bones, crippled, candidates for the grave."[33] It should be remembered that this was written three years before World War II began.

The most serious results of this general situation were evident among Jewish children. A detailed investigation in the town of Ostrog showed that, out of a sample of 386 Jewish children in four out of fifteen "Jewish" streets, 262 were of school age but only 109 attended school. Of the other 153, 12 were ill, 3 were retarded, 6 had no documents for registration, 9 had not enrolled in time, 6 were not accounted for, and 117 could not go to school because they had no clothes or shoes. Of the total of 386, only 67 were healthy; 196 were weak or anemic, 61 were scrofulous. A total of 71 percent of the children were in various stages of undernourishment down to and including starvation.[34] This was the situation three years *before* the establishment of ghettos in Poland. Similar descriptions could be quoted about other areas as well. JDC estimated that about one-third of the Jewish schoolchildren went to school hungry.

Government action, quite apart from official policies, tended to be quite unscrupulous. Polish tax collectors interpreted the law in the most brutal way. Reports came in to JDC of bakers from whom the last bit of flour was taken away in lieu of taxes they could not pay; of horses taken away from peddlers, thus reducing them to complete destitution; of sewing machines taken away from tailors, as well as material left by the customers to be made up into clothes.[35]

This, then, was the situation facing JDC in Poland—a mass catastrophe of the largest Jewish community outside the United States: a hostile government, an anti-Semitic population, and no local economic or political resources to draw upon.

JDC could not send to Poland more than it received from American Jewry. Table 12 shows that from 1934 on—even in the face of the decline in JDC income and expenditure in 1935—the importance of Poland in JDC work increased steadily, in spite of the German emergency. By 1937/8 fully one-third of all JDC work was done in Poland.

This paralleled the attitude of the Jewish Agency, noted earlier, in granting the majority of Palestine immigration certificates to immigrants from Poland, despite the German emergency. The situation described above was constantly brought to the attention of the JDC Executive Committee members in New York. They were torn between the needs of German Jewry, the necessity for supporting German Jewish refugees in various European countries, the need for supporting emigration, the urgent needs of Romania, eastern Czechoslovakia, and Lithuania, the obligation to wind up the Russian work in an organized fashion and, finally, the desperate situation in Poland.

Several problems confronted JDC in Poland. A major problem was whether to enable at least a certain proportion of Polish Jews

TABLE 12

Expenditures by JDC in Poland

Year	Total JDC expenditure (in $)	JDC expenditure in Poland (in $)	Percentage of total
1933	665,754	123,700	18.5
1934	1,382,326	136,280	9.8
1935	983,343	216,532	20.7
1936	1,904,923	464,529	23.7
1937	2,883,759	943,830	32.7
1938	3,799,709	1,245,300	32.7

to emigrate and thus partly alleviate the situation for the rest. In the early 1930s all such ideas were rejected out of hand. "With the doors of the world closed to immigration in the largest measure, Jewish life will have to be reconstituted in the lands in which large Jewish populations abide," declared Hyman in 1934.[36] This was the JDC attitude until 1935/6.

Apart from the obvious difficulties in getting Jewish emigrants accepted anywhere in the world, there was an ideological tendency to see the Jews as loyal citizens, and ultimately integrated members, of their various host nationalities, paralleling what the leaders of JDC considered to be their own experience in America. As a result, those leaders rejected Palestine as even a partial solution to the Polish Jewish problem, though 24,300 Jews emigrated to Palestine in 1935 out of a total Polish Jewish emigration of 30,703. In the 1930s one of the central figures in JDC in New York was George Backer, who was very active in anti-Nazi politics in the United States and was also fairly friendly toward Palestine causes. Even he declared in 1936 that there was no use in glorifying Palestine "until the structure of Jewish life in other countries has been saved."[37]

The Zionists argued that Jewish life in Poland simply could not be saved, but they were hampered by the fact that the British increasingly barred the doors of Palestine to Jewish entry after 1935, and thus removed Palestine as an immediate solution. When Simon Marks of England tried in 1937 to raise funds there for Polish Jewry and intended that these monies reach "the Hechalutz and Zionist groups," Kahn remarked that "these are just the people who have not been very prominent in our work."[38]

After 1935 the attitude of JDC underwent a gradual change. The main reasons for this were that (1) Polish Jews (actually, the Zionist leader Yitzhak Gruenbaum) themselves declared that one million Polish Jews should emigrate; and (2) the Polish government exercised ever-increasing pressure both on Polish Jews and on international bodies to help large numbers of Jews to emigrate. JDC resisted these demands; Hyman complained especially of the

fact that the Jews themselves were expressing what amounted to
"demands for the expulsion of millions."[39]

Labor leaders close to the Bund were more explicit. In Poland
the Bund declared itself opposed to the notion that Jews were an
alien people in their countries of settlement;[40] in the U.S., Vladeck
wrote in the Yiddish socialist paper *Forverts* that "to make the
existence of the Polish Jews possible in Poland, they must stop
looking upon Palestine as the solution to their problem. . . . They
must dedicate their activities to a healthy, free, and better Poland
—and not Palestine." Sholem Asch was certain that once the
Polish government realized that three million Jews could not emigrate and that economic betterment for all of Poland's citizens
should be their aim, the Jews would succeed in maintaining their
position as citizens of Poland.[41] This was echoed by Hyman, who
hoped that the situation in Poland was "only a temporary setback
to democracy and liberal ideals." He still believed in finding a way
"to integrate the Jew with his environment under a liberal and
tolerant system of society."

When the British delegation of Lord Samuel, Lord Bearsted, and
Simon Marks came to the U. S. to discuss the emigration of German Jewry in early 1936, Polish government circles seized the
opportunity to present their demand for the mass emigration of
Polish Jews. Prince Radziwill voiced the demand in the Polish
senate in early February. In October the Polish delegate at the sixth
commission of the League of Nations demanded that countries
other than Palestine be opened for the emigration of European
Jews, so as to allow for an emigration of Polish Jews as well.[42] A
scheme for the yearly emigration of eighty thousand was discussed.
Kahn reacted immediately and stated in a press release that the
scheme was "ill advised," that on principle it was wrong to "single
out Jews for such emigration," and that this was a "discrimination
against the law-abiding Jewish citizens which [he] did not think
possible in Poland."[43]

This indeed was slowly becoming the second line of defense for
JDC: objectively there might be a case for an ordered emigration

from Poland, but Jews should not be singled out. Within an ordered program of emigration, the Jews would play their part in proportion to their numbers.

In early 1937 JDC changed its attitude even further, because by that time there seemed to be hope for a practical plan of emigration. We have seen that Joseph A. Rosen tried to organize the emigration of German and Polish Jews into the Soviet Union. At the same time, there appeared on the horizon another plan for mass emigration—to Madagascar.

Polish interest in that tropical island under French rule was by no means new. In 1926 the Polish ambassador to France, Count Chlapowski, had inquired about the possibility of Polish peasants emigrating there, but the information he received regarding climate and soil conditions convinced him that this was out of the question. However, if it was not suitable for Poles, it might still be good enough for Jews. The French government was quite willing to encourage European immigration into the Malagasy highlands, and the Poles sent a mission there, under Major Lepecki; this mission included two Jews. Lepecki's report was not favorable, and the two Jewish members reported that "there is no possibility for a mass immigration to Madagascar."[44]

The French Colonial Office, for its own reasons, nevertheless began exerting pressure on JDC to lend its support to Jewish settlement in Madagascar or other French possessions. In June 1937 Rosen and Kahn were received by officials at the Colonial Office and assured of French interest and cooperation. Despite Lepecki's report, the Polish foreign minister, Józef Beck, discussed the problem in France and proposed a Jewish emigration of 30,000 families yearly, or 120,000 families (about 500,000–600,000 individuals) within five or six years.[45] Rosen thought Madagascar had possibilities, and he wanted an independent JDC commission to go there to investigate the island. Tentatively JDC allocated $12,000 for such a commission, but it never got under way.[46]

The concrete results of all these developments were practically nil. Despite the change of attitude on JDC's part and the great need

of Polish Jewry to flee Poland, not more than 8,861 Jews emigrated
in 1937; of these 3,423 went to Palestine.⁴⁷ This emigration was
considerably less than the birthrate for Polish Jewry,⁴⁸ and the
Poles had before them the shining example of Nazi Germany,
which had managed to rid itself of a large number of Jews by
forcing them out.

When President Roosevelt called upon the nations of the world
to meet in Evian in July 1938 to discuss the problem of refugees
from Germany, the Polish government also swung into action and
demanded that the Evian Conference discuss the problem of Jewish
emigration from Poland. The Americans and British refused, but
the Poles tried to press the Jews themselves to ask for the inclusion
of the Polish Jewish problem at Evian. In the course of this campaign the Polish ambassador in Washington, Count Potocki, approached the American Jewish Committee and JDC (on June 8,
1938). He asked for an emigration of fifty thousand a year, and
alleged that the relatively small emigration of thirty thousand in
1935 had had a psychologically calming effect on Polish anti-
Semitism.⁴⁹ (Actually, after the "calming effect" of the 1935 emigration, pogrom activity increased sharply in late 1935 and in 1936.
Nevertheless, the argument that emigration would be an effective
way of avoiding anti-Semitic outbursts became a deeply ingrained
belief among Jewish leaders in Poland.)

In a more subtle way the same point was made in discussions
held in New York in October 1937 between the Polish consul
general, Sylvester Gruszka, and JDC. Gruszka also demanded
emigration. He intimated that this would aid the democratic and
liberal wing in the Polish government in their struggle against
Polish reaction, and that therefore the support of American Jewry
for Poland was very important. He asked specifically that the *New
York Times* be persuaded to desist from anti-Polish articles, that
the influx of American Jewish capital into Poland be organized,
and that JDC help in eliminating from the public scene in Poland
those American Jewish organizations that the Poles considered
objectionable. This last referred to the American Federation of

Polish Jews, which was conducting a propaganda campaign with largely political overtones against anti-Semitism. There was considerable Zionist influence on AFPJ, and it was even trying to collect money for Polish causes in the U. S., which in the eyes of JDC was wrong. When Gruszka tried to use the animosity between the two Jewish organizations in order to put them against each other, however, Hyman refused to cooperate. The AFPJ, he told Gruszka, was quite useful, if only they would stop competitive fund raising. He and Kahn "stated very definitely that we could not assent to the idea of permitting any pressure to be brought upon the Jews of Poland in relation to the Federation."[50] At the same time, Gruszka intimated that JDC was after all the source of most of the money sent to Poland, and its cooperation was needed for any development connected with the modernization of Polish industry, the advancement of Polish exports to the U. S., and the emigration of Jews.

In planning its policy in Poland, JDC had to take into account the difference between the utterances of Polish representatives abroad and the actual policy of the Polish government vis-à-vis the Jews. Abroad, the pressure for Jewish emigration was coupled both with plans for the modernization of the Polish economy and with statements expressing the hope that the Jews who would remain in Poland would be assimilated politically and become patriotic Poles. The Jews in Poland were loyal to Poland (if for no other reason than that the alternatives in the 1930s were Nazi Germany or Soviet Russia), but in actual practice the Polish government did not tend to act on such optimistic and relatively friendly premises. The head of the JDC office in Poland, Isaac Giterman, declared quite bluntly—on the basis of very full knowledge of Polish policy toward Jews—that there simply was no possibility of a more liberal treatment of the Jews. Polish anti-Semitism was inherent in the local population, and any minister who treated the Jews fairly would lose his position.[51]

In the face of these obstacles and difficulties, the policy of JDC was intractable and heartrending. In the 1930s JDC continued to

refuse to spend its monies on relief. But that policy could not
always be maintained. There were natural disasters, such as the
floods in Galicia in the summer of 1934, which caused damage
estimated at 1 million zloty ($200,000). The Polish government
established a "nonsectarian" relief committee (with one Jewish
representative) and JDC contributed $10,000, or 5 percent of the
sum that was needed. Then there were man-made disasters. After
each pogrom, JDC stepped in to save whatever could be saved. Its
Free Loan *kassas* were strengthened in localities hit by the outrages, and the child care, health, and educational institutions supported by JDC increased their allocations to help as best they
could. Some of the items that appeared in JDC budgets as constructive help through the support of organizations were in fact
little more than intelligently—indeed, constructively—applied relief to stricken communities.

Generally speaking, however, in its approach to the Polish Jewish problem JDC moved more and more in the direction of the
industrialization plans advanced by Kahn. The sums devoted to
Poland were increasing, and there seemed to be an opportunity for
testing Kahn's plans.

The problem of the industrialization plans was intimately connected with the future of the Free Loan and Reconstruction Foundation loan *kassas*. The older, more conservative loan *kassas* were
able to help those who were in a stronger economic position by
loans with a low rate of interest. We have also seen that the position
of these *kassas* weakened as a result of the 1929 economic crisis.
On paper there were still 680 such institutions in Poland in 1933,
but an indeterminate number of these were in fact inactive. In 1934
it was estimated that only 340 of the 601 still registered were
actually operating. The figures quoted in various JDC sources were
contradictory; but by 1935 only 223 *kassas* were said to be in
operation, and 221 more were inactive.

The Reconstruction Foundation stepped in, and throughout
1935–37 tried hard to reorganize the *kassas*. Their importance lay,
after all, in the fact that large numbers of small traders, artisans,

and small manufacturers, as well as members of the intelligentsia, had recourse to them. Even in early 1936 the number of active members was estimated to be over forty-seven thousand. There was an umbrella organization of these *kassas,* largely influenced by Zionist elements. This group, the Verband, had no financial responsibilities, but was supposed to supervise the *kassas* and to see to it that the rules and regulations were observed. It was not at all efficient.

In the autumn of 1936 Kahn and ICA intervened decisively and declared that they would maintain direct contact with the *kassas* and no longer work through the Verband. Despite the negative experience with the Central Bank in the early 1930s, the Reconstruction Foundation set up a new Central Financial Institution, headed by its own nominees from the conservative and largely assimilated group around the Jewish industrialist Karol Sachs. Sachs received the highest accolade JDC could bestow on a Polish Jew: he was placed "in the class of our own leaders in America."[52]

The institution was set up in May 1937, and from then on the Reconstruction Foundation gave its credits to the *kassas* through it, leaving the Verband to deal with questions of organization and rules. In 1937 the foundation appropriated 1 million zloty ($200,000) to reorganize and revitalize *kassas,* under the prodding of its very effective deputy director, Noel Aronovici. At the same time, the foundation was pursuing an essentially conservative policy. Between 1932 and 1935, during and after the dissolution of the Central Bank, the foundation actually withdrew more monies from the *kassas* than it gave them in credits.[53] This money was not returned to the foundation, but kept in Poland. It was not reinvested, however, until the new Central Financial Institution had been set up in 1937/8. In 1937 the foundation books showed a reserve of $494,000 in cash, and its total expenditure in credits granted that year was considerably less than that. ICA had no real wish to invest the monies in doubtful industrialization plans in Poland, and so the *kassas* carried on with their work of helping those whose economic situation was sound. At the end of 1937, 241 *kassas* were functioning and 161 more were awaiting reorganization; 205 others were defunct and had to be liquidated. At the same time, the Reconstruction Foundation included in its work program loan *kassas* organized by merchants on an occupational rather than general basis. The functioning *kassas* included 37 such merchants' institutions, which were really small merchants' banks; these were quite successful. Kassa membership in Poland at the end of 1937 numbered some sixty-eight thousand.

As we have already seen, the political situation of Polish Jewry began to improve very slightly in early 1939. However, the economic situation was worsening, and the loan *kassas* had to intervene in what really amounted to a prevention of catastrophe rather than reconstruction. While most of the work in this respect was done by the Free Loan *kassas,* the loan *kassas* of the Reconstruction Foundation also played a part. A report in 1939 claimed that in many places the *kassas* had prevented the elimination of Jewish market stalls and bakeries; Jews who had been forced to leave their villages by the pogroms of 1937/8 were now being helped to establish places of business in towns. Certain projects engaged in by the more successful artisans and traders, such as fowl fattening, sawmills, and production of soda, were also being aided by the *kassas.*[54]

Relations between the *kassas* and the Reconstruction Foundation were not always happy. The foundation did supply credits, but only on strict terms. In the harsh conditions of economic crisis in Poland there were occasionally bitter recriminations at the rigid way in which agreements were interpreted. The complaint was even heard that the foundation credits had been collected "harshly and ruthlessly, and many *kassas* have been ruined" by the foundation itself.[55] Against this stood the foundation policy, which was quite clearly "not to save the weak and unsound, but to fortify and strengthen the sound and secure positions."[56]

The main instrument of reconstructive work in Poland was not, however, the loan *kassa* but the Free Loan *kassa.* These institutions, it will be remembered, were JDC creations and had no contact with the Reconstruction Foundation-run enterprises. They became immensely popular as the economic crisis hardened, because they charged almost no interest on loans. There were 676 such *kassas* in Poland in 1933, and 841 by 1939. This meant that in practically every Jewish village there was a *kassa* where impoverished artisans and traders and intellectuals, and to a certain extent workers, could get loans to tide them over difficult times. These loans were very small, averaging about $16. But they often prevented a Jew from becoming a public charge.

The central institution of the *kassas* was the CEKABE,[57] through which credits were channeled to the *kassas;* it also filled the functions exercised by the Verband in regard to the foundation loan *kassas.* The total amounts loaned by the Free Loan *kassas* were at first considerably below those loaned by the foundation *kassas*—in 1934 the latter loaned $38.8 million, whereas the Free Loan *kassas* only loaned $2.2 million—but the number of free loans grew steadily throughout the 1930s. The average sums loaned were paltry, which in itself was an indication of the deteriorating position of the Jews.

While the number of free loans and their general totals were increasing, the Reconstruction Foundation *kassas'* work was declining: in 1936, the foundation *kassas* had loaned $15.8 million, or 40 percent of the 1934 total.

T A B L E 13
Free Loan Kassas *in Poland*[58]

Year	No. of loans	Total amount (in millions of zloty)	Average loans (in zloty)
1933	135,600	10.7	79 ($16)
1934	125,000	11.0	88 ($17.60)
1935	149,214	14.5	97 ($19.40)
1936	163,670	15.0	92 ($18.40)
1937	191,294	18.0	94 ($18.80)
1938	221,226	20.0	90 ($18)

With the relative increase in funds available for Poland, Kahn returned to the idea of industrial and other constructive investments in strategic places. In May 1935 he asked for a special yearly allocation of $100,000 for that purpose. The idea was received favorably by Baerwald, who advanced the project in a memorandum of September of that year.[59] British help was solicited, and the Board of Deputies agreed to participate in the effort.

As early as April 1934 a Jewish Economic Council (known as Wirtschaftsrat) had been founded by CEKABE; it was run by Isaac Giterman. This now swung into action and in 1936 started very cautiously to help in establishing small local crafts and industries, and to supervise them, check the quality of the products, and aid in finding appropriate markets if necessary. This kind of rather plodding but quite effective small-scale work went on throughout 1937 and 1938.

A special subcommittee set up by the Wirtschaftsrat in January 1938, called TER, took over the task of finding export markets for those establishments that needed it. In this, it was hoped, some government help would be obtained. A total of about $410,000 was invested in these ventures directly by JDC; an additional 30–40 percent was found locally. In addition, the call went out to certain expatriate organizations in America, comprised of people who had emigrated from certain localities (Landsmannschaften). These were asked to contribute a minimum of $2,000, which would be matched by JDC. Up to 1938, 250 Landsmannschaften responded, and rather large amounts of JDC money went out to match these small grants. The expenditure was under the surveillance of CEKABE. In 1937 some five thousand families were helped by these small ventures, which included such branches as mechanical weaving (at Choroszcz), carpenter cooperatives (Tarnopol), saddlers' cooperatives (Chelm), and semiagricultural pursuits, such as vegetable farming, the planting of medicinal herbs, and the like.

Another venture of CEKABE was the establishment of small dairies on the outskirts of towns. This work was carried on in 1938. There were 2,088 families that were helped in this way in the first half of the year, but we lack information for the rest of the period, up to the outbreak of the war.[60]

By early 1938 Kahn had accumulated sufficient experience to decide that the experiment had been worthwhile. In January of that year he demanded a yearly allocation of $1 million for this kind of economic reconstruction, and hoped that within five years this would lead to the employment of twenty-three thousand families. It can safely be estimated that up to the end of 1938 JDC had succeeded in finding new employment in these enterprises for about ten thousand families. This in itself was a partial success, and JDC could justly be proud of it. Yet measured by the economic decline of the Jewish population in Poland and by the fact that about one million people there were living at or beyond the edge of starvation, the outcome of the efforts was small indeed. The basic problem of JDC was that with its relatively small resources it could do no more than help those who were above the danger line from sinking below it. JDC was not a government, and it could not solve the problem of the starving million.

For a few years JDC was helped in its efforts by the British Jews. In 1935 British Jews sent close to 40,000 pounds (almost $200,000) to Poland, to be distributed by JDC. This was repeated in 1936. But in 1937 the pro-Zionist and non-Zionist wings in Britain disagreed on aid to Poland, the Zionists favoring such aid. Collections went down, and no more real help was obtained. The help of the British Jews, while it lasted, was important from another angle. JDC and ICA (primarily a British organization) had been very interested in vocational retraining. JDC saw this as one of its main tasks. However, the vocational programs in Poland were distributed among a variety of organizations. ICA ran its own schools, and JDC had to divide its money between three additional groups of schools: those established by ORT, those of an independent organization in Galicia (the former Austrian, southern part of Poland) known as WUZET, and JDC's own schools. There was much criticism of ORT in JDC circles, especially at the Warsaw office. The charge was that ORT was too prone to follow established trade lines such as textiles, fur, and the like, and did not attempt to pioneer in the employment of Jews in the mechanical trades and in new industries (radio, auto repair, etc.). The problem was that when the youngsters finished their training, they had to be given employment in Jewish enterprises—non-Jewish ones would not accept them—and there simply were not many new Jewish industries around. Another problem had to do with the so-called Bursen, or apprentice homes, for those youngsters who were living away from home while learning a trade. This was a real problem, because usually the parents could not afford the expense of paying for lodging, and JDC had to help. It did so, and through various social institutions (TOZ, CENTOS, and the like) it supported a number of homes that were either built or rented to house these young people. By early 1938 there were 17,720 pupils in these vocational schools, which were of varying standards; 3,946 were in ORT schools, 4,714 were in ICA schools, and 6,172 were in schools supported directly by JDC; 2,888 more were at WUZET institutions.

In addition to all this, there was the network of training camps run by Hechalutz, the Zionist organization that prepared pioneers for Palestine. By early 1938 Hechalutz had 16,206 trainees who were working, as Kahn put it, "in a manner still somewhat primitive."[61] Hechalutz had no money, and it had to send its members to farms and shops where the conditions of work were primitive and extremely difficult. Most of the trainees worked in agriculture, the idea being that they would leave Poland as soon as possible.

The British funds in 1935 and 1936 were partly earmarked for Hechalutz, and Kahn supported this allocation. The reason was that while the Hechalutz people were supposedly training for Palestine, the lack of certificates for that country made it extremely doubtful that most of them would ever get there; therefore, they were actually training for future jobs in Poland, a program Kahn favored.[62] Here, too, there was a growing discrepancy between the number of individuals trained for new jobs and the number of jobs available. Large groups of trainees were bound to suffer the hardships of unemployment unless large-scale efforts were made to provide employment through investment in new or old enterprises. But before this problem really became acute, the "final solution" came and solved this and all other problems for Polish Jewry.

JDC tried industrialization and it supported vocational training. But it was not, of course, operating in a vacuum, was not free to operate as it wished. Jewish groups and subgroups were fighting for position in the harsh reality of Poland. One of these struggles was the fight against centralization waged by regional interests, especially in Galicia, which was very poor but had a very proud tradition of culture and independence. Galicia was traditionally under strong Zionist influence, and a group of leaders emerged among whom Alfred Silberschein occupied a place of special importance. Silberschein, a Zionist leader, favored decentralization, and he gained the support of most of the influential circles in Jewish economic life in Galicia. In early 1937, 25 percent of the total Jewish population in Poland lived in Galicia. Yet the Galician Jews were underrepresented in all the economic activities undertaken by JDC. This charge in itself would have remained ineffective had not an organization been founded called the American Committee for Aid of Jews in Galicia, which threatened to solicit funds in competition with JDC.

Early in 1937 JDC asked its Warsaw office for an explanation and proposals, and in April and May 1937 these came. They revealed a difference of opinion between the head of the Warsaw office, Isaac Giterman, and his two chief lieutenants, David Guzik and Leib Neustadt. Neustadt and Guzik were for maximum centralization and were prepared to fight Silberschein's demand that JDC set up special regional organizations for its free loan institutions there. Giterman, on the other hand, acknowledged the fact that Galicia had separate institutions in many areas; a separate CEKABE committee was thereupon established by JDC for Galicia, though only in early 1939. More important, it emerged that a number of local enterprises (probably more than Galicia's proper share) were established there by CEKABE: a chain factory in Stanislawow, a carpenter cooperative in Stryj, two locksmiths' shops in Czortkow, an export furniture shop in Lwów, and so on.⁶³

The question as to whether work for children was relief work exercised some of the minds at the JDC offices. To Kahn, at any rate, it was quite obvious that this was constructive work of the highest order, and he insisted on devoting roughly one-third of his Polish budgets to the support of various types of activities for children. This, of course, was in line with the traditional Jewish approach to social work generally and made JDC popular among the Jewish masses in Eastern Europe. A large percentage of these budgets went to two organizations that dealt mainly with children: CENTOS and TOZ.

The number of children requiring the attention of CENTOS, the child care agency, grew considerably in the 1930s. Only a small number of them could be accepted into institutions providing full-time care; these were mostly either orphans or half orphans. In 1937 there were 8,047 of these youngsters. However, the total number of children that CENTOS looked after, partly or wholly, grew from 15,102 in 1933 to 32,066 in 1937. These included youths in vocational training institutions (they were included as JDC institutions in the figures for vocational training given above) and summer camps.

JDC actually supplied about 12–13 percent of CENTOS's budget, in line with its policy of helping others to help themselves. But these percentages were very important for the men who ran CENTOS. They could then go to the Polish government and municipalities and point to American help (in foreign exchange) as a weighty argument in their demand for Polish contributions. These contributions added another 17 percent to their budget, and the rest was largely covered by membership contributions. This was a unique system of organization whereby CENTOS had over forty-five thousand registered members who owned, and theoretically ran, the organization and its institutions. They were, of course, recruited from the wealthier segments of the Jewish population, and there, too, the fact that CENTOS had been set up by JDC and continued to enjoy its support was adduced as an argument in collection drives.

A similar structure characterized TOZ, though TOZ was smaller and weaker than CENTOS. The task of TOZ was not limited to children; it had to look after the health of the poorer sections of the Jewish population, young and old. It had only 11,191 members in 1937, and its budget was 1.4 million zloty, or less than half of the 3 million zloty budget of CENTOS. But it, too, spread its 142 institutions all over Poland, and tried to introduce modern hygienic methods into slums and poverty-stricken townships and villages. One of its main achievements was the organization of lectures by various types of experts. Its forty-six stations for mothers and babies gave valuable advice at very little cost to large number of women who could not afford to visit doctors. It had six X-ray installations and twenty-nine dental stations, some of them mobile. It ran three Jewish hospitals, thirty-three ambulatory clinics, and twelve anti-TB dispensaries in 1938.

With regard to TOZ, JDC help was relatively larger than with CENTOS and amounted to 28 percent of the TOZ budget. But Polish governmental and municipal help amounted to only 9.4 percent, and the percentage of the budget covered by local Jewish contributions was about the same as for CENTOS. JDC supervised closely the expenditures and general activities in both cases through its Warsaw office.

One of the most important types of work with children encouraged by JDC was the network of summer camps. The reasoning behind this network was that children who suffered privations throughout the year should spend the summer in healthful surroundings, with adequate medical attention and with plenty to eat,

T A B L E 14
Summer Camps in Poland

Year	No. of camps	No. of children
1935	222	37,286
1936	428	58,661
1938	636	102,615

relatively speaking. In 1934 some thirty-five thousand Jewish children went to summer camps supported by JDC-subsidized institutions. These included not only CENTOS and TOZ, but also the various Jewish school networks.

Direct participation of JDC in these camps ranged from 10 percent of the budget in 1936 to 7.2 percent in 1938; but apart from JDC's direct participation, the various organizations that ran the colonies were themselves JDC-controlled or -subsidized or both, and the expenses of these camps were part of their regular budgets.

The problem of starving children could not, of course, be solved by a few weeks of summer vacation. Very large numbers of Jewish children went to school in the mornings without breakfast. The choice was whether to give them something to eat at school or let them go hungry. There was no question as to the response from JDC, despite its opposition in principle to direct relief. In the face of the deteriorating Polish situation and the approach of war in Europe, some JDC officials in New York asked whether some of these expenses could be cut; Kahn lost his usual patience and retorted: "Try to be hard and do not give any money for feeding and clothing and see what will happen. I hear so much about your wanting to be drastic—try it!"[64] They did not.

The problem of Jewish children in Poland was very closely bound up with the question of Jewish culture and religion. JDC's main task was to try to save the economic and social structure of European Jewry; but it could not, and did not want to, close its eyes to cultural and educational problems. Cyrus Adler, head of the American Jewish Committee, served as chairman of JDC's Cultural and Religious Committee. In 1935 he stated: "Hard as the situation is, if no effort is made to save the minds and the souls of the Jewish people, there will not be any Jewish people left to save."[65] There was some truth in that statement, though the danger was less one of immediate cultural assimilation than of physical, economic, and ultimate cultural degradation and decline. As it turned out, the spirit of the Jewish people bore up remarkably well in the face of the most horrendous obstacles.

The first and most urgent problem was that of schooling. Polish schools were making it increasingly difficult for observant Jewish children to attend classes. In the 1930s the special Polish schools where Jewish children were excused from writing on Shabbat began to close down. The same fate awaited Jewish private schools. The pretexts were usually of a purely formal nature, that is, nonobservance of regulations regarding the size of rooms, facilities, and the like that were ignored as far as the Polish schools themselves were concerned. Then there were Jewish schools that had to be renovated for reasons other than the pressure by Polish authorities; these schools, which depended largely on voluntary contributions, were rarely in a position to build or renovate without financial aid. In 1934 Kahn was warning New York that "the schools, once closed, will never be allowed to reopen" by the Poles. "The institutions, fallen to pieces and deteriorated considerably, will cost very much more to restore if they are allowed to go to pieces altogether."[66] In the early 1930s Kahn was experiencing great difficulties in getting allocations for physical facilities for Jewish schools, but the situation eased somewhat later on as a result of increased funds. It was then that he stated his view that schools were as productive as industry and indicated his opposition to those in New York who wanted to increase "productive" investments at the expense of schools.

The Polish Jewish school structure was itself a model of confusion. At the end of 1935 a total of 523,852 children were registered in various types of institutions, government and private, from the primary grades to the age of eighteen. Of these, 343,671 studied in Polish schools, including those where certain allowances were made for Shabbat observance. This accounted for about two-thirds of the Jewish children; the rest, 180,181 children, studied at Jewish institutions of different kinds. The largest of these were the religious primary schools, traditional *chadarim*, where Jewish law and religious observances were the main studies. These schools were said to have close to 50,000 pupils. Some 35,585 girls studied in specially set up, rather primitive religious institutions that paralleled the *chadarim.* About 16,000 boys of high school age studied at various types of yeshivoth (higher institutions of traditional learning); thus over 100,000 children attended 963 religious educational institutions.

Of the rest, the most important were the Tarbuth schools, where most of the subjects were taught in Hebrew rather than Polish or Yiddish, though both the latter languages were also taught. There the stress was on modern secular schooling, with a careful balance of the sciences, humanities, and sports. Needless to say, this network of schools was under Zionist influence. A total of 44,780 children studied in its 269 institutions. These included 9 secondary schools, from which much of the young Zionist leadership between the two world wars in Poland came.

Also Zionist, modern, and religious were the 299 schools of the Yavneh group, which had 15,923 pupils. Yavneh was under the influence of religious Zionist parties.

A special network of Yiddish schools (167 primary and 2 secondary) was organized by circles close to the Bund; this network was called Cisho. A total of 16,486 children studied in those schools; the trend was left-wing, Yiddishist, and anti-Zionist. There was also a small network of 16 schools with 2,343 children (Szulkult), which tried to combine Yiddish with Hebrew. That was the complete picture of Jewish elementary and secondary schooling in Poland.[67]

To this one must add the 167 yeshivoth for young adults, with their 31,735 pupils, who formed the backbone of traditionalist Jewry in Poland. JDC paid special attention to the yeshivoth, mainly because Adler saw in them a certain guarantee for Jewish existence in Europe, and also because the many Orthodox supporters of JDC had the right to expect financial aid for the yeshivoth. Besides the yeshivoth, JDC also supported the Jewish Scientific Institute (YIVO), which had its main center in Vilna. In 1939 a JDC leader said of YIVO that its achievements made "the Hebrew University look childish in accomplishment."[68] This may have been somewhat exaggerated, but there was no doubt that YIVO was an institution of quality and had a right to expect JDC help.

JDC had the choice of supporting all the different trends in Jewish education or none. The schools represented various types of political thinking no less than various trends in education, and JDC could not appear to be partisan to any particular trend. Subsidies therefore went to all types of schools; but the principle of supporting only capital investments, not current budgets, was carefully observed. This was sometimes rather liberally interpreted— for example, when it came to various types of teaching aids; but generally speaking JDC support went toward construction, repairs, acquisition of essential school equipment, and the like.

From 1933 to 1939 JDC school expenditures trebled,[69] and while the total sums were quite small, a great deal was done with them. As in other cases, JDC made its support conditional on the raising of local funds. Without JDC contributions these funds would never have materialized. With them, many schools in Poland either were built or were salvaged for the use of thousands of pupils.

Yet despite all these efforts Jewish schools continued to shut down all over Poland in the late 1930s. In the Cisho network alone, sixty-three schools with eighty-four hundred pupils were closed down by the Polish government between the two world wars, under a variety of pretexts. Kahn suspected that the Poles would attack the Tarbuth network as well. The same pattern that we observed in other areas was repeated here: the funds that JDC had at its disposal in Poland simply did not allow for any radical cure of the massive illness the Jewish economic and social structure was suffering from. Without JDC help, it must be presumed, the situation would have been considerably worse; with it, it was bad enough.

ROMANIA

The situation of the Jews in Eastern Europe outside Poland was similar to that of the Jews inside Poland. Romania was moving in the same direction as Poland, as far as both the general and the Jewish situations were concerned. The Romanian Fascist movement known as the Iron Guard was growing stronger. Under its leader, Corneliu Zelea-Codreanu, it embarked on a campaign of violence that led to the assassination of a Liberal party prime minister by an Iron Guard member in December 1933. From that moment on, Romanian democracy, never very strong, was in constant decline. Until 1937 the Liberals, under Tartarescu, were in power, but their policy became more and more rightist and anti-Semitic under the pressure of a right-wing opposition group that came under the influence of a Fascist leader, Octavian Goga. A prop of the regime against a rightist takeover was King Carol, though he also aspired to dictatorial rule and had in fact attempted —unsuccessfully—to gain absolute power in May 1934. The fact that his mistress, Madame Lupescu, was of Jewish descent increased anti-Semitic tendencies because of the almost universal distaste with which the king's extramarital adventure was regarded. Despite all this, a semblance of parliamentary democracy was maintained until December 1937, when the defeat of the Liberals brought about a sharp turn to the Right and the ascent of Goga to power.

The number of Jews living in Romania was a matter of dispute. Romanian sources tended to exaggerate their estimates in order to prove the supposedly inordinate influence of the Jewish population in the country. In fact, the census of 1930 showed that there were 728,000 Jews in Romania. An investigation into Jewish citizenship in 1939 showed that there were 662,244 Jews. Even if we assume that some Jews managed to escape a census that was intended to deprive them of their citizenship,[70] there could not have been many more than 700,000 Jews in Romania in that year. The figure of 760,000 usually mentioned in Jewish sources represented the absolute maximum and was probably an overestimate.

The Jewish communities throughout the country differed considerably from one another. While the Jews in Bucharest and in some parts of Walachia, Moldavia, and central Transylvania were at least partly westernized and had abandoned the religious way of life, others were living well within the sphere of strict Orthodoxy. In northern Transylvania, around Satu-Mare, Máramarossziget, and Brasov, there lived a poverty-stricken Jewish population clamoring for the kind of help JDC could provide. In Bessarabia, and to a certain extent in Bucovina too, a similar situation existed. In Bessarabia there was a fairly large Jewish agricultural population (about forty thousand persons), whose primitive methods of cultivation exposed it only too often to threats of starvation in years of drought.

In Romania, as in Poland, JDC was able to increase its allocations as the 1930s progressed. Of the sums available, about one-third was spent to feed children in hunger-stricken districts and to maintain summer camps, because Kahn believed that such camps constituted a primary reconstructive task. Help to children was especially important in the Máramarossziget area and in northern Transylvania generally, where just about the only hope for the future seemed to be to save the children from the effects of starvation. Thirteen hundred children were fed in that area in 1933; this grew to five thousand by 1935. As for the summer camps, about 30 percent of their budgets were covered by JDC, the principle being—as in Poland—that the larger proportion of the funds had to be found locally.

In Cluj (Klausenburg), the capital of Transylvania, there was a very effective Jewish child care society, which expanded its work in the 1930s and became a source of pride for JDC. By 1937 it not only ran eighteen recreation and health centers for children, but it also went into vocational training and convinced the ultra-Orthodox groups to open training centers where part of the time was devoted to traditional yeshivah studies and part to carpentry and other pursuits. It also ran four homes for apprentices and permanently supplemented the feeding of over one thousand children. The Cluj group received about one-sixth of its budget from JDC and managed to find the rest locally.[71] The importance of this work stood out against the general backwardness of the country: in 1940, infant mortality in Romania was 188 per thousand, higher than that in India in the same year.[72] Among Jews it was considerably lower.

The summer camp program was also concentrated largely in

T A B L E 15
JDC Allocations in Romania (in $)

Year	Total amount allocated	Amount allocated for children	Percentage of total
1933	16,650		
1936	51,554	18,350	36.6
1937	79,304	24,773	31.3
1938	83,430		

Transylvania. The numbers were fairly constant—about three to four thousand children (thirty-seven hundred in 1937) were given the opportunity to spend their summers in about thirty camps, to whose budget JDC contributed a third.

An especially serious situation developed in Bessarabia, which had a large Jewish peasant population. There was a crop failure in 1935. In December of that year a JDC press release reported "serious famine conditions" which "threaten half of the Jewish population of Bessarabia and part of the population of Moldavia." About thirty thousand Jews were reported to be on the verge of starvation. Kahn authorized the expenditure of $5,000 to start a feeding program. This sum was soon spent, and additional sums had to be sent to Bessarabia throughout the spring of 1936. Medical aid also became necessary because of the spread of skin diseases, and clothes were collected because children had only rags to wear.[73] Paradoxically, the plight of the Jews increased rather than diminished the spread of anti-Semitism, because a "large part of the hunger-stricken area [was] inhabited by German colonists who [were] all under Nazi influence."[74] Peasant unrest became one of the major influences that brought about the rise of the Right under Goga.

Generally speaking, much of the work of JDC in Romania was done by the Reconstruction Foundation loan *kassas,* whose influence in Poland has been discussed. In fact, with the Polish loan *kassas* in the throes of a crisis between 1933 and 1937, much attention was devoted to the Romanian *kassas,* and large sums were invested in Romania.[75] The number of these *kassas* grew, until they reached eighty-one in 1938. Over 52,000 individuals were registered with them; together with their families, this embraced over 25 percent of the Jewish population in the country, and thus the *kassas* became a popular and extremely helpful prop for the shaky Jewish economic situation. They charged only a nominal rate of interest and extended loans that averaged about $70 for relatively long periods of time. As in Poland, this helped small Jewish merchants and craftsmen to withstand temporary setbacks, made it possible to purchase essential equipment or horses for transport, and aided them in their hard struggle against growing competition. A large proportion of these *kassas* operated in Bessarabia (thirty-nine in 1938), the most poverty-stricken area in the country.

Free Loan *kassas* existed in Romania as well. However, contrary to the situation in Poland, these never became popular. Only fifteen such institutions operated in 1935, and their number did not increase in later years.

It should be stressed that, except for regions such as Bessarabia, Romania recovered from the effects of the world economic crisis quicker than did her neighbors. By 1937 she had achieved a budgetary surplus, and exports were rising. However, it was mainly the Romanian middle class and landowners who benefited, while the rising tide of nationalism prevented most minority group members from participating in this economic improvement. These minorities, about 4.5 million people in a nation of 18 million, were not treated equally by the government. Hungarians and Germans, who were a majority among the 4.5 million, were treated better than the rest—Ukrainians, Bulgarians, Greeks, Russians, Gypsies, and Jews. The usual reasons for anti-Semitism were aggravated in Romania. Small trade was, in crucial areas, in Jewish hands—48.3 percent of Romanian Jews engaged in trade[76]—and the economic competition grew by leaps and bounds. The Jews were the least protected of the ethnic minorities and could be dealt with with impunity by economic competitors.

It is therefore not surprising that openly anti-Semitic measures were taken even by the Liberal regime. By late 1935 decrees had already been published limiting the employment of non-Romanians in industry. In late 1936 and early 1937 a series of government decrees said that at least 50 percent of the employees in all industrial or trade establishments must be ethnically Romanian. As the Jews were the only minority among whom trade and industry formed a major part of the occupational structure, the decrees were clearly aimed at them. Worse, the Romanian National Bank instructed all its branches not to rediscount bills of businesses belonging to members of ethnic minorities. Merchants, artisans, and mercantile employees had to pass examinations like the Polish ones or be deprived of their occupations. Apprentices—in a country where the majority of artisans were Jewish—would have to have seven years of Romanian elementary schooling in the future.[77]

The results were a swift deterioration in the Jewish economic position. One after another, Jewish banks outside the JDC *kassa* system were failing. Jewish masters had to accept non-Jewish apprentices for training, both to satisfy the quota for Romanian employees and also because there simply were not enough Jewish apprentices to qualify under the new regulations. Unofficial but effective ostracism operated in the professions too. In 1935 and 1936 no Jewish lawyers were accepted by the Romanian bar; the number of newly accepted Jewish medical students dropped from sixty-six in 1934 to five in 1935 and to none in 1936. In 1937 four Jewish students were accepted by the medical school, but were prevented by force from attending classes.[78]

It was against this background that the extreme rightist government of Octavian Goga came to power on December 28, 1937. The rumors that began to spread among the Jewish population were only too well-founded. The *New York Times* reported on January 20, 1938, that Goga wanted to expel five hundred thousand Jews, that another luminary of the government, Cuza, had said that there would be no expropriation of Jewish property "at present," and that no Christian maids under forty-five would be allowed to work in Jewish homes—this latter statement had been taken straight out of the Nazi Nuremberg laws.

On January 22 a law was passed forcing Jews to submit to a "revision" of citizenship. This was to be completed by February 12 in so-called Old Romania (that is, Moldavia and Walachia) and in the rest of the country fifty days later. Jews had never bothered to establish their residence by documentation. The peace treaty had laid down that people habitually residing in the territories acquired by Romania after World War I would automatically become Romanian citizens. Owing to their lack of documentation to establish habitual residence, the anti-Semitism rampant in courts of justice, their limited knowledge of Romanian culture and language, and the ridiculously short time in which to correct all this, there was pessimism and even panic in Jewish circles. Dr. Wilhelm Filderman, a lawyer and the head of the Romanian Jewish community, who also was JDC's most trusted contact in Romania, estimated that 80 percent of the Jews in "New" Romania would be deprived of their citizenship. At a meeting in France between Filderman and representatives of JDC, ICA, and the Reconstruction Foundation, the conclusion was reached that the coming Romanian elections on March 2, 1938, would be of "vastly greater importance than the hopeless task of mitigating the effects of an anti-Semitic victory." The situation of the Jews in Romania was judged to be a "disaster, even worse than [that] which befell the Jews in Germany."[79]

However, the new decrees were too much even for many of Romania's rightist politicians, including the king. Early in February a juridical committee of the Romanian parliament found the anti-Jewish decrees unconstitutional, and the Goga government resigned on February 10. It had been in power for less than six weeks, but the damage it did was incalculable. In its stead the king established a coalition of Right and Center, with the patriarch Miron Cristea as prime minister. It was in a real sense the king's government that now took over.

The openly anti-Semitic course gave way to a more subtle approach. New decrees were enacted regulating such things as the renovation of shops, requiring state examinations for previously qualified doctors and druggists, forbidding the transfer abroad of funds for the support students who were not of Romanian descent, requiring proof of Romanian citizenship for any foreign transaction, and the like.[80] This was followed by the mass cancellation of the licenses of Jewish petty traders. All big industrial companies were told to name Christian directors. Worst of all, although the summary procedure of depriving Jews of their Romanian national status was abolished, the principle of a revision of citizenship was maintained and the threat of denationalization remained. Kahn fully expected that 150,000 Jews would lose their Romanian citizenship. Most of them would then have no way of earning a living, and there would be a tendency for them to emigrate under government pressure. Yet there seemed to be no alternative to supporting the king, because the most vocal opposition to his rule came from the pro-Nazi Iron Guard.

The situation continued to deteriorate during 1938. In the spring of that year the Romanian government decreed that all cooperative institutions would be incorporated into government cooperatives. This meant the end of the Reconstruction Foundation and Free Loan *kassas*. JDC and its ICA partner tried to prevent this liquidation, and ICA obtained the British government's agreement to intervene with the Romanian government. As a result, the liquidation, which was to have taken place on June 1, 1938, was postponed. In the meantime, Alexander A. Landesco, a prominent member of JDC's Executive Committee, who was of Romanian Jewish origin, went to Bucharest to try to influence the government. At the same time, Hyman intervened with the Romanian minister in Washington. On June 16, 1938, Landesco cabled from Bucharest: "Liquidation cooperatives Romania suspended one year." But on June 23 the minister with whom Landesco had negotiated, Militia Constantinescu, went back on his word and declared that the liquidations would soon begin. Liquidators were in fact appointed on June 28.

ICA and JDC again tried in every possible way to influence the Romanians. The State Department was asked to intervene. On July 21 James C. Dunn of the State Department wrote to Hyman that the Romanians had told the American representative in Bucharest that Landesco had "misunderstood" the Romanian minister: what Constantinescu had meant was not postponement for one year, but one year's time for the cooperatives to liquidate. Since the Romanian government had not received a prompt answer to this generous offer, it was now withdrawing it and would liquidate the cooperatives as required by its laws. The exchange of letters with the State Department continued into August, but the State Department was inclined to blame JDC for not having promptly accepted the Romanian offer and declined to take any further steps in the matter. Fortunately, the remnant of the Romanian *kassas* was saved by a ruling of the Romanian Court of Cassation in March 1939.[81]

In the meantime, denationalization proceeded. Two decrees, on September 15 and December 2, 1938, provided explicitly that all denationalized Jews would henceforth be treated as foreigners and required to obtain certificates of identity that would authorize them to reside in Romania for one year at a time. No licenses for trade, industry, or the professions would normally be issued to such persons. The number of persons affected by these decrees was in the neighborhood of 150,000.[82]

In the wake of these draconian laws, all Jewish organizations of a political nature were ordered closed down. This affected the Union of Romanian Jews led by Filderman and the Jewish political party (Volkspartei). In certain areas of the country Jews were forbidden to use any language except Romanian, even though that was not the language generally spoken there. Economic and political ostracism of Jews reached unheard-of proportions. The only Jewish organization permitted to exist, declared the foreign minister, would be a committee for the emigration of Jews.[83]

Paralleling the development in Poland, Romanian politicians now began an intensified propaganda campaign for Jewish emigration. Illegal immigration into Palestine was encouraged, and further declarations in favor of Jewish emigration were made.

JDC, overwhelmed by the effects of Nazi expansion on Central

European Jewry and deeply worried about the fate of Polish Jewry, which was also facing threats of expulsion, did not know how to deal with the Romanian situation. A memorandum by Noel Aronovici, himself a Romanian Jew, proposed remedies in more or less traditional terms: more homes for apprentices, vocational retraining, establishment of Free Loan *kassas* (despite the fact that the existing ones were being closed down), and aid to children.[84] Indeed, there was very little that JDC could do in this situation except increase their help in the form of thinly disguised relief until the overall situation eased. Attempts by the World Jewish Congress to arouse public opinion by political action at the League of Nations met with no greater success.[85] The feeling of gloom and lack of any real hope found its way into Joseph C. Hyman's speech in September 1938, when he declared: "While we sit here and talk of budgets, of quotas, of campaign agreements, a remorseless torrent sweeps away everything that our brethren have believed in, have prayed for, have fought for, and have built up during their existence."[86] JDC was trying its best to stem the flood, but those who directed its fortunes were well aware not only of the hopelessness of their task but also of the fact that the very foundations of their humanist and liberal philosophy were being swept away.

Finally, as in Poland, the very grimness of the situation was beginning to force upon local Jewry the necessity for unification. As in Poland, JDC in 1939 tried to set up a Central Committee of Romanian Jews, for economic purposes at first. But unlike Poland, negotiations in Romania did not advance beyond a preliminary stage. Nothing had changed by the time war broke out.[87]

CZECHOSLOVAKIA AND HUNGARY

Another area in which JDC spent sizable sums of money and considerable energy was Subcarpathian Russia (or PKR, in Czech initials), the easternmost tip of Czechoslovakia. A mostly Orthodox Jewish community lived there, subsisting on petty trade, agriculture, and forestry. There was a famous Hebrew secondary school at Munkács (Mukachevo) and a number of yeshivoth. In 1933 JDC started a feeding program for children.[88] Occasionally small sums were granted to vocational establishments or small Jewish workshop cooperatives, mainly in the automobile repair and textile branches. Most of this work was done in conjunction with the Jewish Social Institute in Prague and a parallel organization in Bratislava.

In neighboring Hungary, JDC did not operate at all in the 1930s, though it followed developments there with increasing anxiety. The Jewish population in Hungary was actually declining, as a result of numerous conversions among the upper strata of Jewish society and a decline in the birthrate. There were 444,500 Jews in Hungary in 1930. With the annexations of parts of Slovakia and PKR in late 1938 and in March 1939, the Jewish population grew to 725,000 by 1941.

In Hungary proper (as contrasted with PKR), and especially in Budapest, Jews tended to be a prosperous middle-class community. In early 1939 it was estimated that 43 percent of Hungarian commerce was handled by Jews; 49.2 percent of the lawyers and 37.7 percent of the doctors were Jewish. Industry, too, was partly in the hands of Jews.[89] Yet Jews in Hungary were still considered to be strangers, despite the fact that they had lived in the country for many centuries and despite their own keen desire to be regarded as Hungarians. The regime of the archconservative regent, Admiral Horthy, wavered between personal friendship for Jewish elements in the Hungarian aristocracy and anti-Semitism. In May 1938, under the influence of Nazism, Hungarian anti-Semitism won its first great victory in a bill that decreed that by June 1943 not more than 20 percent of people working in any establishment could be Jews. As a result, a large number of Jews were thrown out of their professions.

Hungary's politicians followed the German example closely in other ways too. In late 1938, after the Sudeten crisis in the autumn of that year, the Hungarian government published the text of a second bill, which was finally passed in March 1939. The preamble to that law stated quite explicitly that the Hungarians were outlawing Jews as part of a general movement: "Before the [1938] law was promulgated, only one of the neighboring states, Germany, had taken energetic measures to drive the Jews out of the country. Since that time, however, many other states in Europe have followed this example. . . . The Jewish question is an international problem like many other questions of international interest, such as world traffic, world economy, hygiene, and instruction." An international solution—that is, mass emigration and expulsion by international consent—was consequently desired.

The 1939 bill itself provided for the invalidation of the citizenship of certain classes of Jews who had obtained their Hungarian nationality after 1914; in effect, it revoked the Jewish franchise by instituting a separate Jewish poll in the national and municipal elections; and it barred Jews from positions in the civil service, municipalities, and public corporations, and from working as public notaries and editors-in-chief. The number of Jews in the legal, medical, and engineering professions was limited to 6 percent. Publication of papers owned by Jews was forbidden, and state contracts for Jewish enterprises were withdrawn. Most serious of all was the provision that no trade concessions or licenses could be granted to Jews unless the percentage of Jewish license holders dropped to less than 6 percent.

The definition of a Jew was clearly Nazi in origin: a Jew was a person of Jewish faith, a Christian born of Jewish parentage, or the offspring of a mixed marriage if the Jewish parent had not been baptized before the marriage.

It was quite clear that very soon Hungarian Jewry would be calling for active help from JDC.

THE BALTIC STATES

The Baltic states of Lithuania and Latvia were an area of long-standing JDC interest—especially Lithuania. There, some 153,000 Jews fared better than in Poland. The reasons for this were, briefly, the smaller percentage (7.5 percent) of Jews—Poland had about 10 percent; their declared identification with Lithuanian national aspirations; the more rational economic structure of the country; and a spirit of local Jewish initiative. There was, however, a strong desire on the part of urban middle-class Lithuanians to take over Jewish positions in business, industry, and the professions. This movement received additional impetus from the events in neighboring Germany.

Jewish education was generally in Zionist hands and embraced some 190 elementary schools, in 180 of which Hebrew was taught. A number of Hebrew and Yiddish high schools taught the Jewish national languages as well as Lithuanian. These were considered private schools but received some financial assistance from the state treasury.

The world economic crisis made itself felt in Lithuania as well, however, and JDC recognized the need for action there. The local cooperative movement was quite vigorous, and in 1936 there were eighty-eight cooperatives with close to seventeen thousand members,[90] partially supported by JDC.[91] In addition, there were nineteen Reconstruction Foundation *kassas* in 1937, which gave out fifty-six thousand loans averaging $107 per loan (thus indicating a much higher level of economic operation than in Poland).

Standards of health tended downward, pressure for emigration began to increase, and the JDC allocation to vocational schools went up because of the large demand for training that would prepare Jews for emigration.[92] Emigrants went largely to Palestine and South Africa and caused a slow decline in the Jewish population in Lithuania. While there were no overtly anti-Semitic laws or regulations, local disturbances on the Polish model did occur, though to a lesser degree than in Poland. Kahn summarized the Lithuanian situation by saying that it was "not quite so bad [as in Poland and Latvia], but nevertheless worse than previously."[93]

Latvia was a different case altogether. The ninety-three thousand Jews in that country were being systematically deprived of their means of livelihood by the Karlis Ulmanis dictatorship, which had come to power in 1934. As in other countries, the Jewish population was declining: six thousand had emigrated since 1925 and the birthrate was going down. Jewish factories were being taken over by the state; since 1930 no Jewish doctor had been allowed to practice, and government monopolies based on the Polish model (for the sale of agricultural products, among other things—a major Jewish trade) almost automatically meant not only the pauperization of former Jewish owners, but the sudden unemployment of many Jewish workers as well. With the ruin of the intellectuals and the traders, Jews tended to move into manual work, but the transition was difficult because of the opposition of Lettish workers.

The Jewish educational system was run by the Agudah, the only Jewish body that cooperated with the government. JDC gave very little help, and what it did give was mainly channeled through its credit institutions. As in other countries, by the end of the 1930s, everyone realized that emigration was the only feasible solution—but there was nowhere to go. European Jewry remained trapped.

6

The Beginning of the End

The annexation (anschluss) of Austria on March 13, 1938, placed 185,246 Jews, a large majority of them in Vienna, in German hands.[1] Austrian Jewry was poorer than its German counterpart and less well organized. Large numbers of Austrian Jews were dependent on charity, and JDC had had to support relief operations and loan *kassas* there before 1938. The concentration of Jews in certain branches of the economy was very marked: 90 percent of the advertising industry was Jewish, as were 85 percent of the people in the furniture business; 80 percent of the radio, newspaper, and shoe industries was Jewish. More important—because more obvious—51.6 percent of the doctors and dentists and 62 percent of the lawyers in Vienna were Jews.[2]

This occupational concentration made the Jews both conspicuous and vulnerable. Austrian anti-Semitism was nothing new. At the beginning of the century, Vienna's burgomaster, Karl Lueger, had risen to power on the crest of anti-Semitism; the young Hitler had developed his hatred of Jews in the slums of Vienna during that period.

Viennese Jewry was split into many factions (there were 88 religious congregations and 356 secular organizations in Vienna at the time of the anschluss)[3] and the official community organization

—the Israelitische Kultusgemeinde (IKG)—suffered from considerable internal strife. Two main groups contended for leadership: the Union, a liberal group with strong assimilationist tendencies, in many ways similar to the German Jewish CV; and the Zionists, themselves split into a large number of factions.

Prior to 1934 a third significant group had been the socialists, Jewish members of the strong Austrian Marxist party. The defeat of Austrian socialism, in the February 1934 fighting in Vienna, at the hands of the Austrian proto-Fascist clerical party under Dollfuss endangered the Jews, because by and large Jewish sympathies were with the socialists; eleven out of the thirty arrested socialist leaders were Jews. But two IKG leaders were sent abroad by the government to show the world that no anti-Semitic measures were being planned.

While the political danger receded, economic misery increased. In 1935 JDC sent $20,000 to keep soup kitchens going for the impoverished Jewish proletariat. In 1934 a quarter of Vienna's Jews were on relief. The situation did not improve in 1936/7; in 1937, 35.5 percent of the Jewish working population were unemployed.[4] After the 1934 events the IKG Council was composed of twenty Zionists (sixteen middle class and four socialist-Zionists) and fifteen Union representatives. At the time of the anschluss, the leader of IKG was a Zionist, Dr. Desider Friedmann, and another Zionist, Dr. Josef Löwenherz, was becoming increasingly important.

Despite the popularity of the last chancellor of independent Austria, Kurt von Schuschnigg, the anschluss was welcomed by almost all Austrians. Cardinal Innitzer's advice to all Catholics in this Catholic country to vote for the anschluss in the plebiscite arranged by the Nazis to legalize their seizure of the country, the Nazi promise to ex-socialists that they would be given the positions that Jews held, and the further Nazi promise to end unemployment —all this helped cement Austro-German unity.

From the very start, Nazi anti-Jewish policies in Austria were much more radical than those in Germany. Within a matter of a few months Austria developed a process of Jewish humiliation, discrimination, and expropriation that had taken five years to develop in Germany. However, in many areas the Austrian Nazis went far beyond what had been inflicted upon German Jews up to then. Immediately following the anschluss, "spontaneous" anti-Semitic outrages by the population were encouraged by Nazi stormtroopers. Jews were beaten in public, forced to clean streets under especially humiliating circumstances, and driven out of their apartments. The expropriation of the property of the owners of 26,236 Jewish establishments in Austria started in May and June 1938. By November, 20 to 30 percent of Jewish capital, valued at about 100 million German marks, was in Nazi hands. Old-time Nazis became the new Nazi-nominated managers of the Jewish shops; most of them were uneducated people, and many were members of the Austrian underworld. They had no notion of business methods and speedily brought the firms to ruin.

On March 18 the Gestapo opened a branch in Vienna (Staatspolizeistelle). On that day IKG was officially closed and its leaders arrested. A fine of 300,000 shillings ($40,000) was levied upon the Jews—an amount equivalent to the sum donated to the Schuschnigg government to support it against Germany prior to the anschluss. In March too Adolf Eichmann arrived on the scene; he was responsible to the SD (SS security police) leader of the Danube area on matters pertaining to Jews. He nominated the head of the Palestine office (the Vienna branch of the immigration department of the Jewish Agency), Dr. Alois Rothenberg, to be in charge of Palestine emigration affairs. His main aim was the emigration of Jews, by any and all means, with the greatest possible speed.

The policy of forced emigration had been openly advocated by the SS prior to the anschluss; this seems to have been in line with Hitler's own thinking. On February 10, 1938, the SS journal, *Das Schwarze Korps,* published an article entitled "Where Should We Put the Jews?" [*Wohin mit den Juden?*]. The present rate of emigration, argued the Nazi paper, was not enough. The Jews who remained in Germany were not anxious to have their brethren, "the parasites,"[5] leave their present homes. Only the forced settlement of the Jews in a country to which they would be directed could solve the question—a hint at the Madagascar plans then being publicized by the Polish government.[6] After the anschluss, the leading Nazi daily in Germany, *Der Völkische Beobachter,* wrote on April 26, 1938, that all Jews must be eliminated from Germany by 1942. According to one source, a small experiment in forced emigration was carried out in eastern and western Prussia in 1937, in the areas of Allenstein (Olsztyn) and Schneidemühl (Pila). The victims, a few hundred people in all, were harassed, constantly supervised, robbed of their possessions, and driven to despair. The result was a panic exodus.[7]

After the period of partly organized bestiality, Eichmann allowed the reopening of IKG on May 3, 1938. In a very short time, twenty thousand heads of families applied for emigration permits. This must have represented at least forty to fifty thousand individuals. To further the desire for emigration, the Gestapo arrested about sixteen hundred Jews and sent them to the concentration camps of Dachau and Buchenwald during the first three months of Nazi rule. Many of these were wealthy Jews.[8]

Finally, in August, Löwenherz himself suggested to Eichmann that a central institution be established where the Jews could get all the necessary papers to enable them to leave the country. This was the genesis of Eichmann's famous Zentralstelle für jüdische Auswanderung, the Central Bureau for Jewish Emigration, which made him a paradigm of German efficiency in Jewish matters. Set up on August 26, the Zentralstelle henceforth took care of emigration procedures. Its method of operation was simple: by the time the Jew had gone through its procedures, he was left with no property except his ticket out of the country. All his possessions had been "taken care of" with German thoroughness (part of them, incidentally, went to IKG so that the many poor people who had no property could leave Austria). Also, IKG paid for its many activities, mainly relief and vocational retraining, from the emigrants' money).

The immediate reaction of the JDC central office in New York to the Austrian disaster was consternation and paralysis. Baerwald wrote to Jonah B. Wise a few days after the anschluss that at a meeting with leaders of the American Jewish Committee "everybody reluctantly agreed that nothing much can be done [in] connection [with the] Austrian situation."[9] Kahn, on the other hand, had no hesitation regarding the need for action. Rosen volunteered to go to Vienna, and when he came back to Paris on March 23 he reported having spent several thousand dollars for soup kitchens through friendly officials at the American mission. Of course much more was needed. In the absence, at first, of an officially active IKG, he demanded American government intervention. Baerwald was not so sure; he thought that "the best way for us to proceed is to cool down and to wait for any new developments which may come out of Washington."[10] However, nothing much materialized from that quarter.

In the meantime, Jews were starving and desperate. What aroused public opinion, non-Jewish as well as Jewish, was the plight of the Jews from six small towns in the Austrian province of Burgenland, who were evicted from their homes; some of them found temporary refuge on a boat on the Danube. Neither of the neighboring countries was willing to receive these unfortunates; action was taken against them "as though against the Black Plague."[11]

Meanwhile, JDC's New York office was hoping that a nonsectarian committee could be formed to deal with the situation.[12] When nothing came of it, the decision was taken to step in with as much money as JDC had on hand. Apart from this decision in principle, JDC tried very hard to find an American Jew of some standing who would represent it in Vienna. Further, it did not intend to send dollars into Austria if that could possibly be avoided.

A number of prominent personalities were sent to Vienna during the first months of the anschluss: Joseph A. Rosen, Alexander A. Landesco, Alfred Jaretzki, Jr., David J. Schweitzer of the Paris office, and others. Through them, JDC not only kept in touch with the situation, but was able to contact Nazi agents and try to influence their actions. The driblets of aid that these American Jews were able to bring with them and distribute, largely through the friendliness of Leland Morris, the U. S. consul general, were quite inadequate.[13] On June 11 the Council for German Jewry in London (theoretically representing JDC as well) intervened with the German Embassy in Britain to ask for the introduction of order into emigration proceedings.[14] IKG, reopened on May 3, was desperately trying to cope with the disastrous situation. By that time JDC was clear about its obligation to support Kahn's policy of maximum aid. In June JDC appropriated a sum of $250,000 for Austria. The sum of $431,438 was actually expended in Austria by the end of the year, however, or 10 percent of the total JDC spending for that year.[15]

Emigration through IKG was slow in starting. From the first days of Nazi rule a parallel emigration office operated under the auspices of Frank van Gheel-Gildemeester, son of a Dutch court chaplain, whose actual intentions and connections with the Germans have not quite been cleared up to this day. His main concern was with the so-called non-Aryans, that is, converted Jews or descendants of Jews who fell under the definition of a Jew by Nazi standards. There were at least 150,000 of these in Austria, and Gildemeester claims that 30,000 had emigrated by the summer of 1939.[16]

JDC had to give up its attempt to establish an American Jew as

T A B L E   16[17]
Persons Fed in Vienna in 1938

Month	March	May	June	August	September
No. fed	3,789	9,000	10,995	11,522	13,323; also, 7,000 food packages were sent to people in their homes

its representative in Vienna. Apart from other considerations, the U. S. government was disinclined to sanction such a move. Löwenherz, who soon became the guiding spirit of IKG, was not trusted by JDC; at the end of 1938 Morris C. Troper, who succeeded Kahn as European director of JDC, called him a "Gestapo agent."[18] Yet there was no alternative, and IKG had to be supported. Of the JDC contribution, 60 percent went to emigration. This was not done, however, through a direct contribution of American dollars to the German treasury. The procedure was to pay for the prospective emigrant's tickets and other expenses outside the Reich; in return, money paid by the emigrant to IKG was utilized to cover that institution's expenses. It is true that this cost the Germans nothing —or, as Heydrich put it, Jewish emigration was effected "without any payment by the German side, not even in the form of 'additional exports.' "[19] But Germany did not acquire any foreign currency through this method—and Jewish property was in the Nazis' hands in any case. JDC visitors were treated well by the Gestapo, and the Nazi agents they met became "rather amiable young fellows" when discussing financial arrangements; but the message that they welcomed "our cooperation in getting the Jews out of Austria as quickly as possible," and that emigration "was proceeding at much too slow a rate" was very definite and unmistakable.[20]

Many Jews did not, or could not, wait for any emigration arrangements made by IKG. In the first panic thousands fled Austria, often pushed across the border by Nazis, mainly by SA and SS units. Czechoslovakia, Hungary, and Yugoslavia, countries sharing a common border with Austria, closed their frontiers. Although illegal crossings were particularly dangerous, a small but unknown number of Jews managed to get across. On the other hand, it was relatively easy to get into Italy and Switzerland. Travelers with Austrian passports did not need a visa. During the first few weeks after the anschluss, over three thousand refugees, mostly Jewish, crossed the Swiss border.[21]

Swiss reaction to the flow of refugees was swift. On March 26 the federal Justice and Police Department asked the government

(Bundesrat) to decree that holders of Austrian passports must have entry visas. "We have to defend ourselves with all our strength, even with a measure of callousness [*Rücksichtslosigkeit*] against the influx of foreign Jews, especially from the east, if we wish to avoid creating justified ground for an anti-Semitic movement unworthy of our country."[22] The defense "with all our strength" against refugees fleeing for their lives was eminently successful: on March 28 the Bundesrat decreed that visas were necessary for holders of Austrian passports. On April 8 a circular from the federal police administration informed cantonal police departments that unless there were very weighty reasons for refugees to stay, they had to be told to leave the country at the earliest possible moment. However, these stricter regulations were of no avail, and from about the middle of May 1938 groups of Jews would be brought to the Swiss border, stripped of all their possessions, kept in Nazi jails at the border, and then sent across into Swiss territory at night. A return into Austria meant the immediate threat of concentration-camp treatment. The Swiss police chief, Dr. Heinrich Rothmund, earnestly requested the German government to put an end to these deportations into Switzerland, "which needs these Jews just as little as Germany does."[23] After April 1 there seems to have been an influx of another two thousand refugees who came without visas, plus an additional number of illegals. In addition, there were wealthy refugees, who received official permits to enter the country. In fact, the Swiss consulate in Vienna seems to have been more liberal in granting entry permits than was warranted by the instructions it received from the Swiss government.

A similar influx of Austrian refugees into Western Europe—France, Holland, Luxemburg, and Belgium—created similar reactions there. From Italy, where racist propaganda began under German influence in 1938, desperate refugees were trying to get into Switzerland; apparently some three thousand succeeded in doing so.[24] But as the summer approached all countries in the West began closing their doors to these refugees, and Switzerland began to return to Germany the refugees caught crossing her border illegally.

EVIAN

On March 22, 1938, President Roosevelt invited thirty-three governments to a conference in Europe that was to deal with refugees from Germany and Austria. In his book *While Six Million Died,* Arthur D. Morse traces the origin of this conference to Undersecretary of State Sumner Welles, who suggested in a memorandum that an American initiative on the international level would counteract liberal pressure about the restrictive quota system. The international body that would presumably be set up would take on the responsibility for finding places of settlement for the refugees other than the U. S.[25] This memorandum seems to have represented the thinking of the State Department and its chief officials. Another political reason behind the president's move was probably the anti-isolationist policy it implied. The fate of the refugees was used as a means to other ends rather than as a problem that had to be solved. The fact that until well into June the State Department proved incapable of expressing what it wanted to achieve at the conference indicated that there was little intention to do something tangible for the refugees.[26]

Myron C. Taylor, former chairman of U. S. Steel and a Roman Catholic, was appointed as Roosevelt's representative and given the task of convening and chairing the conference. His appointment was probably intended to demonstrate real American interest in the refugees. At the same time, however, the president made it clear that the U. S. quota system would not be changed; also, all expenditures for emigration and settlement would have to be borne by private agencies. The task of the American government was to exert pressure on Germany to permit the refugees to leave and to influence countries of immigration to receive them.

Two steps were taken in April to supplement the American initiative. First, the administration declared that the Austrian quota would be added to the German quota, and the resulting quota of 27,370, it was hinted, would be filled to a much greater extent than heretofore. Second, it was made clear that the U.S. government believed that the solution to the problem lay in requesting the Germans to allow Jews to bring some of their property with them when they left Germany. If Jews came with money, they had a good chance of being accepted; if they came without funds, all doors would be closed.

Having made his invitation public—in the end South Africa, Iceland, El Salvador, and Italy refused to participate, thus reducing the number of the countries involved to twenty-nine—Roosevelt created an Advisory Committee on Political Refugees. There was marked anxiety not to make it appear that Jewish refugees were involved at all. Indeed, the very word "Jew" was considered to be somehow unmentionable; "political refugees" was the official terminology, despite the obvious fact that the overwhelming majority of the refugees were in fact Jews.

The first meeting of the Advisory Committee was held on April 13 under Roosevelt's chairmanship. Eleven non-Jews and three Jews (Henry Morgenthau, Sr., Bernard M. Baruch, and Stephen S. Wise) participated. Baruch and Morgenthau, of course, belonged to the immediate political family of the president, so that the only political invitee was Wise, head of the American Jewish Congress and the World Jewish Congress, and the acknowledged leader of American Zionism. Naturally, this was a blow to the leadership of the American Jewish Committee and JDC, who made some bitter comments about Wise's membership on the new committee.

Welles had prepared the president against any move to liberalize American immigration policy, but at the meeting one of the Jews, Baruch, went a step further: he was the only one among the participants who opposed the president's initiative. He wondered whether "it would be wise for our government to encourage the idea that more refugees should come here." The fact that this had been preceded by a private visit by Baruch to Roosevelt on the same day would seem to indicate that this "opposition" was prearranged.[27] Roosevelt explained that private agencies would have to pay for all emigration and settlement expenses, because any government appropriation would have to be passed by Congress, and that was not very likely.

McDonald was elected chairman of the new committee, and it was he who proposed that Paul Baerwald be invited to join. The president's letter of invitation to the JDC chairman went out on April 18. In the meantime, the JDC leadership had agreed, at a meeting with American Jewish Committee officers late in March, that large-scale settlement projects were the order of the day.[28] In all matters concerning refugees it was preferable that non-Jews take the lead, in order to avoid anti-Semitic feelings. JDC accepted the government's policy—no questions were asked, no requests were made, no hint of any criticism of the government's attitude was heard. Nothing was said regarding the government's decision to put the burden of expenses on "nongovernmental sources."[29]

At the conference itself, held at Evian, France, between July 6 and July 15, 1938, two main ideas seem to have been in the minds of Taylor and George L. Warren, his executive secretary and chief aide: to try to get countries of immigration to make liberal immigration declarations, and to establish international machinery (directed mainly by the U.S.) that would enter into negotiations with Germany. There were difficulties on both points, however. The statements of the various representatives were discouraging and often tinged with anti-Semitism. For example, the Australian representative declared that "as we have no real racial problem we are not desirous of importing one." Latin American delegates were very restrained—a few countries, like Brazil, Argentina, Colombia, Uruguay, Paraguay, and Peru, offered some prospect for the immigration of agricultural workers or farmers. All made a special point of declaring that no merchants or intellectuals would be allowed in. Nowhere was special legislation to allow immigration being contemplated, and of course in this matter the U.S. example was being followed.

Britain's representative, Lord Winterton, declared that Palestine was temporarily closed to large-scale immigration until a political solution was found. However, he declared, there were prospects for settling refugees in Kenya and other parts of East Africa.[30] This declaration was "an unexpected and welcome gesture."[31] Britain

itself, Winterton said, was not a country of immigration. Yet the
people of the United Kingdom were ready to play their part within
the narrow limits feasible, given the high degree of industrialization
and the large number of unemployed in Britain. European countries emphasized the necessity for emigration overseas, but Holland
and Denmark stressed their relatively liberal policies as transit
countries. Speaking for Switzerland, which had refused to play
host to the conference, the police chief, Dr. Rothmund, insisted
that his country could only be a temporary stopover en route to
other places.[32]

Taylor himself had no illusions regarding the prospect of getting
public governmental declarations welcoming refugees. Although
insisting in his opening speech that governments must act promptly
on the refugee question, he also said that probably no more "could
be expected than that the conference should put into motion the
machinery and correlate it with existing machinery that will, in the
long run, contribute to a practical amelioration of the conditions."[33] The declarations, while far from satisfactory, were not
quite as negative as press criticism at the time and historical accounts since then would have us believe. While we have seen that
some countries of potential refuge refused to consider immigration,
others were willing to accept people under certain conditions. It
was therefore a matter of providing refugees with sufficient means
to make their immigration to those countries attractive to the
governments concerned.[34]

This was by no means easy to achieve. Britain and France were
reluctant to have the refugee question taken out of the League of
Nations, where their influence was paramount. Sir Neil Malcolm,
the League of Nations high commissioner for refugees, displeased
the Americans by stating that government funds were needed and
that private organizations could not possibly bear the burden. He
also spoke his mind regarding the attitude of the governments and
declared that "large-scale immigration and settlement . . . presently
appear impossible."[35] Warren termed his speech "not helpful."[36] In
the end, however, the British and French agreed to the setting up
of an Intergovernmental Committee on Refugees (ICR), which

would be located in London; presumably ICR would swallow up the League committee under Malcolm.

These were not the only problems raised at Evian. Poland and Romania tried to have the conference deal with the emigration of their Jewish populations, but the delegations from Britain and France very energetically rejected all such attempts. The discussions were limited to the subject of persons—termed "involuntary emigrants"—who might be forced out of Germany and Austria in the future and those who had already left but had found no satisfactory place of permanent residence (their number was estimated at thirty thousand). Only in the long run was it proposed to deal with larger aspects of the question, thus including the emigration problem of East European Jewry.

The delegations of German and Austrian Jews, prodded by the Gestapo to make clear to the conferees the necessity of finding havens quickly, made a considerable impression.[37] The Jewish organizations from the free countries, about twenty-one of them, presented a spectacle of disunity and confusion. The Liaison Committee, under Norman Bentwich, drew up a statement, but the individual groups would not forgo their right to make separate appearances; as a result a large number of speeches were made, more or less repeating each other.[38] Jonah B. Wise represented JDC at Evian, and his presentation on July 14 was really a summary of what JDC had achieved up to that time. He emphasized that JDC's resources were limited and based on voluntary contributions, and that it was necessary that the emigrants be able to take out some of their own capital.

In official American eyes the role of JDC was quite important. Prior to Evian, JDC leaders had been invited to an informal meeting with Warren, Prof. Joseph P. Chamberlain, and James G. McDonald, where stress was laid on the pressure that would be brought to bear on Britain to get her to open her possessions to refugee settlement. The point was made that if the British hold back, "they may hurt their present relationship with our government."[39]

It must be stressed that only the World Jewish Congress, represented by Dr. Nahum Goldmann, disregarded the appeals for moderation. It sharply attacked German practices, demanded that the Jewish problem be viewed as a whole, said that Jews fleeing from Eastern Europe should also be helped, and insisted that uncultivated areas be set aside for Jewish settlement. Also, WJC thought that government financing was indispensable because private agencies would not be able to support the emigration by themselves.

JDC was not displeased with the outcome of Evian. In a telephone conversation with Baerwald on July 14, McDonald declared that he was "satisfied they accomplished everything that could be expected under the circumstances."[40] Baerwald agreed. It must be remembered that JDC was privy to Taylor's intentions at the conference to have the U. S. set up ICR, whose task it should be, as Taylor constantly reiterated, to negotiate with the Germans. JDC was sympathetic to this line of thought. Its Paris secretary, Nathan Katz, was asked to prepare for and take part in the discussions at the first ICR meeting in London on August 3, 1938. Taylor's statement on that occasion had been prepared "in Paris with the cooperation of Dr. Kahn and myself," as Katz wrote.[41] Typically, the number of people who would have to be dealt with by ICR in Germany was put at 660,000; this included all persecuted "non-Aryans" and other gentiles, so that the Jewish aspect could be toned down as much as possible.

A small administrative budget, to be paid to ICR by the governments, was agreed to after some haggling, and George Rublee, an American lawyer, was elected director—in fact, prospective negotiator with Germany. An assistant director, Robert Pell, was loaned from the State Department, indicating that these proceedings were considered to be of some importance for American diplomacy.[42] JDC leadership tended to regard the very fact of American and international involvement in the refugee problem as a great step forward. Kahn wrote about "the message of the Evian Conference, the significance of a great gathering which solemnly affirmed the initial responsibility of humanity in the solution of the problems of the refugees."[43]

THE REFUGEES

The immediate results of the conference amounted to nothing. In France, the Austrian disaster evoked a harsh reaction on the part of the government. There were not many refugees in France to start with: at the end of 1937 about seven thousand German Jews lived in France, of whom twenty-five hundred had to be supported.[44] But in early 1938, even before the anschluss, French policy hardened. This was the period of the final collapse of the Popular Front movement and the rise of conservative forces. On March 2 there was a French government proposal to settle ten thousand refugees as agricultural laborers. Those who refused to be settled in this manner would be expelled. The Consistoire Centrale, the main religious authority of French Jewry, agreed in principle that Jews who disobeyed the government's orders should not stay in France. To avoid disaster, Kahn for JDC and Baron Robert de Rothschild for French Jewry suggested that a sum of 3 million francs be set aside for this project. The whole question was aired at a March 27, 1938, meeting of all Jewish organizations, French and non-French, working in France. At that meeting and again in April, the scheme was enlarged to a 20 million franc project; the intent was to settle twelve to fifteen thousand refugees on French lands. Nothing came of it. In the end the French government decided that it did not want to have refugee Jews settle on French soil.

However, at the March meeting, two weeks after the anschluss, a much more dangerous French demand was made known: Philippe Serre, French undersecretary of state for immigration, demanded that the Jews in France collect money for the government, to cover the expense of forcible repatriation of refugees to Germany. Marc Jarblum, a Zionist and the leader of the Fédération des Sociétés Juives, the main organization of East European Jews in France, had told Serre that no Jewish support should be expected for such a proposal. Kahn for JDC and Edouard Oungre for HICEM had given similar answers. But the chairman of the meeting, Prof. William Oualid of the Consistoire, demurred: it was "unwise to give a point-blank refusal"; he proposed that the Jews participate in the cost of repatriation when it was impossible "to obtain a favorable solution." Let it be said to the credit of that particular meeting that Oualid's suggestion failed to get majority approval.[45]

As the refugees from Austria began to pour in, French reaction stiffened even further. On May 2, 1938, the government decreed that all refugees who could not move to other countries and could not get permission to stay in France would henceforth be treated as criminals. Judges were instructed to hand down sentences of one month's imprisonment to such refugees. If after that month the person concerned still could not find another country of refuge within a week of his release from prison, he was to be put in jail for another six months. Children of such "recalcitrant" parents were to be placed in charitable homes.

On October 12, 1938, further instructions were issued to the effect that Austrian refugees in particular should be sent back. They were given four days in which to leave France, and if they did not do so, they were subject to imprisonment for many months.[46]

These draconian measures hit not only refugees from Germany and Austria, but also Polish Jews who were deprived of their citizenship by a Polish decree of March 1938.[47] These people, some of whom had been living in France for ten years or more, were now suddenly subject to arrest and imprisonment because a country, which the younger ones among them had not even seen, had withdrawn its technical protection from them. Finally, on November 12 an amendment to the earlier decrees was published, and the imprisonment was changed into forced residence. Of course, judges were free to assign refugees to closed camps rather than some village or town. Jewish refugees began to be interned in French concentration camps even prior to the Nazi onslaught on France; this internment ultimately contributed to a significant degree to the mass murder of Jews in France by the Germans.

JDC did not have much choice in France; this was the seat of its European office, and Kahn had to support the refugees to the best of JDC's limited ability. The numbers were growing throughout 1938, but in the summer and autumn they were still manageable. In early 1938 there were ten thousand refugees in France; this was to increase to twenty-five thousand in December. JDC spent $130,884 in France in that year, most of it through different French Jewish organizations in support of various aspects of refugee work; it also spent money through HICEM, which was trying to find places of settlement for the refugees. This was no easy task, because as a result of the Evian Conference most governments adopted a "wait and see" attitude. "Many countries are said to have closed their doors in the expectation that through the establishment of the Winterton-Rublee committee, refugees from Germany might bring some money with them."[48] This, of course, was preferable to an influx of destitute refugees. JDC leaders saw that they had to do everything in their power to enable the newly established ICR reach an agreement with the Germans.

The situation in France tended to repeat itself in other countries. Britain experienced a wave of antirefugee protest in some of its most vocal newspapers.

The London *Times* and the *Manchester Guardian* had voiced satisfaction with the outcome of Evian.[49] But there was no necessary contradiction between that and a basically negative attitude to Jewish immigration into Britain. Jews had to find a haven and should be helped to find one—but not in England. "Dreadful, dreadful are the afflictions of Jewish people," cried the *Daily Express* on September 2, 1938, in an article which emphasized that there was no room for them in Britain. The *Evening News* went even further on July 13: "Money we will provide, if need be, but the law of self-preservation demands that the word ENTER be removed from the gate."[50]

In Switzerland, too, the influx of refugees from Austria caused a sharp reaction. Despite the measures taken in March and April, Jews continued to cross the Swiss border. VSIA cared for those that managed to do so and in 1938 erected six camps housing 877 penniless refugees.[51] Throughout July and during the first half of August about 2,300 Jewish refugees managed to cross the border illegally. Since March, Austrian passport holders had had to obtain Swiss visas of entry to get to Switzerland, but a German decree of August 15 announced that as of January 1, 1939, all Austrian passports would be changed into German ones; and German passport holders could enter Switzerland without a visa. The Swiss government therefore took a series of measures against the refugee influx. On August 10 a police circular to border police stations established a policy of refusal of entry to refugees. On the same date the Swiss chief of police submitted a report to his government; in it he stated that refugees who said they would be interned in a concentration camp if they were returned to Germany would not be handed over to the Germans. The problem was what to do with the illegals already in the country. He thought they should be expelled to Germany, but he did not dare to take this step because it might "arouse a tremendous outcry against Switzerland in all civilized countries."[52] A conference of police officials on August 17 confirmed this policy, which was then approved by the Swiss government on the August 19.[53] This latter decision, however, went even further: henceforth there was to be no refugee immigration from Austria at all, thus presumably eliminating all exceptions regarding persons threatened with concentration camps.

The position of Swiss Jewry in all this was quite difficult. At a general meeting of VSIA it was noted that while the situation of the refugees was tragic, Swiss political and economic interests should not be ignored. At the same time, however, the head of SIG, Saly Mayer, very energetically denied rumors regarding supposed communications from the heads of the Swiss Jewish community to the government, to the effect that Swiss Jewry objected to the further entry of refugees into the country. "The law of 'love thy neighbor' is still the guideline for our actions, and we must try to achieve as much as is possible for our brethren who are in trouble."[54]

This was said, however, a month before the anschluss. After that event the situation changed. The economic burden brought on by the sudden influx of thousands of refugees could not be sustained by the tiny Swiss Jewish community. While some of the immigrants went on to other destinations, and others had money at their disposal and did not become a burden to the community, about twenty-four hundred had to be supported by October 1938.[55] SIG stated that it was not capable, technically and financially, of supporting a further influx.[56] On the same day that the Swiss government made its decision to close its borders, August 19, VSIA cabled IKG in Vienna warning it not to send any more illegal refugees (all refugees were illegals, because no Austrian Jew could get a legal entry permit into Switzerland unless he was in transit to another country or had plenty of money in Switzerland).[57] In other words, Swiss Jewry felt that it had to yield to Swiss official pressure and play a part in the official antirefugee policy. By the end of 1938 there were ten to twelve thousand Jewish refugees who could not get beyond Switzerland. Tragedies on the borders became the order of the day; refugees physically resisted expulsion into German hands. But of course such resistance was of no avail.[58]

In its despair Swiss Jewry, through Saly Mayer, turned to JDC. In a cable on August 25 Kahn reported to JDC that Swiss Jews needed 1 million Swiss francs, but that only one-third of the sum could be raised locally. The reaction of New York was that local resources should be tapped first, because JDC's income was not geared to such large-scale emergencies. Then, New York told Kahn, ICR should be approached. "We have constantly in mind that settling such refugee difficulties quickly will encourage pushing many others over frontiers."

But Kahn had a different view. He announced to his head office that he had given emergency support not only in Switzerland, but in Luxemburg, Belgium, and Czechoslovakia. Baerwald thought that these appropriations were "staggering," and objected. Kahn reacted sharply: on August 26 he explained in a curt cable that it was imperative to preserve the goodwill of Jewish and non-Jewish institutions. "[The] entire record [of] JDC activities constitutes [a] precedent supporting such appropriations." He had given the money to the Swiss "to avoid [a] debacle." Baerwald had no wish to quarrel with his European director. In any case, he realized that JDC would have no choice but to support the Europeans as much as possible. On August 28 he assured Kahn that he fully realized "appropriations unavoidable." He added: "Please do not worry. Nothing will be done against your judgment."[59] Indeed, unless they decided to change the director in Europe, JDC in New York had no choice but to confirm the judgment of its Paris office. The increasing force of the crisis in Europe, however, did lead the New York leadership to weigh the possibility of a change in its European personnel.

As far as Switzerland was concerned, Kahn's action turned the country's Jewish aid committee, VSIA, into one of Europe's main recipient of funds. For its six refugee camps and its support of refugees outside the camps, JDC paid a total of $66,000 in 1938. Total JDC expenditures in Switzerland amounted to $72,000, which included small sums given to vocational training institutions as well. These sums fell short of Swiss demands—Saly Mayer wanted a monthly allocation of $57,600, but in the last two months of 1938 JDC allocations to Switzerland were running at a monthly rate of $20,000, which was only a little less than what was being spent in Austria itself. The dollars were converted into Swiss francs at the most favorable rates, and SIG reported that they got 415,449 Swiss francs as a result, or about 33.8 percent of the Swiss Jewish community's total income of 1,820,457 Swiss francs.[60]

Switzerland and France were by no means the only trouble spots in the summer of 1938. In tiny Luxemburg fifty-two Austrian Jews were expelled by the authorities in May. JDC in Paris intervened with the Luxemburg government—a very rare thing for JDC to do —and asked it to prevent further expulsions. Luxemburg thereupon allowed two hundred refugees to enter, with the understanding that JDC would send aid and the refugees would ultimately be moved to other places. The Jewish community in that country numbered only two hundred taxpayers, and the aid committee, Esra, was at the end of its resources by August. When JDC could not send enough money, Esra told the government that it could no longer cope with the Austrian influx, and asked for government restrictions on immigration, without, however, excessive severity. Political refugees, it said, should be treated "more humanely."[61] Probably as a result of this step, Luxemburg closed its borders on August 17. But illegal entry continued. The police used to drive the refugees back into Germany, while those who managed to enter the country were sent over the borders into Belgium and France. In late August JDC undertook to help Esra maintain housing and feeding facilities for refugees. This took care of poor refugees; the Luxemburg government then allowed a thousand people of means to enter the country in late 1938.

Similar problems arose in other European countries. An Italian decree of September 7, 1938, translated the growing racist propaganda—instigated by the Germans and their supporters among Italy's Fascists—into harsh practice. All Jews who had become Italian citizens since 1919 had their citizenship revoked by a stroke of a pen. All foreign Jews who had entered the country since 1919 were supposed to leave Italy within six months. In Holland the borders were officially closed; eleven thousand Jewish refugees had become absorbed in the country's economy, but two thousand were either on relief or preparing for emigration, or both. Throughout 1938 the government gave permission to about two thousand additional Jews—mostly parents of youngsters already working in Holland—to enter the country legally. However, all further attempts to enter Holland were frustrated by strict border controls.

ZBASZYN

On March 25, 1938, the Polish Sejm passed a law according to which any Polish citizen who had not visited Poland for five consecutive years could be deprived of his citizenship, unless his passport was specifically renewed. The original aim of this ruling was

244 : *My Brother's Keeper*

to prevent Polish Jews in Vienna from entering Poland after the German occupation of Austria on March 13, 1938. On June 15 the Polish Telegraphic Agency reported that those Polish Jews from Vienna who had nevertheless succeeded in crossing the Polish border would be put into the Polish concentration camp of Bereza Kartuska.

Among the approximately 500,000 Jews in Germany in 1933, there were 98,747 Jews of foreign nationality. Of these, 56,480 were Polish Jews.[62] Frantic attempts by many of these Jews to avoid being declared stateless were of no avail; their denationalization was to take effect at the end of October 1938. The Nazi government, bent on getting rid of as many Jews as possible, saw the Polish step as a menace to their own anti-Jewish policy. If they did nothing, they might later not be able to expel these Jews into Poland because the Poles would then argue that they were no longer Polish citizens. One of the main planks of the original Nazi party program in 1920 had been to rid Germany of foreigners, and first and foremost this applied to Jews. Ideologically, therefore, there was every reason for the Nazis to prevent the continuation of Polish Jewish residence in Germany.

On October 6 the Polish government decreed that those who did not have their passports renewed by October 29 would lose their Polish citizenship. On October 26 the German Foreign Office requested the Gestapo to evict as many Polish Jews as possible from Germany.[63] The Gestapo obliged with its customary promptness and brutality, and on the night of October 27/8, some seventeen thousand Polish Jews in Germany were rounded up, some of them in their nightclothes. Many were beaten. They were put on special trains and sent to the Polish border. There some of them were forced by the Germans to cross the border illegally; most, however, were simply shunted across the frontier in railway carriages.

Some of the refugees still had families or other connections in Poland and were able to resettle with some measure of ease. Others were less fortunate. People who had left Poland dozens of years before, or had never been to Poland at all but had inherited their

Polish citizenship from their parents, found no place to stay. By early November the JDC office counted 12,800 homeless refugees all over the country. There were small groups of these refugees in the main Jewish centers such as Lodz, Warsaw, and Cracow. Local refugee committees sprang up in these places to look after the people as best they could.

The worst spot, however, was a tiny hamlet of some four thousand inhabitants, Zbaszyn, on the main railroad between Frankfurt on the Oder and Poznań, which was situated on the Polish side of the border with Germany. At the crossing the Germans expelled some ninety-three hundred men, women, and children; nearly four thousand managed to get away into Poland within the first forty-eight hours. The Poles were unwilling to let the rest, some fifty-five hundred, into Poland and forced them to remain in the village. It presented a terrible sight. Since the number of refugees was larger than the total population of the village, they had to be housed in stables, pigsties, and other temporary shelters. November is a very cold month in Poland, and after the first few days there were problems concerning bedding, heating, warm food, sanitation, and medical attention. The refugees themselves were completely helpless, for the Polish government would not allow any of them to leave Zbaszyn for the interior.

Polish Jewry, however, reacted fairly swiftly. On November 4 an aid committee was set up in Warsaw, which collected large amounts of money locally. By July 1939 over 3.5 million zloty had been collected, of which JDC contributed 20 percent.[64] This was besides aid in kind, which during this period amounted to over 1 million zloty more.

The struggle over the Zbaszyn refugees had an importance that transcended mere financial considerations. JDC in Poland found itself pursuing a policy quite different from the one it had practiced throughout the 1930s. Giterman and the famous historian Emanuel Ringelblum, who was a JDC employee, rushed to Zbaszyn immediately on receipt of the news of the refugees' arrival. With local aid, they organized the first help. Throughout the months of

November and December, JDC personnel directly supervised the aid activities at Zbaszyn. The usual roles seemed to be reversed: usually, JDC allocated money and the local committees did the actual work; in this case, the local Warsaw committee provided the bulk of the funds, and JDC personnel did the actual work of organizing and supervising the aid.

At first Giterman's policy at Zbaszyn was not to erect more permanent structures for the refugees, since this might encourage the Polish government to regard Zbaszyn as a permanent refugee camp.[65] However, this policy of trying to pressure the Polish government into doing something penalized the refugees rather than the government, which refused even to provide food. In early December intense cold set in, and there was no choice but to order adequate bedding and food and to construct appropriate shelters. After the first ten days Giterman left and Ringelblum, with a devoted staff of about ten people, stayed on. In the name of JDC he organized food distribution, heating, first aid, distribution of clothes (collected from all over Poland), emigration advice, and similar essential activities. He also saw to it that there was a library, that the schooling of children was organized, that a Talmud Torah for Orthodox children was set up, that concerts and lectures were held. Apparently he even collected historical material on the expulsion of Polish Jews from Germany; unfortunately this material has not reached us.

Despite repeated interventions by the Warsaw committee the Poles let very few of the refugees enter the country, and by the end of the year there were still fifty-two hundred refugees at Zbaszyn.

An aspect of the Zbaszyn crisis was the growing tension between the Polish Jewish committee and JDC. Giterman stated JDC's position in a cable he sent on December 21: "We giving contribution only when approached by local organizations after their funds becoming exhausted." In the U. S., meanwhile, JDC fund raising naturally became geared to the new situation and much money was collected for aid for refugees in Poland. In early 1939 the Warsaw refugee committee complained that only 15 percent of the funds so far had been spent by foreign organizations, including JDC, while all the rest had come from the impoverished Polish Jewish community. In New York, Alexander Kahn, chairman of JDC's Polish Committee, was worried. He stated: "Our position is untenable, when we seek and receive substantial contributions here for assistance to German deportees and negligible sums are expended in the face of such dire need."[66]

Possibly as a result of repeated interventions by the New York office, JDC expenditure for Zbaszyn increased in 1939. By early June there were still four thousand Jews at Zbaszyn, and about $40,000 monthly was needed there. However, JDC in Poland was careful; it was not completely convinced of the correctness of the Warsaw committee's statistics, and besides, additional issues had arisen in the meantime to complicate the problem considerably.

The Polish government was extremely unhappy about the whole situation. Trying to pay the Germans back in their own coin, it threatened to expel German citizens from Poland, especially German Jewish refugees who had arrived from Germany in previous years. In this tragic situation, where the mutual animosity of two anti-Semitic states was typically and brutally expressed by the maltreatment of each other's Jews, a way out was found (at least temporarily) when both countries agreed on January 24, 1939, that no further expulsions would take place, and that the Jewish expellees would be granted limited rights to visit Germany to wind up their affairs there or to arrange for final emigration to other countries.

However, the Poles had learned their lesson effectively. If Germany managed to get rid of her Jews by Gestapo methods, Poland could follow in her footsteps. In early November the government forced the acknowledged head of the Jewish community in Poland, Rabbi Moshe Schorr, to set up the Jewish Emigration and Colonization Committee. The Poles gave this organization the task of collecting 3 million zloty and convincing Jewish organizations abroad to do everything in their power to get large numbers of Polish Jews to emigrate. By and large the Zionists boycotted this committee; but their leaders, Henryk Rosmarin, Anselm Reiss, and Moshe Kleinbaum, were told point-blank that the government no longer considered Palestine as the only emigration goal for Jews from Poland. "If the price paid to Germany for brutalities against the Jews will be taking out the Jews from that country, nothing remains for Poland but to use similar methods with regard to stimulating Jewish emigration from Poland."[67] In line with this approach, and in order to increase the pressure on the Jews, the Polish government also set up a non-Jewish committee of Friends to Promote Jewish Emigration to Madagascar.

The main task of the members of the Jewish committee, aside from collecting money, was to travel abroad and conduct negotiations about the emigration of as many Jews as possible. Within a month, by December 1938, one-third of the required sum of 3 million zloty had been collected from wealthy Jewish individuals in Poland. The new JDC European chairman, Morris C. Troper, saw no possibility of opposing the new Polish attitude. On December 20, 1938, he wrote to Hyman that if the Polish emigration pressure was inevitable, then the committee should at least be in the hands of people amenable to JDC.[68] Schorr and Rosmarin were connected with the American Federation of Polish Jews and the World Jewish Congress. WJC's concept of the unity of the Jewish people all over the world and its endeavor to set up political machinery to represent world Jewry ran counter to JDC's rejection of Jewish nationalism. Also, WJC and AFPJ were trying to collect money in America for Europe's Jews, in competition with JDC. Schorr and Rosmarin were therefore unacceptable, and Troper suggested that three industrialists respected by JDC should be invited to the U.S., one of whom was Karol Sachs, a very wealthy Jewish industrialist from Lodz.

The New York office, as well as the Warsaw JDC office, were not eager to enter into the whole problem of emigration from Poland, at least not under such blatant Polish pressure. There was, it is true, a slow but decisive change of JDC opinion on emigration generally. Polish anti-Semitism seemed less marked in early 1939, and it was believed that the Poles had to "throw something to the wolves."[69] Adler thought it was very easy to tell people not to emigrate when one was a Jew in America. "But if they are legislated out of existence, our only chance is emigration."[70]

The problem was, of course, where to go and how to prepare effectively for emigration. In Poland itself the stress on vocational retraining for occupations that might be useful in applying for entry into overseas countries was nothing new. A report from Galicia in March 1939 stressed that "nowhere are we allowed to grow roots and we are forced to consider our children and youths as future export merchandise. We must try to deliver first quality."[71] Yet in the 1939 world, not even first quality was sufficient. Palestine was almost closed. The Polish quota for the U. S. was about six thousand annually. South American countries were reluctant to accept Jews. The world was unwilling to help the three million Polish Jews.

In this desperate situation desperate remedies were thought of, even in such level-headed circles as those at the JDC offices in New York. George Backer, who was very active with both JDC and the American Jewish Committee, was suggesting to the Poles that they buy a colony, presumably in Africa, where the Jews might settle. The Polish ambassador, he reported, responded enthusiastically.[72]

In the meantime, at the end of January 1939, Rabbi Schorr and others left for London. If they were to come to the U.S., the situation might become difficult for JDC. JDC could not offer any places for emigration, nor could it pay for such a huge enterprise even if there were places to go to. A campaign for emigration might endanger the small-scale but vitally important work that JDC was doing in Poland. No emigration would ensue, and masses of Polish Jews who were now receiving some help through JDC would find themselves abandoned. JDC therefore decided that a visit by the delegation from Poland had to be avoided. In February 1939 Troper reported to Hyman that he had prevented the visit and that the delegation was discussing its problems in London instead. There, apparently, the delegation reported that the Poles had threatened anti-Jewish legislation if no emigration was forthcoming. This legislation would include "revision" of citizenship and the elimination of Jews from the economic and cultural life of Poland.[73] There was not much JDC could do to help.

JDC IN 1938/9

The dramatic developments in Europe caused an internal upheaval in JDC's setup. This reorganization had already started during the last months of Felix M. Warburg's life. When the founder and honorary chairman of JDC died on September 20, 1937, his death was a tremendous blow to the organization, because there were few persons in American Jewish life who could match his humanitarianism, his personal concern with aiding stricken Jews all over the world, and his prestige in the Jewish and non-Jewish world. Paul Baerwald, his close associate in JDC work, became the head of the organization in fact as well as in name. (Years before his death, Warburg had officially ceased active work for JDC, becoming honorary chairman—but in reality he remained the arbiter of the organization's fortunes.)

In 1936/7 JDC grew into a large organization, and the old way of running things no longer seemed adequate. In June 1937 a nucleus of the Executive Committee, called the Administration Committee, was formed to run the day-to-day affairs of JDC. It was composed of those laymen most concerned with its work: James N. Rosenberg, George Backer, Alexander Kahn, Morris C. Troper, Jonah B. Wise, William Rosenwald, Herbert J. Seligman, Mrs. Harriet B. Goldstein, David M. Bressler, and a few others. The JDC office was represented by Hyman, and of course Paul Baerwald almost always participated. Meetings were sporadic at first, but soon weekly meetings became the rule. By the middle of 1939 even the new committee had become too unwieldy, and a small steering committee, composed of fifteen members, began to emerge. More and more, the Executive Committee's meetings became formal occasions, with the real decision-making transferred to the smaller bodies.

In late 1938 and early 1939 committees of laymen were formed to deal with policy decisions on separate areas, whether geographical or other. Cultural, religious, and educational matters had been the province of a special committee ever since the inception of JDC. There was also the Budget and Scope Committee, which dealt with financial planning. Other committees dealt with fund raising, allocations, and other matters. In 1938 the need arose to coordinate activities in different parts of the globe. A committee on refugee countries was therefore formed under Edward M. M. Warburg, Felix M. Warburg's son, who was to take his father's place in the leadership of the organization. Another committee under Alfred Jaretzki, Jr., was formed to deal with Latin America; a committee for Poland and Eastern Europe, under Alexander Kahn, had been in existence for some time.

A similar process began at the European end of JDC's operations. As early as January 1937 Baerwald began admonishing Kahn that he should be in constant consultation with his chief accountant and representative on the Reconstruction Foundation, David J. Schweitzer, and with Joseph A. Rosen. A European Council of JDC was then formed, of which Kahn became chairman and Nathan Katz secretary.[74]

The truth of the matter was that Kahn was getting old; in early 1938 Troper visited the Paris office and reported that Kahn did not seem to be able to manage the whole scope of JDC's affairs; others thought differently. In April 1938 the demand that Kahn be replaced was voiced at an Executive Committee meeting. The main reason advanced seemed logical enough: Kahn was not an American and could not move about in German-occupied countries. JDC had to plan ahead for the eventuality of a German takeover in Czechoslovakia, and an American Jew who knew the American background of JDC would now be the right person to represent the organization in Europe. When Kahn was informed of the decision, he did not object. He moved to New York, became an American citizen, and spent the rest of his extremely active life as a member of the JDC office.[75]

This is perhaps the place to evaluate the contribution of Dr.

Bernhard Kahn to Jewish history in the interwar period. For most of the period between the wars, Kahn was the arbiter of many Jewish economic endeavors in the field of reconstruction and relief. Behind his cold and remote exterior there was a warm heart and an immensely fertile mind. None of his peers, certainly none of his successors in JDC or elsewhere, could equal his knowledge of Judaism, Zionism, economics, history, social work, philosophy, art —or indeed his achievements and interest in a dozen or more fields. His departure in 1938 was, one suspects, inevitable; but with him disappeared one of the great figures of Jewish life—a man whose name rarely if ever appeared on the pages of the press, and whose preoccupation with practical matters never allowed him to devote his time to creative scholarship.

His successor as chairman of JDC's European Council was Morris C. Troper, until then the head of a firm of accountants who had been responsible for checking JDC's accounts. In many ways Troper was Kahn's opposite. A simple man with simple tastes, an efficient administrator, ebullient, he was quite unlike Kahn, the aesthete and polyglot. Troper had a warm heart and—again, unlike Kahn—could express himself publicly much more effectively than the shy German Jew with his foreign accent. The difference lay, among other things, in Kahn's knowing Europe, and that was his strength; Troper's strength lay in his knowledge of America and American Jewry.

In autumn of 1938 Troper went to Europe to take over responsibilities from his predecessor.

THE ''NIGHT OF CRYSTAL''

On November 7, 1938, Herszel Grynszpan, a young Polish Jew whose parents had been deported from Germany to Zbaszyn, fatally wounded Ernst vom Rath, third secretary of the German Embassy in Paris. The occasion provided the Nazis—actually Goebbels—with an excuse to do what had been planned for a long time: organize a large-scale pogrom. On November 9 and 10 almost all synagogues in Germany and Austria were destroyed, windows of

Jewish shops were smashed, goods stolen, large numbers of Jewish homes demolished, men and women beaten, and about ninety-one persons killed. A wave of arrests swept through Germany; thirty-five thousand Jews are estimated to have been shipped to the concentration camps of Dachau, Buchenwald, and Sachsenhausen.[76]

The course of this pogrom, cynically known as the "Night of Crystal" *(Reichskristallnacht),* is too well-known to be dwelt upon here.[77] It so happened, however, that Troper, on his way through Europe with some of the JDC staff, was in Berlin at the time. His report emphasized those aspects that had a specific importance from JDC's point of view, but it also dealt with some of the larger aspects. Some of the facts brought out later by historical research were already contained in it.

Troper mentioned the fact that the SS paper, *Das Schwarze Korps,* had demanded on November 2 that Jews be excluded completely from German life. Ghettoization and confiscation of property were also hinted at, as was forced labor for unemployed Jews. Anti-Jewish disorders had been taking place since mid-September. Troper also knew that special barracks had been prepared in several concentration camps to house those who would ultimately be arrested. As a result of the pogrom in November, the "basis of existence of German Jewry has been wiped out."[78] RV and all the central Jewish institutions, except for the Hilfsverein and the Jewish Cultural League, were closed. Most of the central personalities of German Jewry except for Leo Baeck were among those arrested. In the provinces, many of the public institutions in which JDC had a special interest were destroyed: at Königsberg it was the orphanage, at Karlsruhe the children's home, at Mannheim the old age home, and so on. At Bornsdorf training center the Nazis shot and killed a boy who could not explain why there were thirty-eight persons present instead of the forty who were registered there. Often, Troper reported, the pogrom turned against those who were about to emigrate, as in Stuttgart, where all those who had invitations to see the U. S. consul for their visas were arrested.

The reasons for the pogrom seem to have been the desire to

radicalize the treatment of Jews and force their emigration while robbing them of their property; at the same time, Goebbels, the main instigator of the event, wanted to involve the masses of the German people in the Nazi party's anti-Semitic policy. His success is in doubt: not only was there little enthusiasm outside party and SA circles, but there was an active rivalry with the SS; in the end Goebbels lost out. The SS was opposed to the wild "popular" character of the pogrom. It preferred a more orderly, quiet reign of terror, such as became evident after the pogrom.

One of the results of the pogrom was Göring's decision, at a famous meeting on November 12 with representatives of different groups in the Nazi party and the government, that the Jews should pay an "indemnity" of 1 billion marks to the government. On top of that, they would have to pay the government any sums that were paid to them by insurance companies. In the end, the payment by the Jews came close to 1.25 billion marks.

A series of measures designed to eliminate the Jews from German economic life followed. By January 1, 1939, the only gainful occupation a Jew could follow in the Reich was as employee of a Jewish institution. Jewish businesses and industrial enterprises were forcibly transferred into German hands ("Aryanized"). Doctors, lawyers, businessmen, workers, employees—they were all forbidden to practice their occupations; doctors and dentists were even denied their professional titles and were allowed to treat only Jewish patients.[79] Obviously, reliance on outside support became much more important after the November pogrom than before. And it was clear that JDC would have to take on a major share of the additional burden.

The need for a large-scale fund-raising efforts in the U. S. made itself felt throughout 1938 and reached a climax in November. From below, from the grass roots, there came a demand for the unification of the two main fund-raising efforts: that of JDC and the United Palestine Appeal. The person mainly responsible for bringing the two groups together was Henry Ittleson, a highly influential member of what has loosely been termed the German

Jewish aristocracy of the American East Coast. Under Ittleson's energetic leadership, a meeting took place on November 23 of JDC, UPA, and the the Council of Jewish Federations and Welfare Funds (CJFWF). A combined drive for $20 million was decided upon. The reasons that prompted JDC to agree to a united drive were given by James N. Rosenberg: JDC, he said, "must recognize the powerful desire throughout the country to avoid competing campaigns"; in New York City, joint campaigns had already been adopted by a number of professional groups, and separate fund raising was harmful "from the American point of view"[80]—he probably meant that separate efforts in the face of the German threat were somehow unpatriotic.

The United Jewish Appeal was finally set up in December, and JDC very definitely played the leading part in it. It was to get almost 50 percent of the funds collected, the rest being shared mainly by UPA and the National Coordinating Committee, the agency for absorbing and settling new immigrants in the U. S., which was very closely linked to JDC.

JDC was, in effect, pushed into the new agreement. Its experience with the UJA of 1934/5 had not been happy, and memories of it were still very fresh. Zionists had then been collecting only for Palestine, JDC Executive Committee members argued, but they still had expected JDC to contribute to Palestine directly or indirectly through the support of Palestine-centered organizations in Europe and the payment of the emigrées' transportation to Palestine. In 1938/9, the increase in the level of Nazi persecutions and the growing misery in Eastern Europe could have absorbed JDC funds many times over. "At no time has the Budget and Scope Committee [of JDC] during these years of cumulative tragedy been authorized to adopt a budget bearing any close relation to the amounts deemed necessary even for the minimum requirements," complained Edwin I. Goldwasser, JDC's treasurer, in late October 1938.[81] The upbuilding of Palestine was all very well, but Jews in Europe were starving and persecuted—and they, JDC felt, had first claim on whatever funds were available.

Jews in the United States, however, were beginning to think differently. They saw that the Jews of Europe were not the only ones endangered; their own position and that of the U.S. might well be in jeopardy. This obviously was no time for interorganizational rivalry. Also, it was much more convenient (and also more profitable from the fund raiser's point of view)—to campaign once yearly for all overseas needs. There was clear pressure from below, for which the CJFWF was the mouthpiece.

There still remained the problem, minor but vexatious, of the separate fund-raising efforts of smaller groups that might compete with the larger campaign. The struggle over this question with ORT was becoming a ritual. In early 1938 a public statement was prepared attacking ORT for its separate fund-raising plans, and showing that 67 percent of its budget in 1937—$130,000—had really come from JDC.[82] In the end, as always, more moderate counsels prevailed. The prepared statement was not issued, ORT received another allocation, and the threat of separate fund raising was removed.

In the wake of the November pogroms, a wave of panic emigration swept Germany and Austria. Internees in concentration camps would be released if they undertook to leave Germany within a specified, and very short, time. If they did not, they were threatened with rearrest, which often meant death. The Austrian example was followed; "police and party authorities insist that the practices which worked successfully in Vienna in forcing Jews out of the country should likewise be applied in Berlin and throughout the country."[83]

The many thousands now leaving the Reich had to be supported, as well as those staying behind. During the first weeks after the pogrom, emigration was partly stalled as a result of the disorganization of Jewish institutions in Germany. A case in point was the large debt that the Hilfsverein, which dealt with emigration to countries other than Palestine, had run up with steamship companies (about 55,000 marks); now it could not repay this money because of the large-scale confiscations of Jewish property and the billion-mark fine.[84]

By the middle of December it was estimated that one-third of the Jewish male working population was still in the concentration camps; the process of release had only just begun.[85] German government subsidies to Jewish welfare and schooling were stopped. Most of the twenty thousand Jewish children of school age had to turn to the 140 Jewish schools. These were now dependent upon Jewish support only.[86] Support was also required for four thousand trainees in vocational retraining institutions in Germany and as many as twenty-four thousand in Austria. Some of these groups, especially the more serious ones that were preparing for agricultural pursuits in South America or Palestine, had been brutally hit by the pogrom. Nevertheless, it was thought that vocational retraining increased the chances for emigration, and there were long waiting lists for these institutions.

Generally speaking, the German Jewish organizations and their Austrian counterparts were laboring under a terrific strain. The process of concentration in large cities was proceeding apace, and the small communities were disbanding. In its 1939 report, the Reichsvereinigung (successor to RV) reported that in Prussia it had previously had 743 communities and that now 109 had disbanded, 572 were in the process of dissolution, and 62 were still operating.[87] This meant additional financial burdens, diminished incomes, and more suffering and heartbreak. The numbers of those requiring immediate help in Germany and Austria was constantly increasing, as can be seen from Table 17.

To deal with all these problems there was RV—the Reichsvertretung, founded, as we have seen, in 1933 as a result of Jewish initiative. It appears that the Germans were slowly working toward

---

T A B L E   17[88]
Persons Fed Daily in Public Kitchens in 1939

Country	January	May	July
Germany	23,308	32,000	
Austria	22,227	36,207	34,206

the abolition of this last vestige of independence. The November pogrom was a good occasion, from their point of view, to break with the past. Immediately after the pogrom the Nazis decided not to allow RV to be reconstituted. However, there were divided counsels among them as to the precise form of organization that should be forced on the Jews. In January, Göring still thought that the Jewish central organization should be an adjunct to the new central emigration bureau that he had in mind. But other ideas prevailed, and on February 17, 1939, the Jewish newssheet, *Jüdisches Nachrichtenblatt,* the only Jewish "paper" that the Nazis allowed to appear, announced that a new central organization of German Jewry would be set up, the Reichsvereinigung der Juden in Deutschland, whose members would be nominated by the Gestapo. However, it was not until July 4, 1939, that the official announcement establishing the new RVE came out. This was largely owing to internal squabbling between German ministries. But the crisis also brought forth some ugly squabbles between the Berlin community, led by the conservative liberal Heinrich Stahl, and the old leadership of RV. Things were brought to a head in April, when Stahl went to the Gestapo to ask for its help in asserting his pretensions to leadership of the Jewish community. The Gestapo apparently did not intervene directly, but in the new RVE, Stahl was made copresident with Rabbi Leo Baeck.[89]

JDC was informed of what was going on in Germany; it could only deplore internal differences at such critical times. It was not aware, of course, of the intrigues of the Stahl group, but whenever the Baeck-Hirsch-Lilienthal group of leaders required it, JDC sup-

T A B L E 18[90]
JDC Expenditures in Germany and Austria in 1938 and 1939 (in $)

Year	Total JDC expenditures	In Germany	In Austria
1938	3,799,709	686,000	431,438
1939	8,447,221	978,102	

ported them to the best of its ability. It must be remembered that people like Baerwald, Kahn, and Max M. Warburg (Felix's brother, who finally emigrated to the U. S. in 1938) knew the German Jewish leadership intimately and had confidence in the group that had founded and led RV since 1933. Indeed, Max Warburg had been the initiator of RV, had taken a decisive part in setting up its leadership, and had been to a great extent the arbiter of its policies.

In light of this grim situation—and also, it must be added, as a result of increased income—JDC was able to increase its financial support for German Jews. A part of that support came through the Quakers, who, as always in times of stress, cooperated closely with JDC. In February 1939 JDC voted a sum of $100,000 to be spent by the American Friends Service Committee, "provided that no publicity whatsoever should be given to this grant, and with the provision that there should be taken into account the reluctance on the part of the contributors to JDC to have American dollars go into Germany."[91] The Friends were inclined to spend this money to help "non-Aryans," that is, people not connected with the official Jewish community but considered to be Jews by the Nazis. Through perhaps overcareful management only $26,908 of this money was spent before war broke out in September.

EMIGRATION AND FLIGHT

Total Jewish emigration from Germany, Austria, and the Czech lands (Bohemia and Moravia) after October 1938 is not easy to reconstruct. The figures given in Table 19 probably do not include many "non-Aryans," who should really be included. But they may serve as an estimate based on material in JDC files.

Large-scale emigration started immediately after the November pogrom; the figures were staggering compared with those for earlier emigration. This time JDC had no hesitations—its leaders had learned the lesson of the previous years, as had the leadership of HIAS and HICEM, the two emigrating organizations supported

T A B L E 19[92]

Estimate of Jewish Emigration in 1938 and 1939

Year	From Germany	From Austria	From Bohemia and Moravia	From Danzig	Total for year
1938	35,369	62,958	15,000	3,900	117,200
1939	68,000	54,451	20,000*	1,600	144,000
Total					261,000

*Various JDC sources estimated that out of the twenty thousand, five thousand were German and Austrian refugees.

by JDC. There were few illusions left. At a meeting of some of the wealthy contributors to JDC at the end of 1938, James G. McDonald said that "to many people in Europe to crush a Jew is no more unworthy or reprehensible than to step on vermin and crush the life out of such creatures. The war that the Nazis are waging is not a war against the Jews of Germany, but against all Jews, whose influence must be obliterated and who themselves should either be exterminated or driven out of all civilized lands." In concluding his talk he added: "If you think that because you live in the United States you are immune, you are very foolish."[93] Unfortunately, what the people who listened to McDonald thought of his remarks is not recorded. But words that today sound like prophecies, yet were totally unacceptable before the events of November, were listened to attentively (if sceptically) afterward.

The problem of mass emigration from Germany and Austria was compounded by the addition of yet another victim of Nazi barbarism: Czechoslovakia. In late September 1938 the Western powers had betrayed the Czechs to Hitler at Munich. In early October the German-speaking border lands of Bohemia and Moravia, the so-called Sudeten areas, were occupied by the Germans. Soon afterward the Hungarians took southern Slovakia and southern Subcarpathia, while the Poles occupied an area near Těšín. The democratic character of the Czechoslovak republic was destroyed, Slovakia became autonomous, and nationalist and near-Fascist tendencies increased. "Do not ask us for humanity," officials are reported to have said. "We were not treated with humanity."[94] The number of Czech refugees from the occupied Sudeten areas was estimated at between 180,000 and 200,000. Of these, about 15,000 were Jews. In addition, there were 5,000 to 6,000 refugees from Germany and Austria still in the country.

About two-thirds of all these refugees lacked means of subsistence and had to be supported. To find work in the new, smaller Czechoslovakia was a practical impossibility; anti-Semitism was rampant, and Jews were attacked as a foreign, germanizing element (most of them spoke German). Jews themselves were expected to formulate anti-Jewish laws. In colleges and universities Jews either were not admitted or, if already registered, were thrown out under various pretexts. As a result, tremendous efforts were made by Jews —refugees and natives alike—to leave the country. On January 27, 1939, the rightist government of Rudolf Beran issued a proclamation demanding a speedy emigration of foreign refugees; it also proclaimed that the government would review the status of those who had acquired citizenship since World War I—a measure expressly directed at the Jews.

In this chaotic and dangerous situation a central organization of Jewish communities was set up in Prague under the chairmanship of Dr. Josef Popper. In the Czech lands Marie Schmolka headed HICEM, dealing with emigration. The Jewish Social Institute, the chief aid organization, had to care for 1,290 persons immediately. To all other persons, the Czech government gave an allowance of 8 crowns (about 30 cents) a day; those who could not manage were put into camps. In the Czech lands 118,000 Jews were now crowded; they were threatened with the fate of German Jewry.[95] Of the 136,000 Jews who had been in Slovakia in 1930, 88,951 remained in 1940; some had emigrated, but the rest had become Hungarian Jews as a result of the 1938 annexations.[96] In early 1939 a social committee (Zentrales Soziales Fürsorgekommittee) was working in Bratislava under Dr. Robert K. Füredi and Mrs. Gizi Fleischmann, who was to become during the war one of the great heroines of the Jewish tragedy. In January 1939 this committee was supporting a foreign refugee population of 3,064 who had to be fed daily.[97]

One of the main problems arising from the Sudeten crisis was the terrible plight of thousands of Jews who were driven—by Germans, Slovaks, Hungarians, Poles, and even Czechs—into no-man's-land, the small areas between the new borders. Two thousand such unfortunates were driven by the Slovaks into a no-man's-land near Kosice, a town which passed into Hungarian hands. The Hungarians drove most of them back. In the end some three hundred refugees, largely stateless and Slovak Jews, spent the Slovak autumn in the open, without shelter, food, or medical aid. A great deal of money was spent providing them with basic necessities. After many interventions, Slovakia finally accepted most of these refugees.[98] Hundreds more were reported to be in the Austro-Moravian border areas, between the new Sudeten frontier and the Bohemian heartland and on other borders.[99] It is next to impossible to establish the total number, but there could not have been less than three to four thousand persons. It was not until January 1939, more than three months after Munich, that the last of these people finally found a country that would harbor them, mostly in refugee camps.[100]

Then final disaster struck. On March 15, 1939, Germany occupied the Czech lands; Slovakia became "independent" under a German protectorate; and Subcarpathia was annexed by Hungary. In Prague, Marie Schmolka was arrested by the Nazis immediately after they entered the city; she was not released until May.

JDC policy in Czechoslovakia was to support the two social committees in Prague and Bratislava. Prior to March, JDC was providing 40 percent of the budget of the Prague Social Institute. After March it gave more than 50 percent.[101] Large-scale aid had to be given to Slovakia to support the 2,938 refugees who were completely dependent on outside help.[102] In the Czech lands an arrangement similar to that in Germany and Austria was worked out, whereby American dollars would not go into German coffers but would cover the costs of emigration, while the emigrants' money would be used to cover local needs. But in Slovakia the new authorities would not accept these arrangements, and immediate help was essential. Reluctantly, Troper cabled his head office on June 15, 1939, that a one-time transfer of $20,000 to the Slovak National Bank was unavoidable; on the 16th, New York cabled agreement.[103] In Prague, JDC support was, as we have seen, indirect, but it ran at a monthly rate of about $33,000.

The main concern of the committees and of JDC was, of course, to aid as many people to emigrate as possible at the greatest speed. Prior to March 15 there was a great deal of competition from Sudeten German opponents of Nazism and from Czechs who wished to leave the country. Nevertheless, by the end of 1939 about thirty-five thousand Jews managed to leave the Czech lands. This was facilitated by a British government-supported fund, the Lord Mayor's Fund, which had 4 million pounds at its disposal. Despite the fact that the fund was largely used for Czech internal requirements, small amounts were used for Jewish refugee emigration. England was the main destination of the emigrants; representatives of British groups, Quakers and others, did a tremendous job in Prague, sifting and processing applications; the staff of the British Embassy in Prague was also very helpful.

Nevertheless, there were difficulties. In the panic that the occupation of the country brought, people simply tried to flee without bothering to obtain visas. A train with 160 Jews went across Germany in April, only to be stopped by the Dutch because the emigrants did not have any visas of final destination. The Gestapo declared that if the train was still in Germany by a fixed deadline —April 29—the refugees would be arrested. It was only through a waiving of formalities by the British that these people were saved.[104]

Illegal emigration to Palestine also flourished; other persons crossed the border into Poland as Czech refugees, only to be threatened by the Poles with deportation back into the Gestapo's hands.[105] The Germans were pressing for Jewish emigration by the same methods that had been so successful elsewhere, and in July 1939 they established in Prague a branch office of the Central Bureau for Jewish Emigration. After March, too, the tragedies of small groups in no-man's-land were repeated. Germans were expelling Jews from the Czech lands, and on the Polish border the scenes of autumn 1938 took place once again. In all these cases the Prague Social Institute had to intervene to keep the people alive.[106] When the curtain came down on the unhappy country in September 1939, the fate of Czech Jewry had become identical to that of Germany and Austria.

Where could the Jews of Central Europe have gone? No country was willing to accept panic-stricken Jewish refugees without the necessary and delaying prerequisites of form-filling and careful scrutiny. No country really wanted penniless Jews.

In France the shock of November produced a much greater readiness among local Jewry to come to the aid of refugees. A new central coordinating committee (Comité Central de Réfugiés) was set up under Robert de Rothschild. They approached the government and demanded the acceptance of ten thousand Jewish children (as in England); the committee also asked, in vain, for the abolition of the May 1938 decree against refugees. Although they were not crowned with much success, in these actions French Jewry at last was showing "greater energy and devotion than before."[107]

Government reaction was not favorable. Refugees crossing illegally from Germany into Alsace were pushed over the border to Switzerland and then deported to Germany. OSE, with its three homes for 185 children (there was no money for more homes), was saddled with hundreds of refugee children "without their parents or with parents imprisoned for failing to obey expulsion orders. . . . Most of them were between the ages of five and ten."[108] The number of refugees at the end of 1938 was twenty-five thousand, including two thousand who came from Czechoslovakia in March 1939.

The main burden of supporting these desperate people fell to the

Comité d'Assistance aux Réfugiés (CAR)—founded in 1936—under Albert Levy and Robert de Rothschild. In early 1939 it supported 10,378 persons. Persecution—there is no other word for it —by the French authorities reached new heights; refugees were arrested for periods up to one year, and "many who have undergone this punishment have been expelled."[109] Work permits were almost impossible to get, and vocational retraining did not touch more than a fraction of the people: in January 1939 the Reclassement Professionel, a French Jewish agency, was training 224 persons, and ORT was training 476.[110]

In 1939, 13,500 Jews are estimated to have emigrated into France.[111] With the growing hostility of the French government to Jewish refugees, there was a meeting in June 1939 between the main agencies dealing with the problem—JDC, the Alliance Israélite Universelle, other French committees, and the World Jewish Congress. The main problem that was discussed was whether to start a public campaign in France to air the issue. The majority of those present, including Troper for JDC, were against such a course; it was still felt that the best way to approach the problem would be through quiet diplomacy. Dr. Goldmann for WJC and Marc Jarblum for the Fédération des Sociétés Juives, who demanded a public campaign, were in the minority.[112]

JDC rejected the notion that the issue of Jewish suffering should be aired in public so as to make it a political issue. On the other hand, JDC continued to aid French organizations, and especially CAR, to an ever-increasing degree. France was, after all, the main land of immigration on the European continent. And despite the fact that JDC was highly critical of French Jewry for the small sums being collected in France, it poured as much money as it could into France in order to be of as much help as possible. In 1938, $130,884 was spent in France, and in 1939, $589,000.[113]

Another country of immigration in Europe was Belgium. Prior to November 1938 there were about 13,300 Jewish refugees in the country, of whom some 3,000 in Brussels required help.[114] The government declared that all those arriving illegally after August

27, 1938, would be expelled. But in actual fact there seem to have been no expulsions. Between November 10 and the end of the year, about 3,000 more refugees arrived, all of them illegally. By the end of January 1939 there were 7,500 people who had to be supported —3,000 in Antwerp and 4,500 in Brussels.

JDC action in Belgium was much more speedy than elsewhere because it was obvious that, of all the West European countries, Belgium had the relatively poorest community. In December 1938 JDC gave $10,000 to meet the rising costs of maintaining the refugees; but this covered about one-sixth of the actual cost, and only $20,000 could be raised locally per month. In January, JDC gave $20,000. But that was not enough, and Professor Max Gottschalk, head of the Brussels Jewish aid committee, told Troper that he might have to tell the government that his committee could no longer look after the refugees. This insufficient help had to be further reduced, and that at a time when JDC estimated that 95 percent of the refugees were undernourished and that tuberculosis was on the increase.

In March the Belgian government was told that the committee's resources were at an end. At that time there were already twenty-five thousand German, Austrian, and Czech Jewish refugees in the country, of whom ten thousand had to be supported; four hundred more were entering the country illegally every week. The government's attitude was hardening, and even legal entrants who overstayed their time faced deportation.[115]

However, possibly as a result of Gottschalk's intervention, the government relented to a considerable degree. It increased its budget by 6 million Belgian francs (about $20,000), which enabled three thousand refugees to receive a government allowance. Camps were opened to house the newcomers. The principle that Jewish organizations were the only ones responsible for Jewish refugees was, at least in Belgium, overcome. Until July 15, 1939, all those fleeing from Germany were allowed to remain; after that date they risked expulsion unless they were political refugees.

JDC increased its allocations to $40,000 in April, $60,000 in

August, and $80,000 in September. As a result, JDC expenditure rose from a mere $106,000 in 1938 to $694,000 in 1939.[116] By the summer of 1939 two-thirds of the refugee expenditure in Belgium was covered by JDC.

A similar influx of refugees came into Holland. At the end of 1938 Mrs. van Tijn's Committee for Jewish Refugees counted seven thousand refugees in Holland, including about eighteen hundred who had arrived at the end of the year after the November pogrom. Officially, no more people were supposed to come in after November 11, but a 1 million guilder guarantee by CJR prolonged the time limit to December 23.[117] After that date the Dutch police became very strict and did not hesitate to deport entrants who were without visas. Nevertheless, the number of Jewish refugees in Holland in early 1939 grew by about seven thousand because quite a number of German Jews had obtained legal entry permits by showing that they had relatives who were already living in the country.

Refugees continued to pour in through 1939. In order to care both for illegals who had been allowed to stay and for legal entrants who had no means of support, the government set up three camps for 600 persons. One of these camps was at Westerbork, the future deportation center, from which most of Dutch Jews went to their deaths in 1942–44. JDC supported Mrs. van Tijn's committee as it had done in previous years, especially its Wieringen project, where 270 youngsters were receiving agricultural training in 1939, and the other Hechalutz training centers, where another 330 were preparing for Palestine. Most of these young people never saw the country of their destination—many were sent to their deaths in Nazi camps; others were to form the nucleus for one of the Jewish resistance groups in France during the war.

Switzerland occupied a special place in the events outlined here. The November pogrom was preceded by a German-Swiss agreement on September 29, 1938, regarding the special marking of passports of German Jews with a large red "J." The accusation was later leveled against the chief of the Swiss alien police, Dr. Heinrich Rothmund, that he had initiated the branding of Jews by this

268 : *My Brother's Keeper*

special passport symbol by suggesting the idea to the Nazis. Be that
as it may, it is quite clear that the Swiss police chief—and, what
is more important, the Swiss government—gladly accepted the
regulation that discriminated so blatantly between Jews and non-
Jews, because it made it impossible for German Jews to enter
Switzerland without a visa; "pure" Germans were, of course, free
to enter Switzerland with no formalities. The only German demand to which the Swiss objected—not too strongly, it must be
said, but with sufficient vigor to make the Germans abandon the
idea—was that Swiss Jews wishing to visit Germany be required
to obtain a visa and have their passports marked in some special
way.[118]

The new provision, which went into effect in November, prevented large-scale immigration by Jews into Switzerland. In early
1939 there were some 10,000 Jewish refugees in the country, of
whom 3,062 were supported by VSIA.[119] The Swiss police, backed
by the government, were not content with preventing an influx of
German Jews, however; they felt they had to prevent the immigration of persecuted Jews from all other countries in Europe. After
January 20, 1939, therefore, all prospective immigrants into Switzerland were required to obtain visas; a similar provision was
introduced on March 15 for holders of Czechoslovakian passports.
As a result of these restrictive measures, the numbers of Jewish
refugees decreased, and by the outbreak of war there were about
5,000 Jewish refugees in Switzerland.[120] However, 300 children
were admitted as a special gesture.

Despite the seemingly easier situation, the problem of caring for
the refugees was very difficult for the Swiss Jewish community,
which numbered about 18,000. A total of 810 persons were accom-
modated in sixteen small camps, where they were completely dependent on VSIA help.[121] The Swiss were very strict about denying
working permits to the refugees. Unless the refugee had money, he
had to turn for support to JDC-supported VSIA. VSIA, in cooperation with HICEM, also had to try to help as many Jews as possible
to emigrate. This, too, cost money. Total VSIA expenditure for

1939 came to 3,688,185 francs, of which JDC contributed over 50 percent (over $470,000). By September 1939 JDC had sent $315,000 to VSIA, at a monthly rate of $35,000.[122]

JDC had to intervene in other countries in Europe as well. A steady stream of refugees had been entering Italy. At the end of 1938 there were some six thousand German and Austrian Jews there, and they were not treated too badly. But as we have already seen a decree of September 7, 1938, issued as a result largely of German influence on the Italian Fascist regime, stated that anyone who had acquired Italian citizenship in recent years would have to leave the country by March 12, 1939. Apart from the six thousand refugees, this also affected nine thousand older immigrants into Italy. JDC tried its best to influence the Italian government to desist from its declared intentions, and in early February, Troper contacted Myron C. Taylor, who promised to do his best to change the Italians' intentions. Earlier, an influential Anglo-Scots banker, Sir Andrew McFadeyan, a partner of Sigmund Warburg's in London, also promised JDC to use his influence with the Italians.[123] While it is impossible to say whether all these efforts had any effect, it is clear that by the time the fateful March 12 came, half of the fifteen thousand Jews had left Italy; between March and September, another twenty-five hundred left. In the end, about four thousand people stayed behind and were not molested by the authorities. Most of the emigrants went to the Americas, and quite a number went to Nice. Apart from the Jewish organizations, the Friends were again effective in aiding the emigrating Jews (many of whom pretended to be Catholics) get to South American countries.[124]

On the Continent there was scarcely a country that did not accept some refugees, but the numbers were small and many obstacles were put in their way. In early 1939 there were still about 2,000 refugees in Yugoslavia, although by now many had been expelled. JDC sent small sums of money to aid the Zagreb community, which organized some help (JDC sent $4,300). Sweden took about 2,000 people, and so did Bulgaria. There were between 16,000 and

18,000 refugees in Poland (these were discussed above in connection with the Zbaszyn episode). Norway accepted 2,000. There were 350 in Luxemburg, 600 in Greece, 200 in Finland, 1,000 in Latvia, and so on. Even in Albania there were 150 Jewish refugees from Central Europe. JDC did not—could not—intervene in all these countries. In some, like the Scandinavian countries, there were well-organized communities or reasonably friendly governments. There was no way to transmit money safely to certain places, but wherever it was possible, JDC fulfilled its usual role.

Great Britain was a special case as far as the refugees were concerned. In the wake of the November pogrom, Britain's refugee population grew to 13,500 by January 1939. However, both government and public opinion were under a special kind of moral pressure. To a certain degree the government felt responsible for the Munich settlement and for the events that followed. Then there was Palestine, where since October 1938 it had been clear that a pro-Arab compromise that would put an end to Jewish immigration was planned. In early December the government turned a deaf ear to the demand of the Jewish Agency to allow the immigration of ten thousand children from Germany and Austria to Palestine.[125] But it felt that an alternative should be offered. The alternative was to create a sanctuary for children in the United Kingdom itself. In addition, an arrangement was offered whereby Jewish women could come to Britain to work as domestic servants. Other visas for adults with good recommendations could also be obtained. By the end of 1939 there were between 63,000 and 65,000 refugees in Britain. Of these, 9,354 were children and 15,000 were domestic servants.[126]

This large-scale acceptance of Jewish refugees, while welcomed by a large part of the British public, did not go completely unchallenged.[127] But the climate in Britain in early 1939, and especially later, as it became clear that Hitler would not keep the promise he gave at Munich, was no longer unfavorable to the refugees. Many —seven to eight thousand—were liberated from concentration camps on the strength of British entry permits.

The Council for German Jewry started its collection after the

November pogrom. It collected 850,000 pounds up to the outbreak of war. Of this very large sum, 286,000 pounds were allocated for the care of refugees in England; 145,270 pounds were not allocated at the time but were used later, during the war, to support refugees in Britain. The rest went to support work in Palestine, Shanghai, and other places.

Others were also making financial efforts. Under Earl Baldwin's leadership, the Baldwin Fund for Refugees was founded; it collected 400,000 pounds. It was estimated that 90 percent of the contributors to this fund were Jews; 50 percent of the money collected went to support the work of the Council for German Jewry.[128] A number of smaller Christian committees were coordinated under the leadership of Lord Hailey in the Christian Council for Refugees. The Council for German Jewry itself was transformed; in February, Lord Samuel resigned and Lord Reading became chairman. With this change all pretence that the council represented the American organizations, and especially JDC, came to an end. It became officially what it had long been in fact: a purely British institution, which cooperated with JDC but in no sense represented it.

One of the more fruitful ideas advanced at that hectic time by those favoring the entry of Jewish refugees into Britain was to create large camps for adults and children where the refugees could remain until more permanent homes were found for them. Kahn cabled that the idea was in the "meantime [to] erect camps [and] training centers wherever possible for [the] young generation."[129] The largest such camp was opened at Richborough (Kitchener Camp). Of course, the acceptance of refugees into Britain was considered largely a temporary measure, and most, if not all, refugees were expected ultimately to emigrate to other countries.[130]

During the last months before the outbreak of war, illegal immigration was attempted even into Britain on a small scale. It is symptomatic that British sailors were reported to have facilitated such immigration and that British judges were inclined to recommend that such immigrants not be deported.[131]

One of the main characteristics of the mass emigration of

1938/9, and one intimately connected with Britain, was the emigration of unaccompanied children. JDC had nothing to do with the immigration of adults into Britain, but it played a significant part in the attempts to save as many children as possible from German-occupied lands before the war (and it was to play a similar role during the war itself).

The movement to save the children started in England. Between March 1936 and November 1938, 471 children from Germany, 55 percent of them Jewish (many of the rest were probably "non-Aryans"), were brought there and cared for by an Inter-Aid Committee supported by the Council for German Jewry. The Friends and other Christian groups also participated in this committee. After the November 17, 1938, pogrom, Lord Samuel became chairman of a subcommittee that was to promote the migration of children. On November 21 a delegation of the Council for German Jewry and the Inter-Aid Committee was received by the home secretary, who promised his support in getting the children into Britain. That same evening he announced his support in the House of Commons. As a result, the Movement for the Care of Children from Germany was organized, which undertook to guarantee that the children would not become public charges and that they would reemigrate before they reached the age of eighteen or when their training in Britain was completed.

Two summer camps for youth at Harwich and Lowestoft were used to provide immediate accommodations. In Germany, Austria, and the Czech lands, Jewish organizations and such groups as the Quakers set up procedures to get the children to Britain. JDC had no direct contact with this work in Britain, but through its cooperating committees in Europe it was involved in sending the children to the safety of England.

A plea by Mrs. van Tijn to accept large numbers of children into the United States could not be answered affirmatively. The U. S. organization for placing refugee children was limited both by the strictness of the quota laws and by its own limitations. In November 1938 it could take 326 children, but of these, 177 children in

Germany already had their affidavits; so that the U.S. could at that point consider the immigration of only 149 children. By contrast, other European countries did follow the British example. Holland accepted 1,850 children, Belgium took 800, France took 700, and Sweden 250. Of this total of close to 13,000 children, 2,336 came from Austria, about 8,000 from Germany, and the rest from Danzig and the Czech lands.[132]

When one looks at the total monetary effort expended by JDC in aiding refugees in the different countries, the figures are quite impressive. In 1938 and especially in 1939 there is something of a quantitative jump as compared with previous years. In 1939 over three-eighths of the JDC expenditures were devoted to what was known in JDC jargon as "the refugee countries."

THE RUBLEE-SCHACHT EPISODE AND THE COORDINATING FOUNDATION

The Evian Conference took place in July 1938. In August, ICR held its first meeting, and George Rublee became its director. Then the Sudeten crisis of September 1938 had prevented further progress. The Germans were not eager to negotiate at that time. ICR and the Jewish organizations that placed their hopes in it, on the other hand, assumed that a breakthrough on the emigration front was possible only if negotiations with Germany led to an orderly emigration of Jews from that country, and if emigrants were al-

---

T A B L E   20[133]
JDC Expenditures in "Refugee Countries"

Year	1933	1934	1935	1936	1937	1938	1939
Total spent (in thousands of $)	182	467	149*	311†	428	858.2‡	3,243‡

*R14, 1935 report gives $205,000.
†R13, 1936 report gives $239,820.
‡The figures for 1938 and 1939 are appropriations, not expenditures.

lowed to take some capital with them and thus make themselves more welcome in the host countries. In the debate on refugees in the British House of Commons on November 21, 1938, the home secretary pointedly referred to the fact that the eleven thousand refugees from Hitler who had been admitted to Britain had already provided employment for fifteen thousand Britons. Other countries had similar expectations. The proper way to go about emigration, argued Max M. Warburg, was "to find jobs for German Jews on [a] similar social standard and similar level of living as they had before."[134] The problem was, who would pay for it?

JDC became convinced soon after Evian that emigration "must in the final analysis be financed with funds from German Jews themselves, for which it will be necessary that an international agreement with Reich authorities be reached permitting emigrants to take out some of their money."[135] It was for this reason that JDC so wholeheartedly supported Rublee, and as late as December 1938 saw in Evian "some consolation."[136]

The second point, to which JDC became converted as 1938 drew to an end and 1939 began, was even more important. Private means, voluntary organizations—these were well and good, but they would not be able to settle Jews in difficult new countries. Established countries of settlement were closing their doors. If there was to be mass resettlement, government funds would have to be forthcoming.[137]

In the autumn of 1938 Rublee was cooling his heels in London. On October 27 he presented his own ideas on how the emigration of German Jews should be organized. It appears that these ideas were influenced by the diplomatic contacts taking place in Berlin between members of the British and American embassies and German authorities, mainly those connected with Göring's office. At any rate, Rublee's proposals were almost identical with those known later as the Schacht plan. It is also likely that German Jews were involved in transmitting the German proposals.

The content of these proposals was that 1.5 billion German marks, or 25 percent of the total assets of German Jewry (estimated at 6 billion marks, or $2.4 billion), would be set up as a trust fund in Germany. Jews abroad would raise an equivalent sum in foreign currency, which nominally would be a loan to the emigrants. The money abroad would pay for the actual emigration and settlement. German emigrants would repay the capital and the interest in the form of German goods that they would take with them and sell abroad, thus in effect increasing German exports. However, this would have to be over and above the "normal" level of German exports (whatever that meant). At any rate, Schacht spoke of "additional exports" in this connection.

This plan was apparently conceived by a high Austrian Nazi economic official, Dr. Hans Fischböck, who suggested it to Göring. Göring in turn appears to have brought it to the attention of Hjalmar Schacht, Germany's economic wizard who was at that time the head of the Reichsbank. Schacht went to London in November and presented the plan to Winterton and Rublee. Further negotiations were to take place with Fischböck, but Schacht apparently wanted time to present the proposals to Hitler. He appears to have done this on January 2, 1939, and he received Hitler's approval.[138]

Jews almost unanimously rejected the Schacht plan, as did many non-Jews. As a result of this opposition, new negotiations were started that January in Berlin. With the help of Montagu Norman of the Bank of England, contact was established with the Germans; then Rublee himself came and talked with Schacht. Ribbentrop objected to these talks, but the Schacht-Göring group overcame that opposition. Schacht's new proposal was much more favorable to the Jews: the idea of "additional exports" was dropped, and the money in the trust fund would simply be used to buy equipment for Jews with which they could hope to start new lives outside Germany. This might boost German exports incidentally, but no foreign currency would accrue to the Reich treasury. Transport and freight expenses would also be covered by these funds, insofar as German vessels or other means of transport were used. The Jewish corporation that would be set up abroad would pay for all the other expenses. There would be no necessary connection between that corporation and the trust fund, which was to be run by a directorate of three: two Germans and one non-German.

One hundred fifty thousand Jews of working age would settle abroad, to be followed by 250,000 dependents; 200,000 others would remain behind and be supported out of Jewish capital other than that in the trust fund. The Germans promised that these people would not be molested. For these 200,000, some Jewish businesses might be reopened, and "Jews outside of Germany would not be called upon to support their coreligionists in the Reich."[139] As soon as the scheme was started, Jews would be released from the concentration camps.

At the same time, negotiations were opened between Germany and Poland, and the Poles declared themselves willing to take back into Poland four to five thousand Polish Jews from Germany, if they came with 70 percent of their property.[140]

In the midst of the negotiations, on January 21, Rublee was informed that Schacht had been dismissed from his post by Hitler, but that an official by the name of Helmut Wohlthat had been nominated by Göring—in his capacity as Germany's economic dictator—to continue the negotiations. In a personal interview on January 23,[141] Göring assured Rublee that the German government was serious in its intentions to see the negotiations through.

Public opinion in Britain and the U. S. was divided on the new plan; so were the Jews. Although the majority of the Zionists remained opposed to the plan despite the improved conditions, personalities like Stephen S. Wise and Louis Lipsky voiced approval. JDC hesitated. Its labor component was very definitely against what became to be known as the Rublee plan. The Jewish Labor Committee had joined with the American Jewish Congress in supporting the boycott of German goods, and at the JDC leadership meetings, Adolph Held, a leading journalist of the labor wing, voiced opposition to the scheme. The counterpart organization that the Jews were supposed to set up would, Held thought, recognize the right of the German government to expropriate Jewish property and would destroy the boycott.[142] However, it was quite clear that unless some Jewish counterpart to the trust fund was set up, the whole scheme was unworkable. This again raised the whole problem of private organizations arranging for the mass settlement of hundreds of thousands of people with voluntary contributions —and JDC was convinced that this was impossible.

At the same time, Jewish leaders in Britain were much less hesitant and were pressing for the establishment of a Coordinating Foundation that would fulfill two main tasks: it would serve as a secretariat in directing emigrants to various places of settlement and it would invest money in settlement projects.

The Rublee plan had the full support of the American State Department. Rublee himself resigned on February 13, 1939, having—as he thought—accomplished his mission. The directorship of ICR was taken over by Sir Herbert Emerson, the League of Nations high commissioner for refugees. Myron C. Taylor was again called to help the U.S. government, and beginning in March a most extraordinary campaign was waged by the president, the State Department, and Taylor, to press American Jewish organizations into accepting the Rublee plan and setting up the Coordinating Foundation together with British Jews.

As a result of concerted pressure, a first meeting of Taylor with Lewis L. Strauss, Henry Ittleson, Albert D. Lasker, Harold Linder, and Joseph C. Hyman took place on March 28, 1939. A second "informal meeting of Jews" was held on April 15.[143] At this meeting in the chambers of Roosevelt's friend Judge Rosenman, the leadership of JDC and the American Jewish Committee, as well as prominent Zionists like Wise and Robert Szold, decided to negotiate with Taylor. An aide-mémoire drawn up as a result of the meeting stated that "we should take no steps that directly or by implication would give recognition by the Jewish community as such to the validity of any expropriation of private property or of the requirement that German citizens who are Jews [sic!] shall be driven into exile. We should particularly refrain from undertaking, as a Jewish group, any step which might tend to induce any other government to follow the German program." The matter was not just Jewish, and if Taylor insisted on forming an organization to implement the Rublee plan, this should be done "under general and not Jewish auspices." Further, the problem was of such magnitude "as to place it beyond the power of individuals alone to solve, and to make it a subject for the concern and active aid of governments."

Meetings with Taylor followed. Taylor disregarded the Jewish reservations and chose to regard the Jewish attitude as favorable to the creation of the Coordinating Foundation. He agreed with their reservations, he said, and the foundation should be set up forthwith. But to the State Department he reported that there was great reluctance in Jewish circles because of the fear that the Jews, with their own hands, might create that ogre of anti-Semitic propaganda called "international Jewry," against which Hitler was rampaging.

But the Jews were already relenting. On April 29 forty-one Jewish leaders met and agreed to Taylor's demands. Nevertheless, Roosevelt requested that a Jewish delegation meet with him. The meeting took place on May 4, with Baerwald, Ittleson, Strauss, Proskauer, Sol Stroock, and Samuel I. Rosenman representing the Jews, and Welles and Moffat representing the State Department. The president urged the Jewish leaders to set up the foundation as quickly as possible. In response, JDC—obviously the Jewish group most immediately concerned—decided on May 30 to send two representatives to London to negotiate with the British regarding the establishment of the foundation. Paul Baerwald and Harold Linder agreed to go on the delicate mission.[144]

Into this crisis-ridden atmosphere there burst the *St. Louis* affair. The story has been told elsewhere[145] and a bare outline will suffice here.

The *St. Louis,* a German ship of the Hamburg America Line, sailing under a very considerate and liberal captain, Gustav Schroeder, left Germany on May 13, 1939, with 930 Jewish emigrants. They were all going to Havana with legal Cuban visas issued by

the person responsible for immigration in the Cuban government
—except for twenty-two persons who had decided not to rely solely
on the visas and had had them verified in Cuba at additional cost
to themselves. By the time the ship reached Cuba, the ordinary
visas had been declared invalid. Later, the JDC committee dealing
with the affair came to the conclusion that the government of
President Bru of Cuba had never intended to permit the refugees
to land. The person who had issued the visas, a Colonel Benites,
supported the faction of the Cuban chief of staff, Fulgencio Batista,
a rival of President Bru's. Bru apparently thought that to refuse
permission for the landing would be a good way to fight Batista,
who, through Benites, had hoped to collect large bribes from the
refugees. It may be that Bru was willing to accept the refugees if
JDC paid very large sums not only to the government treasury but
also to his private pocket—both factions were asking for about
$450,000 in addition to the official ransom money of $500,000 to
the government. JDC was prepared to pay up to $500,000 to the
Cubans, but since there were no additional handouts of any size,
Bru refused to let the refugees land. Apparently the State Department was of no great help either, because it informed the lawyer
representing JDC in Cuba, Lawrence Berenson, that the Cubans
were merely bluffing and that JDC should not offer them too
much.[146]

The *St. Louis* affair put JDC on the horns of a very real dilemma.
JDC was painfully aware that if it paid a huge ransom for the 907
Jews with Benites visas (one had committed suicide), who headed
back to Europe on the *St. Louis* on June 6, other Latin American
governments would probably learn the lesson and exact equal if not
larger sums. The total JDC income was to rise to $8.1 million in
1939, but ransom monies of $1 million for 900 refugees would
exhaust the JDC treasury in no time. This of course was quite apart
from the fact that JDC had never agreed to pay ransom to unscrupulous operators for innocent human beings.

What moved JDC to go against its own better judgment was the
tremendous pressure from its contributors, who saw, perhaps

rightly, that this was a test case and a symbol and that every effort had to be made to save the passengers. Members of the JDC staff and leading laymen worked literally around the clock to try to find places of refuge for the ship, which was slowly making its way back across the Atlantic to Germany. In the end Troper in Paris contacted Max Gottschalk in Brussels and Mrs. van Tijn in Holland, who intervened with their respective governments; in France, Jules Braunschvig went to the French Foreign Ministry to persuade them to accept some of the refugees. All this occurred on June 10. In the meantime, Paul Baerwald was active in London, where the British government also agreed to accept some of the refugees. Finally the *St. Louis* passengers were landed: 181 in Holland, 288 in Britain, 214 in Belgium, and 224 in France.[147] In all these countries JDC undertook to support the *St. Louis* refugees. In 1939, $500,000 was appropriated for this purpose. JDC was to carry this obligation for a long time, until those who were not deported to Nazi death camps finally found permanent havens.

Another element that influenced the discussions regarding the establishment of the Coordinating Foundation was the situation in Palestine. On May 17, 1939, the British published their White Paper on Palestine, which declared that Britain intended to hand over the Palestinian Jewish minority to the Arabs there within ten years. Another seventy-five thousand Jews would be allowed to enter the country within five years; after that further Jewish immigration would be subject to Arab consent (that is, it would cease). With this, the Zionist experiment was to come to an end.

To counteract this blow, the British government published, on the same day, the *Report of the British Guiana Refugee Commission to the Advisory Committee on Political Refugees Appointed by the President of the United States.*[148] The British had suggested British Guiana as a possible area of Jewish settlement in late 1938, after they had determined to their own satisfaction the course they would pursue in Palestine.[149] JDC, desperately searching for areas of settlement, had sent Joseph A. Rosen to represent it on a special commission that investigated British Guiana between February 14 and April 19, 1939. Rosen fell ill immediately after his arrival, and his signature on the report does not have any real meaning. Two other members of the commission were British.

The commission reported that small areas of settlement might possibly be developed in the more remote parts of the colony, and that a small group of three to five thousand young and sturdy settlers should be chosen to start an experimental colony. It also said that British Guiana "is not an ideal place for refugees from middle European countries" and that no immediate large-scale settlement was possible; there did exist a potentiality for settlement. In short, the remote tropical colony might be a good dumping ground for European Jews, but a longer period of time and a trial settlement were needed to find out whether people could actually live there. In light of the country's checkered history in later years, it seems highly doubtful that Jews would have been welcome there at all. Baerwald and others in JDC tried for some time afterward to defend the Guiana venture,[150] until finally the project disappeared from view, as did so many others at the time.

The British, of course, vehemently denied all allegations that their policies in Palestine and Guiana were in any way connected. At a meeting on British Guiana held on June 22, 1939, Malcolm MacDonald, the British colonial secretary, clearly stated that any colonization would require investment of private Jewish money on a very large scale. From his statements it emerges that he thought of the Coordinating Foundation primarily as an organization to get the Guiana project going. He hinted that if no Jewish money was forthcoming, Britain might have to reconsider her whole refugee policy—a very thinly veiled threat of reprisals against refugees trying to enter Britain.[151]

The negotiations in London made another fact clear: it was doubtful if any money at all would be forthcoming from British Jews. The reason was that British Jewry was contributing very large sums to refugee absorption in Britain and elsewhere; American Jewry was richer and larger, and so far had contributed proportionately less than had British Jewry. JDC at first thought that its preliminary contribution to the Coordinating Foundation would be $500,000; this was a reasonable sum, if one remembers that the total income in 1939 was $8.1 million. But two weeks later half a million dollars was pledged to the support of the *St. Louis* refugees, so that one-eighth of JDC's money was now gone. Pressure by President Roosevelt caused JDC to reconsider its contribution. On June 6 it decided on a risky step: it would provide $1 million and would set up the foundation whether the British participated or not—a complete reversal of JDC's position in March. The lack of realism in these negotiations is perhaps made clearer if one remembers that the foundation, with its $1 million in capital, was to serve as a counterpart to the trust fund in Germany with its $600 million.[152] At a meeting of the Administration Committee, Rosenberg stated the reason for accepting the additional burden: there should be no uncertainty "as to our readiness to carry through a commitment which in effect was desired by Mr. Taylor and the president."[153]

In the wake of the June 6 decision, another informal meeting of Jewish leaders was convened on June 17. At this meeting Wise voiced hesitation regarding the step taken by JDC; but only Joseph Tennenbaum of the American Federation of Polish Jews and the American Jewish Congress, a leading proponent of the boycott movement and later to be a historian of the holocaust, voted against the JDC action, on the grounds that the Coordinating Foundation would finance German exports and hinder the anti-German boycott.[154]

In the meantime, Baerwald and later Linder were negotiating with British Jews and non-Jews in London and with Emerson of ICR. It soon became apparent to them that they were, in fact, negotiating with the British government. Between June 5 and June 7 Baerwald met Wohlthat, who had come to London ostensibly to attend a conference on whaling.[155] Informed of the negotiations in London, Wohlthat expressed the German government's willingness to carry on negotiations with even a purely American foundation, in case the talks between American and British Jews broke down. In such a case, Wohlthat stated that "probably from 5 to 10 percent of the Jewish assets in Germany would be turned over to the trust fund there."[156] Though we lack the documentary evidence to prove it, it seems that the talks with Wohlthat convinced JDC that this was a project that had to be pursued with the greatest energy. JDC had come full circle.

The basic difference of opinion with British Jews lay in the fact that JDC was unwilling to spend money on settlement schemes that were too expensive to be implemented without governmental help. Also, in New York a delegation from the American Jewish Congress and the Jewish Labor Committee met with JDC leaders on July 13 and demanded that the Coordinating Foundation charter clearly declare that no foreign currency would accrue to the Germans and no additional exports would result from the foundation's operations.[157]

The British government, possibly at the suggestion of Sir Herbert Emerson, then went a step further. On July 19 the Foreign Office declared in a communique that, contrary to its previous policy, the British government would be prepared to participate in settlement projects, provided other governments were ready to do the same.[158] The charter of the Coordinating Foundation made it clear that the new organization would be quite independent of anything that happened in Germany, that it would facilitate emigration and settlement and "provide land services"—whatever that meant—and facilities for emigrants. While it was not expressly stated that it would engage in colonization, this was hinted at broadly. A hesitant JDC signed the charter on July 19. The next day, July 20, it was published. Six weeks later, on September 1, it was killed with the first shots fired in World War II.

One of the perplexing questions that came out of the complicated negotiations in the spring and summer of 1939 is this: Why should the president of the United States have been so insistent that American Jews spend large sums of money to settle Jewish emigrants in as yet undefined and remote places? Why should he have been so concerned that an agreement be reached between American and British Jews? The president's humanitarianism, while not itself in doubt, was always tempered with political astuteness. The Coordinating Foundation, from Roosevelt's point of view, must have had a political purpose, possibly that of gaining international prestige by attempting a settlement of the refugee problem—outside of the U. S., of course.

The second problem is no less vexing, but relatively easier to answer: Did the Germans really intend to implement some such scheme as the Rublee plan? It seems quite clear that Hitler was informed in detail of the negotiations with Rublee. Schacht's dismissal in January does not seem to have had any connection with the Rublee plan. True, there was a rivalry between Ribbentrop on one hand and Schacht and Göring on the other. In January a circular letter from Ribbentrop declared that the Jewish emigration problem was for all practical purposes insoluble, and a more radical solution was hinted at.[159] But the negotiations proceeded despite Ribbentrop's objections.[160] In his famous instructions to Frick, Nazi minister of the interior, on January 24, Göring expressly included among the members of the planned central bureau of Jewish emigration Helmut Wohlthat, whom he designated as the man responsible for the Rublee plan negotiations.

It appears that the plan became a bone of contention between Göring and the SS. Heydrich, Himmler's chief deputy, declared on February 11 that the implementation of the Rublee plan was by no means certain, so that forced emigration should in the meantime be continued. Hitler himself—as opposed to his henchmen—may have already been thinking in terms of the destruction of the Jews, as evinced in his famous speech to the Reichstag on January 30, 1939, and even more clearly in a talk with the Czech foreign minister, Chvalkovsky, on January 21, where he threatened to eliminate the Jews of Europe. In the meantime, extermination was impractical, and any method of expulsion that produced results was good.[161] On the whole, it seems that the Nazis took this plan seriously and were willing to consider it as a possible solution to the Jewish question. Meanwhile, this did not prevent them, as long as there was no agreement on emigration, from intensifying their persecutions and driving out people who had no money or visas. But it would be wrong to assume from this behavior that they had scrapped the Rublee plan.

One author expresses regret at the fact that the Coordinating Foundation was set up so late, that valuable time was lost, and "that so little was accomplished in the year before the war began."[162] The evidence does not seem to support this conclusion. Voluntary Jewish sources were quite unable to collect the vast sums of money necessary for the foundation's successful operation; areas of settlement were not, in fact, available, and to arrange for settlement in places like the U. S., Australia, South America, or even Palestine would have required time. Time was certainly not available between January and September 1939. Had the foundation been set up in January, nothing much could have been done before the outbreak of the war. At the end of September, with close to two million Polish Jews in the hands of the Nazis, Hitler and the SS turned to other solutions for the Jewish question. The foundation passed into history.

German Jewry, it must be added, was very bitter about the negotiations. It felt the whole weight of Heydrich's cold terror directed against itself. The "negotiations of the Evian committee," wrote the Hilfsverein to Lord Samuel on February 10, "have definitely done more harm than good."[163]

In May some representatives of German Jewry were allowed to go to London; they were expected to come back with some positive replies regarding places of settlement and the setting up of the Coordinating Foundation. They came back with empty hands, having been callously rebuffed by the heads of ICR. Emerson, the ICR director, even refused to give them a letter stating that every effort was being made to help German Jewry.[164]

ILLEGAL MIGRATION

The tragedy of Jewish emigration caused the appearance of what was to become, for a whole decade, a phenomenon identified with the plight of Jews: illegal migration. As early as July 1934 the first illegal immigrant ship to Palestine, the *Velos,* made a successful run with 330 Hechalutz trainees from Poland. In September of that year the *Velos* tried a second time, but the British prevented a landing; the 310 passengers[165] attempted to find a haven "at several ports" but nowhere were they allowed to enter. Finally they returned to Poland and obtained legal permits to enter Palestine. HICEM requested that JDC support the passengers, but Kahn refused. "We could not contribute to this cause as it was a case of illegal smuggling of immigrants to Palestine."[166]

Efforts to start illegal immigration to Palestine began again in January 1938.[167] This was done partly by the Histadruth (the Palestine General Jewish Federation of Labor), partly by the Revisionists, the opponents of the official Zionist movement, and partly by private persons and various political groups. The official Zionist bodies were split on the question; some of the American and British Zionists were opposed to illegal efforts, at least as long as there was the slightest hope of an accommodation with Britain.

In early 1939 JDC was approached by the different groups engaged in organizing the immigration movement to Palestine. "JDC was ready to put up 5,000 pounds if the Council [for German Jewry] and Simon Marks's group put up a like amount each and if the Council would share in the responsibility."[168] This meant that JDC would participate only if the whole matter became open, public, and, ipso facto, legal. Naturally, this did not happen, and JDC help was not forthcoming. Troper stated that "we must continue to take the attitude that JDC can take no part in this emigration." The local committees (who were not part of JDC in any case), such as Mrs. van Tijn's group in Holland or Mrs. Schmolka's group in Prague, "can do so if they wish."[169] This essentially was JDC's policy right up to the outbreak of the war.

With this position established in principle, there arose a question that could not be easily answered. One could have a set policy, yet not be able to close one's eyes to the misery and the suffering of the people who could not manage to get through to Palestine. JDC

was committed to helping people regardless of the politics involved. Moreover, even ICR, through its British director, Emerson, expressly allowed "giving relief for humanitarian reasons to
those who were stranded through the rejection of the transports"
while warning the "responsible organizations not to give any direct
help to such transports."[170] Some of the situations that arose were
tragic indeed. In early July 1939 the S.S. *Rim* caught fire, and its
772 passengers were landed on a Greek island. Other ships, mismanaged by their organizers, ran out of fuel or food, or were
caught by the British and had to remain in Greek waters without
provisions. By July 1939, $9,000 had been spent by JDC to help
feed these people, largely through the good offices of the Athens
Jewish community, which administered the relief.

JDC was watching the situation carefully. It received reports
and detailed information on boats filled with people trying to save
themselves by getting into Palestine; if these efforts failed, JDC
might have to step in with food and clothes and blankets, while still
maintaining its noninvolvement in the political aspects of the situation.[171]

Palestine was by no means the only goal of boats bearing illegal
immigrants. At about the same time that attempts to reach Palestine were being made, refugees without visas were trying to get to
the Latin American countries. This movement appears to have
started as early as September 1938, when 43 passengers on the S.S.
Iberia vainly tried to enter Mexico and were finally allowed to land
at Havana. A similar journey by the S.S. *Orinoco* in October with
300 passengers ended in the same way. All this of course cost
money: Cuban officials had to be bribed. Cuba remained one of the
main havens throughout the period, largely because of the venality
of its officials. For various reasons, Venezuela, Colombia, Chile,
Costa Rica, and Bolivia also accepted visaless refugees from time
to time. A list prepared at JDC offices in March 1939 counted
twenty-three boats with 1,740 passengers who somehow had to be
squeezed into Latin America without proper documents. Not all
these ships managed to land their human cargo. The S.S. *General*

Martin, for instance, leaving Boulogne with 25 visaless passengers in early February, had to return to Europe with the refugees aboard. The same happened to the 40 passengers on the S.S. *Caparcona* in late March.[172]

JDC had to pay a high proportion of the bribes, thinly disguised as landing money or living expenses for the refugees. Often, too, the passengers held forged visas, or the visas were genuine but the receiving country had suddenly invalidated them—as happened with the *St. Louis.* To arrange matters, money had to change hands, and JDC simply could not pay those sums. On March 15 Baerwald sent a cable to Europe asking for a meeting of the main emigrating agencies to consider what should be done. It was, he said, "quite clear [that the] resources [of] private philanthropic bodies [were] strained [to the] utmost . . . even [by the] more normal [and] orderly emigration under [the] supervision [of] responsible bureaus."[173] The dumping of refugees was resulting in panic migration and exploitation by unscrupulous steamship agencies, lawyers, and venal officials. Alarming problems were arising: indefinite maintenance of the refugees, huge guarantees that were quite beyond the financial capabilities of private bodies such as JDC, and the specter of a more or less permanent threat of blackmail, endangering the operations of different agencies. Both the steamship companies and the Germans would know that the Jewish organizations might protest but would pay in the end.

The other agencies—HICEM, ICA, the Council for German Jewry—were in the same quandary. There was no real solution as long as the countries of immigration were closed. Partly as a result of this panic emigration, most Latin American countries did in fact close their borders in early 1939. Opinions in JDC were divided. Alexander Kahn was one of those who declared that JDC simply "had to help them as far as our means can last, because I do not think we will be forgiven if we take the harsh [line of] policy that we will not help. When the next batch of 100 comes we will have to do it anyway." The other view was expressed by Rosenberg, who argued against agreeing to the expulsion of Jews from Europe. If one allowed the Germans to "eliminate" their Jews, the Poles and Romanians were going to follow suit. In the minds of German officials, also "there is a notion that American Jewry can meet all sorts of emergencies." One had to say no to the refugees. "After all we are in a world war and there are times when you have to sacrifice some of your troops. And these unfortunates are some of our troops."[174] JDC did not follow Rosenberg's counsel. It accepted the policy proposed by Alexander Kahn, but tried to pay as little as possible in bribes; and except in the case of the *St. Louis* it declined to offer ransom money.

During and after the *St. Louis* affair, illegal immigration into Latin America continued. Besides the *St. Louis,* two small boats arrived at Havana: the S.S. *Flandre,* a French boat with ninety-six refugees, and the S.S. *Orduna,* a British boat with about forty people. Like the *St. Louis* passengers, they were refused permission to land. They too returned to Europe and were accepted by the four countries that had received the others.

JDC had to support the Latin American Jewish communities that were trying to care for the refugees from Europe. In December 1938 it sent a former German Jewish social worker to Latin America to establish contact with the communities there. These contacts bore fruit in early 1939. The Havana Refugee Committee was brought under the influence of the New York National Coordinating Committee, later the National Refugee Service. Other committees received direct aid from JDC and dispensed it according to set rules to those who needed it. In 1939, $600,000 was appropriated for this work, which affected about sixty-eight thousand Jewish refugees from Nazi Europe.[175]

In a world of closed borders and hostile officialdom,[176] the Jews of Germany and Austria were ready to clutch at straws. One such straw was Shanghai. In 1937 Shanghai was divided between the international settlement, which was run by the foreign powers (who had, in fact, been ruling the city during the period of the disintegration of the Chinese state), and the Chinese part of the city, which had just been conquered by the Japanese. There was no

290 : *My Brother's Keeper*

requirement for an entry visa into the city. IKG became aware of
this fact in Vienna in the summer of 1938. The problem was to pay
the fares to Shanghai, usually by a German or Italian boat; later,
a rail connection via the USSR into Manchuria and thence to
Shanghai would also be attempted. Shanghai became a place of
refuge, especially for those people who, threatened with arrest and
a concentration camp, could find no other place of emigration.

The Jewish community in Shanghai was made up of two main
elements: a wealthy aristocracy comprised mainly of Iraqi Jews
(among them were members of the famous Sassoon and Kaddouri
families), and Russian Jews who had come from Manchuria after
World War I. Since the rise of Hitler to power, some German Jews
had also arrived, mainly members of the professions. The different
groups maintained separate social and cultural lives and evinced
little mutual sympathy for one another.

The situation of the few German Jewish refugees had attracted
the attention of JDC toward the end of 1937. At that time Judge
Harry A. Hollzer of Los Angeles, a respected JDC stalwart, drew
the attention of JDC to Shanghai—his brother, Joseph Hollzer,
who was the head of a Jewish Relief Committee there, had provided him with some distinctly disturbing information. In early
1938 there were some five hundred destitute Jews in the city, not
all of them German Jews. But in London the Joint Foreign Committee of the Board of Deputies and the Anglo-Jewish Association
decided that Shanghai was "not a matter about which any Jewish
community outside of Shanghai and Hong Kong need be troubled."[177] The truth of the matter was that the rich Jews of Shanghai
were able, but not very willing, to look after the few refugees who
were then in the city. From London it seemed ridiculous to send
money to a place like Shanghai.

JDC could not take this kind of attitude. Not only Hollzer, but
also other people turned to JDC. In February 1938 the New York
office empowered Kahn to look into the matter, though Shanghai
was hardly included in Europe, which was Kahn's proper field of
activity.[178] JDC records indicate that during 1938, $5,000 was ap-
propriated for refugee work in Shanghai.

After November 1938 people began streaming into the Far Eastern metropolis. By June 1939 there were ten thousand refugees in the city, and by the time war broke out in Europe there were close to eighteen thousand. Most of them found refuge in the Chinese part of the city. Unemployment was the rule rather than the exception, because Europeans could not compete with the Chinese for work. In early February the British, American, and French consuls drew "the attention [of] their governments to [the] refugee situation, particularly to [the] necessity [for] relief funds." The U. S. government of course turned to JDC. In JDC the opinion was that "as [the] matter came to us from [the] State Department, we must be prepared to be helpful."[179] The Council for German Jewry in London also provided help in the form of 5,000 pounds; but the main burden fell on JDC, which sent $60,000 to Shanghai before September.

Attempts to stop the influx into Shanghai were made by all the responsible bodies dealing with emigration. But the Jewish agencies in Germany and Austria refused to cooperate. In March 1939 the Hilfsverein in Berlin answered with a plea to "trust us when we tell you that we are unable to diminish the emigration from Germany and that the only possibility to prevent our people from going to such places as Shanghai lies in finding some more constructive opportunities for emigration."[180] Gestapo pressure was definitely more convincing than anything JDC could say.

The paradox of the Shanghai situation—viewed with the benefit of hindsight—lies in the fact that what was in 1938/9 considered the utmost cruelty, namely, forced emigration, turned out to be a blessing in disguise, though the disguise may often have been very heavy indeed. The refugees in Shanghai, the illegal immigrants who were pushed onto boats to Palestine or Latin America by their desperation, often under direct Gestapo pressure—all of them managed to survive the holocaust. The ones who stayed behind did not. Yet among leaders of German Jewry in 1939, who had a clear feeling of approaching doom, it was thought to be more dignified for a Jew to suffer death in Europe than to die of starvation in

Shanghai.[181] The truth is that the people in Shanghai did not die of starvation—in large part thanks to JDC.

During the last week in August 1939 a unique conference called by JDC and HICEM took place in Paris. Paralleling the Zionist Congress that was taking place at the same time in Switzerland, the meeting was attended by about fifty Jewish leaders of social agencies throughout Europe. Saly Mayer for Switzerland, Max Gottschalk, Gertrude van Tijn, Isaac Giterman, and many others attended. The general subject was the war, which everybody was expecting. JDC was keeping its bank balances low and was distributing funds to its cooperating committees so that they would have something in hand should the war come. At the last moment the various committees were told that in case of war they could spend money for six months at the same monthly rate as during the first six months of 1939. This was to become standard JDC practice during the war.

But the practical subjects of money and help were not the only things discussed. The people who met in Paris in August 1939 knew that they were facing possible death. Yet they went back to their stations, with heavy hearts but with the clear feeling that they were responsible for others and could not abandon them.[182]

THE END IN POLAND

Perhaps the most difficult of all the tasks that JDC faced in the summer of 1939 was that of maintaining its work in Poland. The situation there had changed somewhat in favor of the Jews when Neville Chamberlain announced Britain's unilateral guarantee to Poland on March 31, 1939. The anti-Jewish pressure by the Polish government had apparently been influenced by Poland's active concurrence in Nazi Germany's foreign policy: she had participated in the rape of Czechoslovakia in 1938, and she had agreed to Germany's anti-Soviet policy. She was led by a group of mediocre colonels who were stifling whatever remained in Poland of her great democratic tradition.

In April 1939 Poland very suddenly became an ally of democratic Britain, because the Nazi dictator demanded the annexation
of Danzig and was threatening the dismemberment of Poland.
Anti-Semitism could therefore no longer be considered a foreign
policy asset. Nevertheless, Colonel Beck, the Polish foreign minister, asked the British to help solve the Jewish emigration problem
in Poland and Romania.

The careful British answer was given on April 6, 1939.[183] In it
His Majesty's government declared its readiness to examine with
the governments concerned what it termed "particular problems in
Poland and Romania which are part of a larger problem." Such an
examination was not conducted prior to the outbreak of war. After
the war began, it ceased to be necessary.

The change in atmosphere was felt at Zbaszyn, too. Restriction
on the movement of refugees from there into Poland were eased.
Groups of people, mainly young persons who could prove that they
had work waiting for them, or persons who had a chance to emigrate, were allowed into the country. At the end of May 1939
thirty-five hundred refugees remained in Zbaszyn. At the outbreak
of the war, the two thousand Jews still there were overrun by the
Germans advancing into Poland.

As a result of the increasing enmity between Germany and
Poland, the Germans tried to repeat the action of October 1938.
In early June 1939 they attempted to chase two thousand Polish
Jews over the border at Zbaszyn, but the Poles prevented them.
The sufferings of the Polish Jews who were the victims of this act
are beyond description. On June 23, the newspapers reported,
hundreds of these unfortunates were shuttled back and forth at the
frontier near the town of Rybnik. In the end, some managed to get
into Poland. But most of them became victims of Nazi brutality;
anyone who could not be expelled was sent to a concentration
camp.

Polish pressure on emigration was coupled with increasingly
shameless and open acts of coercion against Jews in political and
financial matters. In the spring of 1939 the Polish government

asked for a Polish Defense Loan, to be raised "voluntarily" throughout the country. The Jews were forced to participate in the loan in a manner that was far beyond their capacity. By ruthless methods that amounted to capital taxation, Jews were forced to pay 150 million of the 400 million zloty that were raised throughout the country. This occurred in May 1939. As a result, there was a sharp increase in Jewish business bankruptcies. Jews who refused to pay very large assessments were summarily arrested.[184] In the summer of 1939 JDC was faced with economic emergencies in Poland that seemed grim indeed.

One of the ways to counteract the dangers facing Polish Jews was to encourage the establishment of effective Jewish bodies in Poland. As we have seen, there were no generally recognized Jewish representative bodies in the country. JDC's aim of helping Jews to help themselves could not be effectively promoted under such conditions. The primary cause for this situation lay in the political competition between the many different ideological trends and movements, and in the seemingly insurmountable differences in approach between them. In June 1937 the provisional Representation of Polish Jewry, composed of Zionists and Agudists, was established at the level of the Polish Sejm, but it was short-lived. The World Jewish Congress established a Polish branch in February 1938. But this was formed only of Zionist bodies and was thus ineffective as an overall unifying factor. In any case, JDC would have opposed the WJC branch in Poland, in line with its general philosophy.

JDC therefore embarked on its own schemes to create something resembling a common front of Jewish interests. The first problem was how to hand over major JDC functions in Poland to local groups, thus promoting greater local independence. The subject seems to have been discussed in detail for the first time in July 1938, during a meeting there between Kahn and the heads of the Warsaw office. In a rather sharp and formal letter on August 11, Kahn declared that now it would have to be decided whether the Free Loan *kassas* should continue to operate under direct JDC management or be transformed into independent organizations along the lines of CENTOS and TOZ. With most of the constructive work concentrated in the Free Loan *kassas,* such a transformation would in effect hand over most of the JDC program in Poland to a local body. The second proposal, also broached in Kahn's letter,[185] was for the establishment of a supervisory economic committee "composed of leading Jewish personalities in commerce, banking, industry, and craftmanship." This committee would grant subsidies, subject to JDC approval. Kahn wanted this committee to be set up by the end of 1938.

In October 1938 Morris C. Troper took over Kahn's functions in Europe. The new European chairman of JDC visited Poland in November and found himself in full agreement with his predecessor. JDC, he thought, still controlled the Polish Jews "in a manner and to an extent far beyond what might be expected from a foreign organization." He found a "subservience in relationships" between the local organizations and the JDC office, which he thought was harmful.[186]

Progress was fairly rapid on the first of the two problems dealt with in Kahn's August 1938 letter. In Poland, CEKABE, which had long been recognized by JDC as the central institution dealing with the Free Loan *kassas,* was now given the sole responsibility for all matters affecting this most important aspect of JDC work. Troper could report to Hyman in early March 1939 that the *kassas* were being handed over and that JDC was reserving for itself a purely supervisory function, justified by the fact that it provided the credits necessary for maintaining and expanding the work. Membership on the board of CEKABE included Assimilationists and Zionists and, of course, Giterman as the JDC representative.[187]

The problem of handing over most of the JDC functions to a Polish Central Committee was very complicated. JDC conducted these negotiations with a group of industrialists headed by Karol Sachs. It seems, however, that Giterman and his Warsaw colleagues were not very happy about this development. Troper was inclined to attribute this opposition to Giterman's desire to maintain his predominant position as the JDC representative. He also hinted that there was some jealousy within the JDC office over Giterman's position.[188] But the evidence suggests that Giterman was not in agreement with the idea of going beyond the established political bodies and relying mainly on a group of rich men—whose practical activities up to that time had not been very outstanding and whose ability to unite Polish Jewry behind their leadership was doubtful. The first list of prospective Central Committee members submitted by Sachs in September 1938 was indeed indicative of a trend: not a single leader of the main factions was included except Rabbi Lewin, president of the Agudah.

JDC could not agree to such one-sided proposals. But negotiations continued, and early in 1939 it was clear that the leaders of the Central Financial Institution of the Reconstruction Foundation loan *kassas,* who were identical with the group of wealthy men around Sachs, had been "charged by us" (as David J. Schweitzer put it somewhat grandiloquently) to form the committee "that will practically take over the functions of our present JDC office in Warsaw."[189] In February a new list was submitted by Sachs to the JDC office in Paris. This time the list was much more balanced, though here too about one-half the committee was composed of the Sachs group. The Zionists and even the World Jewish Congress were included, but the Agudah and the Bund were not.[190] In addition, the committee was to include representatives of the main JDC-supported organizations in Poland, such as CENTOS, TOZ, CEKABE, and so on.

In the meantime, as we have seen, the Polish government had set up the Jewish emigration committee; on it were some of the people that had been proposed for the Central Committee. Most of Polish Jewry, especially the Bundists and the Zionists, rejected the emigration committee as a body imposed on the Jews by the government, and the individuals who were on it were suspect in the eyes of the Jewish public. Since some of them were also candidates for membership on the Central Committee, this added complication held up negotiations.

Another very serious problem arose concerning the participation of the Bund. The Bund, as we have already seen, was gaining strength in Poland in 1938/9. As Alexander Kahn put it: "There was a time when the Zionist group could give money to help people to emigrate to Palestine. They were the angels then." Now there was no possibility of emigrating to Palestine because of the British restrictions. That, in Kahn's view, explained the rise of the Bund, "which politically is the strongest expression of the dissatisfaction of the people."[191]

The Bund was opposed on principle to cooperating with a group of Jewish capitalists and Zionist leaders. Yet some of the greatest economic and cultural achievements of Polish Jewry were connected with the Bund, and it could not simply be ignored by JDC. "Whatever work is being done by these [working-class] groups, especially by the Bund, the largest party, be it their extensive school organization, their sanatoriums, their other social and economic activity, it is done well and most efficiently."[192] This opinion was repeatedly supported by Bernhard and Alexander Kahn in New York.

On the other hand, the Polish government, which was aware of the negotiations concerning the Central Committee, tried to influence JDC to cut off its relations with the Bund. One of the leaders of JDC, Edwin Goldwasser, had a talk on the subject with the Polish consul general in New York in July 1939. Said Alexander Kahn: "The consul made a statement that there was a strong feeling in Polish circles that JDC in Poland was closely identified with the Bund, which is considered as a Communist organization dominated by the Russian Communist party. It is natural to assume, therefore, that any special support extended by JDC to the Bund as such will not be viewed favorably by the Polish authorities. Of course," Kahn added, "we here know that the Bund is a socialist group and is opposed to Communism."[193]

Besides its intervention in New York, the Polish government also tried to influence, and even intimidate, JDC representatives in Poland. Police chiefs and the press attempted to put pressure on

persons connected with JDC in Poland to prevent further support
of the Bund. On July 17, 1939, Giterman himself was asked to
appear before the political department of the government commissioner of Warsaw. Nothing was said that would violate good taste,
but the hints were broad and clearly understood.[194]

JDC did not succumb to this pressure. But the Bund was not a
very easy organization to deal with. In early June one of its leaders,
Mauricy Orzech, visited Troper in Paris and conducted negotiations with him. The Bund had just been victorious in municipal
elections in Poland, and Orzech thought, Troper reported, "that
the other Jewish political bodies had practically no political influence or representative capacity and would either gradually wane or
die out completely." Not only did the Bund refuse to cooperate
with capitalists and Zionists in a Central Committee, but it was
clear that since all the other organizations would soon die out
anyway, there was no apparent reason why the Bund should make
any concessions. Troper had to argue Orzech out of his extraordinary and completely unrealistic position. Earlier in 1939 a compromise had been reached to the effect that the Bund would not
sabotage the actions of a Central Committee established by JDC.
A year after it was established the question of the Bund's cooperation with it would be renegotiated. Now, in June 1939, this arrangement seemed out of date. A new compromise was therefore
suggested by Troper whereby the Bund would establish a permanent body whose task it would be to negotiate with the new Central
Committee. However, only those activities of the new committee
that directly affected the Bund or one of its subsidiary organizations would be discussed. The Bund would not be a part of the
committee or concern itself with its overall policies. Orzech accepted this and returned to Poland to obtain the assent of his
organization.[195] There were indications during the summer of 1939
that the compromise was acceptable to the Bund leadership.

Behind the negotiations with the Bund were negotiations within
JDC also. At the Warsaw office Leib Neustadt supported the
claims of the Bund. He thought that its establishments and organi-

zations were models of efficiency and that they, rather than their capitalist counterparts, should receive JDC support. In New York the labor representatives were, of course, inclined to support such a position. Indeed, the Bund organizations managed to do a great deal with very little money. By way of comparison, Troper himself had to write of TER, the export subcommittee of the Economic Council (Wirtschaftsrat) supported by JDC, that it is "under the difficulty that they get orders which they cannot fill and they have to do all they can to prevent people from coming from abroad so that they should not be disillusioned. I thought it best to give them some money so that they would have something to show."[196]

Giterman was not as enthusiastic about the Bund as his colleague was. But he, too, thought that it would be highly unfair to stop supporting the Bund's establishments when the Central Committee was set up, and he therefore supported the compromise suggested by Troper.

Negotiations regarding the Central Committee were carried on with great intensity during the summer of 1939. Troper realized that the problem had to be solved speedily, and he put the whole prestige of JDC behind efforts to reach a satisfactory conclusion. The groups in Poland, both the political groupings and the large social organizations such as CENTOS, TOZ, CEKABE, and others, feared that their affairs would be handed over to a committee that would lean toward one side or another and be less impartial than the JDC office in Warsaw had been. JDC had to put great pressure on the groups to agree to conduct their own affairs alone rather than continue under JDC auspices.

In July a final JDC proposal was worked out. The Central Committee would represent Jewish communal activity "in its entirety." Article 3 of the proposed constitution stated that the committee would coordinate the activities of the federated organizations and "represent their interests," organize and carry out fund raising in Poland, seek financial support abroad, and generally "consider or initiate new proposals for dealing with social and economic welfare needs of a national scope." In other words, what was proposed was an umbrella organization of Polish Jewry, which undoubtedly would have the tendency to become involved in more than economic and social problems. Membership in the committee, as carefully proposed by JDC, consisted of twenty persons; more would be added later. These twenty comprised well-known Zionist and Orthodox leaders, as well as the group of industrialists around Sachs, who would serve as chairman of the committee. Left-wing Zionists were also represented, and the Bund would be taken care of by the Troper-Orzech compromise.[197]

These efforts to establish a Polish Central Committee were typical of a trend in JDC thinking. In effect JDC was almost coercing Polish Jewry to establish a unified front, at least in the economic and social spheres, though it was clear that such a front would have political overtones. JDC was trying its best to reduce its own role in Poland and hand over its work to others. There was an interesting contradiction in its attitudes. On one hand, it continued its detailed supervision of economic and social organizations in Poland; its rather patronizing attitude did not materially change. At the same time, it was trying almost desperately to disengage itself from day-to-day supervision and give the Polish Jews a feeling of responsibility and leadership, so that ultimately they would take over its work.

There was an even greater and more significant paradox. In New York, JDC leadership was in 1939 still concentrated in the hands of the same group that had been at the helm in the early 1930s. The prevalent view was still that the Polish Jews were "coreligionists." The idea of a Jewish national group was viewed with scepticism, at best. Yet here was JDC actually organizing Polish Jewry, for the first time in centuries, as one body, as a national group within the Polish state. Zionists, Bundists, and Agudists had failed to unify Polish Jewry. It was left to an apolitical, philanthropic American Jewish agency, working on general Jewish and humanitarian principles, to attempt the unification of Polish Jewry. Had it succeeded, it is at least possible that Polish Jewry would have been better prepared to meet the horrors that were in store for it.

As it was, the fate of the Central Committee of Polish Jews was symbolic of the situation of Polish Jewry generally. JDC in New York received a telegram, signed by Raphael Szereszewski, a former senator, a banker, and one of the group of industrialists mentioned above, that the Central Committee had been established. The date was September 2, 1939.[198] Twenty-four hours earlier German troops had crossed the borders of Poland. World War II had begun. It was too late.

Conclusion

Morris C. Troper had said at the 1938 JDC annual meeting that to foresee the expenditures for JDC was, in a sense, to forecast the course of history. There seems little doubt that during the decade 1929–39, the course of JDC's history was to a large extent the course of the history of the Jewish people in Europe. JDC had started out in 1929 with the idea of finishing a job that had been started in 1914. By 1931 it had become clear to the leaders of the organization that JDC could not be disbanded. The economic crisis in the U. S. had almost killed JDC. But it survived and was ready to meet, though it never had enough money, the terrible disasters that befell the Jews of Europe in the 1930s.

In a very real sense, JDC undertook a Sisyphean task. With relatively little money it tried, against all odds, to save the crumbling economic structure of the Jewish people in Eastern Europe; then it tried to save the Jews of Central Europe from the effects of the Nazi onslaught. Certainly it suffered from the shortsightedness of its leaders; certainly it made mistakes, did not realize the gravity of situations until it was too late—but did not others fail as well, without trying to do a fraction as much as JDC?

It can be cogently argued that the attempts of JDC to reform the Jewish economy in Poland were foredoomed to failure. With hindsight it is possible to criticize severely the investment of so much money and goodwill in Soviet Russia. JDC's opposition to Zionists merits careful analysis. Its hesitations regarding the emigration of German Jewry from 1933 to 1935 can also be criticized. Yet with all that, JDC could look upon that terrible decade as a period of trial in which it had on the whole stood the test, to the best of its limited possibilities.

There have been few Jewish leaders and thinkers who judged their times with more perspicacity and lucidity than Bernhard Kahn, or with more human warmth than Felix M. Warburg. JDC could not dispense more help to Europe than American Jewry was willing to provide. It never hid any facts from the American Jewish public. It always demanded more funds than it got. It did not keep those funds in banks, but spent them to help the needy, feed the hungry, clothe the naked. There were never enough funds, and too often the answer to a plea for assistance had to be no. But critics rarely criticized what JDC was doing—usually the criticism was directed at what JDC should have done and did not do (largely because it lacked the means). It tried to meet the emergencies as they arose. JDC, together with HICEM and others, was involved in the emigration of some 440,000[1] Jews from Central Europe: 281,900 from "old" Germany, 117,000 from Austria, 35,000 from the Czech lands, and 5,500 from Danzig. It had relieved the suffering of many more in Europe. It proved to them that the Jewish people in America cared, that they were not alone. It answered the voice of conscience—which is more than can be said of many in that time.

Appendix

Income and Expenditure of JDC: 1914–1939

JDC accounts were meticulously audited, and consequently accurate figures for general income and expenditure are available. However, when it came to expenditures in particular countries, questions arose as to what to include in them. Should HICEM expenditures in France be included in accordance with the proportion of HICEM funds originating from the JDC budget? Should emigration from one country to another be registered under the country of emigration or the country of immigration? For these and other reasons there are very considerable discrepancies between the figures for individual areas. The following are the overall figures.

Year	JDC Income (in $)	JDC Expenditures (in $)
1914		61,000
1915	6,167,091	1,904,749
1916		4,249,561
1917	4,603,153	2,827,785
1918	5,813,751	5,894,687
1919	13,574,593	11,606,706
1920	13,840,700	11,189,264
1921	6,006,978	5,023,988
1922	9,081,038	9,635,303
1923	4,956,953	6,071,040
1924	579,077	3,940,114
1925	206,195	1,966,558
1926	4,481,985	4,892,025
1927	4,583,760	4,987,610
1928	3,522,660	2,812,304
1929	1,632,288	1,645,898

1930	1,175,733	1,387,118
1931	741,705	958,760
1932	385,225	340,815
1933	1,151,728	665,754
1934	1,402,198	1,382,326
1935	917,749	983,343
1936	2,340,385	1,904,923
1937	2,952,185	2,883,759
1938	4,021,641	3,799,878
1939	8,138,755	8,490,516

These figures are based on the annual reports of the organization. Tables 5 and 12 in the text give the figures for Germany and Poland in the 1930s. The following are some of the chief areas of expenditure of JDC in 1938 and 1939 (in $).

Year	Germany	Poland	France	Austria	Holland
1938	486,000	1,245,000	130,884	431,438	128,248
1939	978,102	845,000*	589,000	255,374	439,000

These figures are, as stated above, not completely reliable. Where diverging sets of figures were given, the lowest estimate was usually taken. The main sources are 39—Germany, reports; Executive Committee, 1/26/39; R21—1939 draft; R9, aid for overseas.

*For the period up to September 1, 1939.

Notes

Unless otherwise indicated, all references in the footnotes are to the JDC archive in New York. The archive is composed of two parts: one at the JDC Central Office (presently at 60 East 42nd Street) and one in a warehouse in Brooklyn. Very little use could be made of the second part of the JDC archive, because of the technical and physical conditions at the warehouse. Files from that source that have been quoted were transferred to the main office. The files at the office are now in the process of organization, but the material for the 1930s has not been registered yet. In the course of research for the present book, some of the material has been provisionally registered and numbers given.

Files of the Agro-Joint, which are kept separately at the office, have been marked AJ. Files for the 1929–33 period—also kept separately at the office —have been given numbers with no specific letter or figure markings. Files for the 1933–45 period are also kept separately and have been given coded numbers; for example, 44–2, indicates that the file is in cabinet 44, file no. 2. This is true for those cabinets which have been marked and for which index cards were prepared by me for the JDC archive. Cabinets that I did not work through for the archive have a number; the file, having no card and no number, has been described according to the heading on the file (e.g., 29—Germany, refugees). Files that have no numbers at all were taken from the warehouse and transferred to the office, but were not placed in a cabinet by the time the research was terminated. "Excom"—Executive Committee meetings—files are kept in a separate cabinet, as are those of the Administrative Committee (AC). Additional material is kept at the JDC Library in special cabinets. Files marked "R," followed by a number, refer to reports; these are included in the 1933–45 material at the archive, but again are kept separately.

INTRODUCTION

1. Most of this introductory chapter is based on an unpublished manuscript by Herman Bernstein, "The History of American Jewish Relief," written in 1928, now in the JDC Library. Oscar Handlin, *A Continuing Task* (New York, 1964), and Herbert Agar, *The Saving Remnant* (New York, 1960), have also been used.

2. Bernstein, op. cit., p. 161.

3. Ibid., p. 178.

4. Jacob Lestschinsky, *Crisis, Catastrophe and Survival* (London, 1946); Mark Wischnitzer, *Die Juden in der Welt* (Berlin, 1935), p. 225.

5. Bernstein, op. cit., p. 257. See also Zosa Szajkowski's articles dealing with the problems of JDC remittances in the *American Jewish Historical Quarterly* 17, nos. 1–3.

6. Handlin, op. cit., p. 52.

CHAPTER 1

1. AJ (Agro-Joint files) 36, 4/30/28.

2. File 1, 7/25/29.

3. Nathan Reich, JDC *Primer* (1945), JDC Library.

4. File 39, 11/18/31.

5. File 42.

6. R. Mahler, "Jews in Public Service and the Liberal Professions in Poland, 1918–39," *Jewish Social Studies* 6, no. 4 (October 1944).

7. Ibid.

8. Landau reports, 1929–31, file 139.

9. Cited by Faust in *Book of American Federation of Polish Jews,* 25th annual convention, June 11–12, 1933.

10. TOZ had a medical staff of 397 in 1929. It ran thirty-one hospitals, twenty-one anti-TB clinics, and twenty-six dental clinics. JDC contributed 337,000 zloty to its 2 million zloty budget. In its summer camps there were 7,820 children in 1927, 7,633 in 1928, and 6,427 in 1929.

11. There were 540 Orthodox schools for boys and 148 (Beth Yaacov) schools for girls, with over 81,000 pupils (the girls received only ten hours of schooling a week); Orthodox yeshivoth had 18,298 pupils, and evening classes were visited by another 6,700—a total of over 106,000 pupils. The 471 Hebrew-oriented Tarbuth schools had 44,370 pupils, and 210 Yiddishist schools had 19,500 pupils; altogether some 170,000 pupils visited Jewish schools (see Executive Committee, 12/4/30).

12. File 42, 7/10/29.

13. File 19, 6/22/32; annual report by Aronovici.

14. File 20.

15. File 31, foundation council meeting, 1/26/31.

16. A similar proposal to Alter's was submitted by Moses Burgin of the Central Committee of Jewish Artisans in Warsaw in 1931.

17. File 127, 5/3/30. The facts and figures about the social conditions of Polish Jews are based on Kahn's reports—the figures about Lodz, specifically, on his "condensed report," April 1935, 44–5, pp. 14–15.

18. File 42, 1/20/30, Hyman to James A. Becker.

19. Executive Committee, 11/11/31.

20. 1931 report on Poland, JDC Library.

21. File 36, work of the AJDC in 1932.

22. File 19, 5/22/32.

23. File 26, 5/3/31.

24. File 121, 9/30/32.

25. Executive Committee, 12/4/32.

26. Executive Committee, 11/11/31.

27. File 39, 11/18/31.

28. File 121, 2/24/31.

29. Thus the Ministry of Education had a budget of 300 million zloty in 1930/1. Out of that sum, the Jews got 242,593 zloty, or less than one-tenth of 1 percent. In 1931/2, they got 189,011 zloty; in 1932/3, 201,000, and in 1933/4, 197,000.

30. ORT received $46,000 in 1926, $154,000 in 1927, $80,200 in 1928, and $49,800 in 1929.

31. File 13, 8/21/31.

32. File 39, 11/18/31.

33. File 70.

34. Report by Bressler and Hyman on Europe, 1930, JDC Library.

35. Executive Committee, Kahn, 11/11/31.

CHAPTER 2

1. *Na agrarnom fronte,* 1925, nos. 5–6; *Sobrania Zakonov,* 1925, no. 69; 1928, no. 21.

2. AJ, Grower memorandum, 4/26/29.

3. AJ 39, 3/30/28, pp. 1–2.

4. The statistics regarding Jews in Russian agriculture are contradictory. According to the 1926 census, there were about 150,000 Jewish peasants and their families. Dr. Grower's report of September 1929, however, mentions 130,557 persons (AJ 64). A report of March 1928 quotes

the figure of 35,514 Jewish families, which multiplied by four to account for family members would give a figure of about 150,000. But it seems that the statistics included thousands of small Jewish holdings on the outskirts of villages in the Pale of Settlement, which should not really be included in statistics of farmers. The numbers settled by Agro-Joint also appear uncertain. In March 1928, Agro-Joint claimed to have settled 10,000 families, yet another compilation quotes a figure of 7,600 by the end of 1928. A report of September 1929 mentions 12,988 families as having been settled by Agro-Joint (AJ 39, AJ 2). Here the figures seem to include those Jewish colonists not in Agro-Joint colonies who were helped by Agro-Joint at various times. The 5,646 families in the text is the lowest figure.

5. AJ 2, 5/26/26.
6. AJ 51.
7. AJ 19, F.M. Warburg to J.A. Rosen, 12/17/30.
8. AJ 81, to Alfred W. Saperston.
9. AJ 19 (confidential, hereafter CON), 1928.
10. AJ 82, 12/11/29.
11. AJ 2, 4/26/29.
12. AJ 160, Mirkin memorandum, 2/12/30.
13. AJ 11. Yet a report by Rosen on 2/13/30 claims that over 3,000 families had been settled in 1929 (AJ 2). The lower figure has been accepted as nearer to the truth.
14. AJ 4.
15. AJ 2, 2/13/30, p. 3.
16. AJ 2, 11/24/29.
17. AJ 2, 11/12/31 (press conference).
18. AJ 64.
19. AJ 5.
20. Ibid.
21. AJ 64, 2/13/30.
22. AJ 160, Mirkin memorandum, 2/12/30.
23. AJ 2, 2/13/30, p. 3.
24. AJ 2, 11/12/31 (press conference).
25. AJ 58.
26. AJ 2.
27. *Emes* of 3/25/32, cited by the *Chicago Chronicle* of 7/22/32.
28. AJ 66, 10/8/31.
29. AJ 2, 2/13/30, p. 3.
30. AJ 5, 4/14/30.
31. Norman Bentwich in *B'nai B'rith Magazine,* February 1932.
32. AJ 2, Rosen's letter, March 1936.

33. AJ 20.
34. AJ 2, Rosen's letter, March 1936.
35. AJ 4.
36. AJ 59, JTA report, December 1930.
37. AJ 11, 1/30/31.
38. AJ 11, AJ 90.
39. The total amount of interest the Soviets would have had to pay on the $4,725,000 until the end of 1935 was $627,000. This they accepted as payment from AMSOJEFS. In addition, AMSOJEFS handed back to the Soviets Soviet bonds in the amount of $1,848,000 out of the $4,725,000 in bonds that the Soviets had given AMSOJEFS when they received the money from America. Together, these two sums came to $2,475,000 which AMSOJEFS owed the Soviet government. For these bonds and waiver of interest which was worth dollar payment, the Soviets issued new bonds ($2,475,000) which, together with the $2,877,000 in bonds that had remained in the hands of AMSOJEFS after the $1,848,000 had been paid, made for a total of $5,352,000 in Soviet bonds, which were partly repaid and partly returned by agreement by the end of 1940. The 1933 agreement was, of course, extremely favorable to AMSOJEFS.
40. AJ 2, 4/14/34.
41. AJ 11, 4/30/31.
42. AJ 66, 10/8/31.
43. AJ 173, 2/14/32.
44. AJ 23, 1/26/35.
45. AJ 86, 6/20/35.
46. AJ 13, 6/15/35.
47. AJ 2, 11/12/31 (press conference).
48. AJ 86, 6/20/35.
49. AJ 99.
50. Ibid.
51. AJ 35a.
52. AJ 22.
53. AJ 25, 2/20/40.
54. AJ 66, 10/8/31.
55. AJ 62a, February 1938.
56. Executive Committee, 9/20/38.
57. *Palestine Post,* 3/3/38.
58. AJ—uncatalogued materials; file: Russia, settlement of emigrants, 1935, draft verbatim notes of informal meeting, 6/15/35, Rosen's speech, p. 3.
59. AJ 2, reports, résumé by M.A. Leavitt, 3/20/45.

60. Based on AJ 2, reports, résumé by B. Hahn, 10/31/44; ibid., statement of Russian activities, 3/16/34; file 35a, report by M.C. Troper, 12/10/36.

CHAPTER 3

1. Arthur Hays Sulzberger to Max J. Kohler, 5/29/33, CON 21.
2. James N. Rosenberg at Board of Directors meeting, 7/11/33.
3. Dr. Bernhard Kahn at an Executive Committee meeting, 6/27/33.
4. Kahn cable to New York, 3/19/33, 14–47.
5. Eduard Baerwald to New York, 3/19/33, ibid.
6. Kahn to New York, 4/1/33, ibid.
7. Meeting at the home of Paul Baerwald, 4/6/33, ibid.
8. F. M. Warburg to Lord Reading, 4/22/33, ibid.
9. 25—Hilfsverein der deutschen Juden, Dr. Kahn's material, 1931–40, memo of 6/27/33.
10. J. C. Hyman to Judge Irving Lehman, 7/14/33, R19.
11. Kahn, 4/28/33, 14–47.
12. See K. Y. Ball-Kaduri, "The National Representation of Jews in Germany," in *Yad Vashem Studies* (Jerusalem, 1958), 2:159 ff.; Max Grunewald, "The Beginning of the Reichsvertretung," in *Leo Baeck Yearbook* (London, 1956), 1:57 ff. See also Leo Baeck's reminiscences in the same volume.
13. Werner Senator, 8/15/33: "Bemerkungen zu einem wirtschaftlichen Verhandlungsprogram der deutschen Juden," 14–47.
14. Dr. Joseph A. Rosen to Kahn, June 1933, Executive Committee meetings.
15. See note 9 above.
16. From 29—ZA statistical section, 1933 reports. A total of 61.33 percent of German Jews were engaged in trade, and 24.4 percent in industry and crafts. A further 5.6 percent were professionals. Of the 160,000 people who were engaged in trade, more than half, 89,368, were owners of trading establishments, 52,869 were employees, and only 2,913 were workers; 14,956 were family members of the owners.
17. "The Position of the Jews in Germany," 4/28/33, 14–47.
18. Lutz-Eugen Reutter, *Die Hilfstätigkeit katholischer Organisationen und kirchlicher Stellen für die im naz.-soz. Deutschland Verfolgten,* 2d ed. (Hamburg, 1970), p. 9.
19. Werner Rosenstock, "Exodus 1933–1939," in *Leo Baeck Yearbook* (London, 1956), 1:373–90. The author bases his article on one by Dr. Kurt Zielenzieger in the December 1937 issue of the London journal *Population.*

20. Mitteilungen an die jüdischen Reformgemeinde zu Berlin, 5/1/33, 26—Gen. & Emerg. Germany, "J".
21. *CV-Zeitung,* 5/9/35, and *Jewish Chronicle,* 5/24/35.
22. *Jewish Chronicle,* 10/11/35, p. 11.
23. Memorandum, Hyman to Paul Baerwald, 4/23/35, 14–46.
24. Executive Committee, 5/4/36.
25. J.C. Hyman in annual report, 1934; and Executive Committee, 10/9/35, speech by Hyman.
26. Executive Committee, 1/4/34, speech by Dr. Kahn.
27. J. A. Rosen at Board of Directors, 6/13/34.
28. "Summary of Activities of JDC since 1933" (11/25/35), pamphlet. Also, Jonah B. Wise's "Report on the Situation of Jews in Germany" (February 1934), pamphlet, where he says, "The half million Jews still in Germany realize that for the great mass of them, their fate and future lie within Germany."
29. Executive Committee, 1/4/34.
30. Executive Committee, 5/22/35.
31. J.C. Hyman to Oscar Janowsky, 11/24/37, R13.
32. *Jewish Chronicle,* 2/24/33.
33. Based on Nathan Reich, *Primer,* p. 98; draft report for 1936—R13; and Hyman's report to the National Council of JDC, 4/13/35.
34. Werner T. Angress, "Auswandererlehrgut Gross-Breesen," in *Leo Baeck Yearbook* (1965), 10:168 ff.
35. David J. Schweitzer at Board of Directors, 1/4/36; "Training and Retraining outside Germany", 8–1; and "Statement of Reconstructive and Emigration Activities Carried on in Germany," no date, 14–64.
36. Statistics, R43.
37. Memo of Arbeitsgemeinschaft für Kinder-und Jugendalijah to ZA, 7/14/33, 14–48.
38. Hyman to Billikopf, 1/18/34, 14–54.
39. Dr. Lowenstein at Executive Committee, 5/22/35; and 24—German Jewish children's aid, 1934–44.
40. Executive Committee, 4/14/37.
41. Kahn to Baerwald, 2/23/34, 14–58.
42. *Primer,* p. 98; see also 1934 annual report.
43. An ordinance against the attendance of Jewish children in German schools was published on April 1, 1936, but was not rigidly enforced for quite some time after that.
44. Kahn, "Report and Bulletin," January 1936, R15; out of the total amount collected in Germany by all Jewish organizations, Kahn estimated that 8 million marks were given to "welfare," presumably child care, medical care, old age care, and relief.

45. Memo on JDC activities in behalf of German Jewry, 10/24/33, 14–47.

46. Executive Committee, 5/25/33.

47. 14–47.

48. 14–46; and Warburg archives at Cincinnati (hereafter, WAC), Box 316 (d), interview of James G. McDonald with Dr. Fritz Dreyser, vice-president of the Reichsbank. It was apparently at this meeting that the final details were thrashed out and the Germans consented to the implementation of the scheme.

49. Based on the following main sources: 28–30—ZA reports for 1935 and 1936; 28–3 for the 1937 RV (ZA) budget; R22—ZA report for 1934; R19—annual report for 1933; R16—annual report for 1934, and Kahn's report for 1934, 1/3/35; R15—Kahn's "bulletin" for I.1936; R13—draft of 1936 report, 5/28/37, and Baerwald's letter to F. M. Warburg, 3/3/37; Executive Committee meetings of 1/4/34, 3/6/35, 2/10/36, 12/9/37; summary by E. M. M. Morrissey on 3/2/36 in WAC, Box 345 (a). The figures unfortunately show fairly wide discrepancies, sometimes of over $10,000. The problem of the exchange rates had a great deal to do with this; we have relied chiefly on summaries made after the close of each year, for internal purposes, and have disregarded claims made in public.

50. Kahn to JDC, September 1938, 9–27.

51. 22—Gen. & Emerg. Germany, AFSC.

52. 29—Gen. & Emerg. Germany, nonsectarian relief.

53. 15–32.

54. 15–3 (10/26/36); 25—Gen. & Emerg. Germany, INTRIA, esp. Kahn's letter to Hyman, 8/25/36.

55. Ibid.

56. Ibid.

57. *Primer,* p. 97; 24—Gen. & Emerg. Germany, Foundation, 1933–39; 26—Gen. & Emerg. Germany, Lists, etc. 1935/6; 28–30—ZA report, 1936.

58. Kahn report, 3/28/34, in WAC, Box 321 (b).

59. *CV-Blaetter für Deutschtum und Judentum,* 1/10/35, by Dr. Emil Herzfeld. (Fate played a trick on Dr. Herzfeld: ultimately he had to settle in Palestine, where he lived out his days in national Jewish Tel Aviv.) The declaration in support of Hitler's foreign policy was made in November 1933; see Grunewald, op. cit., pp. 57 ff.

60. Executive Committee, 3/26/35; Hyman said in his contribution to a summary for 1934 (R53): "The hope of Jewish leaders to find an orderly, constructive transformation of a segment of Jewish life, especially for the youth, within the borders of Germany itself, to be supplemented by a carefully nurtured preparation of waves of annual emigration, has

been disappointed, since training is permitted only for emigration, immediate or ultimate." B. C. Vladeck, a Labor member of the JDC Executive Committee, put a socialist interpretation on the same ideas when, in a discussion with the Zionist Berl Locker (12/23/35—WAC, Box 323 [d]), he said that "there is a vast underground movement in Germany of 'Aryans,' socialists, etc., who are fighting the Fascist regime and that the Jew must fight along with them." Therefore, the task of progressive Jews in Germany was to stay where they were.

61. *Jewish Chronicle*, 1/13/35. On the eighteenth, the *Chronicle* reported that a man named Herr Fischel had come all the way from Buenos Aires, his fare paid by the German consulate, to vote for Germany.

62. Ibid., 1/11/35. Interview of *La Croix* with Naumann.

63. P. 11, in an article called "Eine Nummer des Stuermer."

64. *CV-Zeitung*, 1/31/35.

65. Ibid., "Zur Wahrung unserer Ehre bleibt uns nichts als feierlicher Protest."

66. Ibid., 2/14/35, p. 11.

67. Quoted in *Jewish Chronicle*, 3/15/35.

68. *Informationsblätter der RV*, 9/22/35.

69. *Jewish Chronicle*, 5/17/35, quoting *Der Völkische Beobachter*.

70. Executive Committee, 9/23/37.

71. Hyman to Janowsky, 11/24/37, R13.

72. The statistics are taken from an article by Max Birnbaum in the *Jüdisches Gemeindeblatt für die Synagogengemeinden in Preussen und Norddeutschland*, 4/4/1938. Hyman to Kahn, 10/11/35, CON. 2; Hyman explained his position in an article published in the 1937 *Proceedings* of the National Conference of Jewish Social Welfare in the *Jewish Social Service Quarterly* (R12). Non-Zionists, he said, see nothing wrong in supporting Communism if this would help millions of Jews to find their feet in a new Russian economy; at the same time they can support "the building up of a great Jewish settlement of refuge and of cultural development in Palestine and yet decline to regard themselves as actually or potentially elements of a Jewish nation with its center in Palestine." While Palestine was capable of absorbing masses of immigrants, they do "deprecate the constant emphasis on Palestine by certain groups," as a Jewish national movement. The major goal of non-Zionists was "the integration of Jews with the life of their lands of birth or adoption."

73. Kahn to Hyman, 11/3/35, CON 2.

74. 28–30—ZA report 1938.

75. Felix M. Warburg at a meeting at the home of Ittleson, 4/29/37, R13.

76. Executive Committee, 1/20/38; Kahn on Germany, WAC, Box 327 (c), November 1935.

CHAPTER 4

1. R17, 10/19/34—JDC memorandum from Paris to JDC Allocation Committee; this stated that in 1933, 59,300 persons had fled, of whom 51,000 were Jews. By April 1934 these figures were reported to have grown to 63,400 and 54,500 respectively. The JDC Report for 1933 (R19) says that 52,365 Jews fled Germany in 1933.

2. See chapter 3, note 19.

3. Norman Bentwich, *They Found Refuge* (London, 1965), pp. 14 ff.

4. Charles J. Liebman reported to Warburg on August 30, 1933 (WAC, Box 303 [c]), that the British had so far raised an average of $3 per British Jew, compared to $.50 for French Jews and $.24 for U.S. Jews.

5. Comité National de Secours aux Réfugiés Allemands.

6. L (JDC Library) 13—report for 1933 and the first months of 1934.

7. *Foreign Relations of the United States* (1933), 3:366.

8. WAC, Box 303 (b), Morgenthau to Hull, 10/18/33.

9. 14–47, 10/12/33, 10/13/33.

10. The High Commission's budget in 1934/5 was $138,000, of which JDC covered $41,250 (CBF contributed $21,250; ICA, $40,000; the rest was paid by UPA and some smaller contributors).

11. 14–46, 1/17/34, memo of Nathan Katz.

12. WAC, Box 316 (b); Norman Bentwich, British Zionist and McDonald's deputy, was said to have stated that the power to control Jewish affairs must not be vested in a small group of American Jews.

13. WAC, Box 316 (e), 11/17/34, McDonald to Cecil.

14. See above, p. 126.

15. WAC, Box 316 (a), 7/7/34, report by McDonald. Of the 7,500 persons, 600–700 were academic teachers, 5,200–5,500 were professionals (engineers, doctors, lawyers, etc.), and the rest were students.

16. On ECF and REC, see 28–1; Executive Committee, 9/20/34; R52 (current reports). By the end of 1938 ECF had spent a total of $136,072, and REC, $463,297. REC's ventures included the purchase of forty-five thousand acres of land in Costa Rica, at the instance of Samuel Zamurray, president of the United Fruit Company. This land had to be sold again after it was discovered that it was not suitable for settlement. REC also supported the International Student Service in Geneva and gave some small sums of money to HICEM for the transportation of refugees to Latin America.

17. 14–46, 8/31/34, Goldsmid to Schiff; also Executive Committee file, meeting at the Harmonie Club, 6/14/35.

18. R16; HICEM's budget in 1934 was $428,500, of which ICA covered $179,500, and JDC $165,000.

19. *Jewish Chronicle,* 4/10/36, article by Dr. Arthur Ruppin, in the special supplement, p. v. The period covered by Ruppin's statistics was April 1933 to October 1935.

20. WAC, Box 321 (b), 2/3/34.

21. R14, 1935 JDC report.

22. WAC, Box 316 (c), McDonald to Warburg, 5/5/34.

23. WAC, Box 304 (c), Warburg to Goldsmid, 10/26/33.

24. 14–46, Hyman to Rosenberg, 4/13/34.

25. Arthur D. Morse, *While Six Million Died* (New York, 1968), p. 135.

26. WAC, Box 324 (a), McDonald to Warburg, 10/29/34.

27. WAC, Box 336 (c), 11/1/35.

28. Ibid.

29. There is no mention of Roosevelt's letter in Morse's book.

30. Morse, op. cit., pp. 189–90; also WAC, Box 324 (a), exchange of letters between McDonald and Warburg, 10/10/35, 10/21/35.

31. WAC, Box 316 (d), McDonald to Warburg, 8/16/34.

32. JDC Library, London meeting of governing body, 11/1–2/34.

33. R16.

34. WAC, Box 323 (c), Kahn to Warburg, 10/30/35.

35. WAC, Box 324 (a), McDonald to Mrs. Roosevelt, 7/24/35.

36. WAC, Box 324 (a), McDonald to Warburg, 9/9/35.

37. Dated 12/27/35; see *Jewish Chronicle,* 1/3/35.

38. Quoted in Morse, op. cit., p. 191.

39. Dr. Kahn's material, file Hilfsverein, 1932–1935, Kahn to Hyman, 5/11/34.

40. Gen. & Emerg. Germany, refugees 1934/5, German Commission report (translated), signed by Prof. Georg Bernhard, Dr. Sammy Gronemann, and Dr. Oscar Cohn, among others.

41. R22, 1934 draft report.

42. R16, Kahn report, 1/3/35.

43. Executive Committee, 1/7/35; cf. also 1/4/34.

44. See note 39 above; Kahn letter, 10/26/34.

45. R16, JDC monthly bulletin, nos. 1 & 2, 3/6/35; ibid., nos. 3 & 4, 6/3/35.

46. R14, Kahn's report for 1935, Jan. 1936.

47. In Paris there had been a committee known as the Assistance

Medicale aux Enfants run by a lady doctor, a refugee from Germany, with the help of her lover, another German refugee. She used the name of the Baroness de Rothschild for raising money without bothering to inform that lady of the fact, and provided medical assistance to some twelve hundred infants and small children (R16, May 1935 report). She also received some JDC funds. One day her lover's wife turned up and found the couple at the Assistance Medicale. The lovers escaped through the window, the wife committed suicide, the baroness discovered that for two years she had been the head of a fairly well-known institution, and the Assistance Medicale dissolved. What happened to the children who had received its help is not recorded (R15, Kahn to Morrissey, 3/1/36). Similarly, an organization called Renouveau, purporting to train youngsters under the influence of religious Zionism, came to an ignominious end (28–9).

48. Dr. Kahn's material, file Hilfsverein, 1936–1939, Kahn to Baerwald, 6/18/36.

49. WAC, Box 324 (a), McDonald to Warburg, 11/21/35.

50. 15–7, for a summary of the correspondence and reports on the delegation's visit. See also Bentwich, op. cit., pp. 30 ff. The origins of the plan can be traced to May 1935 at least, when a similar plan was submitted to JDC by Max Kreutzberger, secretary of ZA (Executive Committee, 5/22/35). He spoke of an emigration of fifteen to twenty thousand annually, half of whom would go to Palestine. The idea seems therefore to have emanated from German Jewry itself and been accepted by McDonald, who then obtained the agreement of CBF leaders in London to support it.

51. Ibid.

52. Executive Committee, 2/10/36; 15–11, Rosenwald memo, 2/1/36. Cf. also *Forverts,* 2/17/35.

53. 15–3, Kahn to New York, 4/3/36; Baerwald to Samuel, 4/7/36; Warburg to Bentwich, 4/6/36. As to Warburg's statement that the British had allocated all their funds to Palestine, the situation by the end of October 1936 was that of the 721,035 pounds collected by them in Britain, 392,000 pounds had been allocated, of which 51 percent went to Palestine (see Council of German Jewry, interim report, 10/30/36, JDC Library). Cf. also Executive Committee, 5/4/36.

54. JC—1/10/36, 1/31/36.

55. Executive Committee, 7/2/36, report by David Bressler.

56. Executive Committee, 4/14/36.

57. R13, Warburg at a meeting at the St. Regis Hotel, 4/29/37; Executive Committee, 9/27/37.

58. WAC, Box 252, Marshall to Weizmann, 12/4/29.

59. WAC, Box 252, Warburg to Magnes, 10/9/29.

60. Files 107–17 (period up to 1933).

61. R10, report of the Emergency Fund, 1936, by Maurice Hexter. Cf. also interview with Judge Jonah J. Goldstein (H).

62. Sources: 15–2, Max Birnbaum; Rosenstock, op. cit, pp. 15–32, HOG report on immigration to Palestine. The figures included "tourists" who stayed on in Palestine and were later legalized by the government. If we combine the above figures with those in Table 7, we will see that Palestine absorbed approximately 18.4 percent of total Jewish emigration from Germany in 1933, 36.8 percent in 1934, 35.4 percent in 1935, 31.5 percent in 1936, 14.2 percent in 1937, and 12 percent in 1938. The figures may have to be revised upwards very slightly to take into account illegal immigration to Palestine in those years. Between 1933 and the end of 1938 about 165,000 Jews left Germany, and of these about 45,000, or 27.2 percent, entered Palestine.

63. 14–51, CBF Allocation Committee meeting, 5/7/34.

64. 42—Palestine immigration, 1938–43.

65. 42—Palestine, general, 1933–38.

66. 15–32.

67. 14–46, Statement of Policy, 4/20/34.

68. JDC Library, National Council meeting, 4/13/35.

69. Executive Committee, 9/23/37.

70. Zosa Szajkowski, "Budgeting American Overseas Relief, 1919–1939," *American Jewish Historical Quarterly* 59, no. 1 (September 1969): 87 ff., 110.

71. Ibid., p. 88, quoting from letter of Caroline Flexner (10/29/35) to Herbert H. Lehman. Also Executive Committee, 10/9/35.

72. Joseph C. Hyman, "Jewish Problems and Activities Overseas," *Proceedings* of the National Conference of Jewish Social Welfare, 1937.

73. Morse, op. cit.; Henry L. Feingold, *Politics of Rescue* (New Brunswick, N.J., 1969); David S. Wyman, *Paper Walls* (Amherst, Mass., 1968).

74. See Germany—AFSC file.

75. R13, 1936 draft report, and ibid., 1937 and 1938 reports.

76. R19. For statistical material on Holland, see also JDC report for 1934, and JDC report for 1933 and the first months of 1934, both in the JDC Library. Also R16, monthly bulletin nos. 1 & 2, 3/6/35.

77. 30—Germany, refugees 1934/5, van Tijn memo, 7/22/34.

78. Ibid., Kahn report, 8/22/34.

79. Oral testimony (H) of Mrs. van Tijn (1968). Cf. also Mrs. van

Tijn's memoirs (manuscript), p. 8; thanks are hereby expressed for permission to use this valuable source.

80. Germany, organizations and institutions, "C"—Holland, letter to Kahn, 1/7/34. Executive Committee, 3/26/35, where Jonah B. Wise declared that the Dutch Committee "needs assistance and should get it. They work efficiently and constructively." See also R14, Kahn's report for 1935, in January 1936; and sources in note 79 above.

81. Sources: 34—Germany, refugees in Holland, 1941/2; Holland—report 1936. It appears that these figures included a part of HICEM expenditures in Holland, because JDC contributed to HICEM expenses. Between 1933 and 1936 the total expenditure of the Dutch Committee came to 1,690,537 Dutch guilders, of which JDC's direct contribution came to 334,677, or 20 percent. HICEM's expenses came to 189,608, and CBF contributed 57,040; the rest was covered by money raised from Dutch Jewry.

82. 31—Refugees, 1939/42; for other figures quoted in the text, see Executive Committee, 11/24/36, and sources for Table 10.

83. Expenditures in 1934 came to $16,589; these had risen to $94,000 in 1938, and jumped to $649,000 in 1939 (34—Germany, refugees in Holland, 1941/2).

84. R9, JDC report: "Aid to Jews Overseas," 1939 and the first six months of 1940; and 31—Refugees, 1939–1942.

85. Gertrude van Tijn, "Werkdorf Nieuwesluis," in *Leo Baeck Yearbook* (London, 1969), 14:182–99.

86. Carl Ludwig, *Die Flüchtlingspolitik der Schweiz seit 1933 bis zur Gegenwart, Bericht an den Bundesrat* (Zurich, n. d. [1957]), p. 60.

87. Ibid., p. 65.

88. SIG, Festschrift zum 50 jährigen Bestehen (Zurich, n. d. [1954]), p. 13 (Dr. Leo Littmann, 50 Jahre Gemeindebund).

89. Ludwig, op. cit., p. 55.

90. Ibid., pp. 59–60.

91. Ibid., p. 69. Ludwig shows that this was not the only case when such statements were made by Swiss Jewish leaders.

92. Ibid., p. 70.

93. R14, Kahn report of January 1936 for 1935. About three hundred persons were actually being cared for, on the average, by VSIA. JDC expenditures in Switzerland came to $7,010 in 1935, $4,200 in 1936, and $4,935 in 1937. Some hospitals and cultural enterprises were supported.

94. R16, monthly bulletin, March-April 1935.

95. Executive Committee, 3/26/35.

96. JDC Library 13, 1933/4 report. See also Kurt R. Grossmann,

Emigration (Frankfurt, 1969), pp. 41 ff. Also R14, Kahn report for 1935.

97. 12–14, report by Neville Laski, 10/15/34.

98. Ibid., report 11/4/37.

99. Ibid., Kahn at a meeting in Paris, 12/12/37: "Man darf nicht zeigen, und dies besonders in Danzig wegen dessen internationaler Lage, dass sobald die Juden durch die Regierung bedrückt werden, gleich jüdische Organisationen zur Stelle sind, die mithelfen, dass die Juden den Platz räumen."

100. Ibid., Giterman report of 12/30/38: "A Jewish community has started the dangerous adventure of deporting their own members from Danzig." Giterman warned JDC "not to assume any responsibility for this adventure." The text of this document is an English translation of the original, which is missing.

101. Eliahu Stern's Ph.D. thesis at the Hebrew University, on the Danzig community, should clarify these points before long.

CHAPTER 5

1. A. Tartakower, "Yiddishe Politik und Yiddishe Kultur in Poilen," in *Allgemeine Encyclopedie*, article "Yiden." See also *Jewish Chronicle*, 9/28/36, p. 24, where figures for the 1936 communal elections show that the Bund obtained fifteen out of forty-six seats, various Zionist parties got eighteen, and the Agudah, ten.

2. R14, Kahn material, November 1936; and Hans Roos, *Geschichte der Polnischen Nation 1916–1960* (Stuttgart, 1961), p. 144. Poland's economic policy had not changed since the late 1920s; it was still wedded to the idea of a state capitalism, and it continued to utilize government monopolies to evict Jews from their occupations.

3. *Jewish Chronicle*, 3/22/35, p. 22.

4. Ibid., 12/20/35, 1/17/36. R61—report on Poland, February 1939, 46—report 1938; special bulletin of AJC, 2/1/38.

5. Large amounts of material on the pogroms are available at the JDC archives, files R13, R52, R60, 8–21, 14–5, 46—reports 1936, 1937, 1938. See also WAC, Boxes 345 and 366. The quotation is taken from Kahn's report, 6/7/37, in R52. See also *Jewish Chronicle* 4/19, 5/3, 5/10, 6/14, 9/6, 11/2, 12/6, 12/13/35; 3/13, 3/27/36; et seq.

6. R13—Hyman's report to the Budget and Scope Committee, 6/27/37; see also WAC, Box 366 (a).

7. *New York Times*, 2/7/37; R10—American Jewish Committee review of the European situation, 3/30/39 (by Moses Moskowitz).

8. WAC, Box 366 (f).

9. "Jews have been deserting many villages en masse and going to the cities, their property burned down and their very lives endangered"—JDC Executive Committee (ECO), 9/23/37.

10. 44–3, cable 3/20/38; ibid., 8–21.

11. R61, February 1939.

12. JDC, 45—publicity, Warszawski Dziennik Narodowy, 4/14/38; R28—*Fortnightly Digest,* no. 14 (5/1/38, et seq.).

13. See note 11 above.

14. 45—publicity, bulletin, 3/10/30; thus a bloody pogrom in Dobrzyn caused "many Jews to be wounded," etc.; at the same time the pogroms did not cease elsewhere.

15. 44–4, memo, 5/1/39.

16. 46—reports 1936/7—Catholic Press Agency statement, 1/25/36, Moskowitz-Schneiderman report, March 1937.

17. Lukomski in *Sprawy Katolicke,* Lomza, 11/10/36, and Kerwalski in *Gazetta Swiateczna,* no. 2915 (1936); 46—report.

18. CON-17, 7/1/38, memo by Raymond L. Bull of the Foreign Policy Association to the American Jewish Committee.

19. R14, Kahn material, November 1936; Raphael Mahler, *Jews in Poland between the Two World Wars* (Hebrew) (Tel Aviv, 1968), p. 15.

20. 44–29, memo 1/30/39.

21. R50, "Situation of the Jews in Eastern Europe," memo of the Paris JDC office, June 1938. The figure of 3,310,000 appears in "General Survey of Political and Economic Conditions in Poland in 1938" (12/3/38), in 46—report 1938.

22. Mahler, op. cit., pp. 46 ff. Only 37 percent of the Jews were economically active, compared to 42.5 percent of the non-Jews (excluding agriculture). This meant that given the same income, the Jew was worse off because he had to feed more mouths. Seen in another way, this was a form of concealed unemployment.

23. The total in industry and handicrafts were 506,990. Without the workers, there were 229,435. This included 22,367 home workers. The total number of Jewish employers was 75,362. This figure included industrialists. By all accounts, therefore, the number of Jewish artisans cannot have been less and was probably more than 200,000.

24. WAC, Box 323 (c), Kahn's report on Poland, 5/22/35.

25. Rabbi Schorr of Warsaw in the *Jewish Chronicle,* 1/18/35, p. 20: "Not less than one-third of the entire Jewish population of Poland was today dependent on charity in some form or other."

26. *Jewish Chronicle,* 1/8/37.

27. JDC Library—American Federation of Polish Jews, 25th annual convention, June 11–12, 1933.

28. Abraham G. Duker, "The Situation of the Jews in Poland," *Newsletter* of the Conference on Jewish Relations, April 1936.

29. 44–4, memorandum re Poland, 5/1/39.

30. 44–6.

31. R14, November 1936, Schweitzer report.

32. See note 29 above.

33. "The Mourner at the Marriage Fete," October 1936, in WAC, Box 366 (c).

34. 45—CENTOS, report, October 1937.

35. R16, 11/23/1935, "Notes and Source Material for Committee on Poland and Eastern Europe."

36. R17—Hyman's draft report to the Executive Committee, 8/24/34.

37. R15—Backer report, 4/27/36.

38. 44–3—Kahn to Baerwald, 1/17/37.

39. R13, Hyman to Budget and Scope, 6/27/37.

40. *Jewish Chronicle,* 5/15/36, p. 19.

41. Executive Committee, 5/18/37. Hyman to Oscar Janowsky, 11/24/37, R13.

42. 46—reports 1936/7, October 1936 (the name of the delegate was Tytus Komarinski); and ITA, 12/12/36.

43. R14, press release, 2/1/36.

44. Marcell Olivier, "Madagascar—Terre d'Asile?," *Illustration,* February 19, 1938, pp. 197–98.

45. ITA, 12/6/37; 44–29 Rosen and Kahn to Liebman, 6/12/37.

46. CON-2, 8/18/36, Rosen to Lehman.

47. 44–29, HICEM report.

48. About thirty thousand a year.

49. Conversation between Potocki, Waldman, and Hyman, 6/8/38, CON-2.

50. Conversation between Gruszka, Kahn, and Hyman, 10/17/37, CON-2.

51. 44–6—Neville Laski report, August 1934.

52. R10, Troper report, 2/17/39.

53. Between 1932 and 1934, 745,000 zloty were granted in credits and 2,394,000 zloty received in repayment (46—reports 36/7, memorandum of 9/30/37).

54. R60, report of 4/18/39.

55. Raphael Szereszewsky, quoted in a report of the Reconstruction Foundation, 5/22/36, WAC, Box 347 (d).

56. 44–21, Alexander Kahn report, 12/9/37.

57. Polish initials for the Central Society for Free Credit and Furthering of Productive Work among the Jewish Population in Poland.

58. The figures are rather problematic. There are divergencies in the reports and between one report and another. It must be remembered that there were self-help institutions approximating the JDC-supported *kassas* in almost every locality, and many of these were not recognized by CEKABE. Reports from the localities were not always accurate.

59. Kahn to Warburg, 5/11/35, 15–33; and 44–5, Baerwald memo, 9/18/35.

60. 46—report 1938. In 1937 Jacob Lestschinsky produced an industrialization plan of Polish Jewry for Simon Marks, which was based on the same principles as Kahn's plans: "Not to save the weak and unsound, but to fortify and strengthen the sound and secure positions." The plan would cost $4 million, of which $3 million would come from abroad. See 44–21, Committee on Poland, 12/9/37.

61. Kahn's lecture at Cincinnati, 1/10/38, R12.

62. R15, 3/29/36, Kahn report.

63. 14–39.

64. 44–21, Kahn's letter, 7/25/39.

65. Executive Committee, 3/26/35.

66. R17, letter by Kahn, 11/3/34.

67. All the figures are taken from a detailed report by Neustadt, dated 5/10/36, "Jewish Private and Public Instruction in Poland," 46—reports.

68. 44–21, Committee on Poland, 4/11/39.

69. From $44,000 to $121,000.

70. *New York Times,* 11/26/39.

71. R62; the budget for 1937 was 3,767,565 lei; JDC participation in this came to 638,382 lei.

72. "The Era of Violence," *The New Cambridge Modern History,* 12:49.

73. Executive Committee, 12/20/35; R15, "Report and Bulletin," January and April 1936. *Jewish Chronicle,* 1/3/36.

74. Kahn to Hyman, 1/15/36, Gen. & Emerg. Romania, 1933–37.

75. In 1934 the foundation invested $36,820 in Poland and $156,349 in Romania. In 1935, $137,500 was invested in Romania; in 1936, $220,-000.

76. R50, "Situation of the Jews in Eastern Europe," report for June 1938; 32.8 percent of the Jews were engaged in industry, 4.1 percent in agriculture, and 2.7 percent in the professions.

77. R48, report from Romania, 1/19/37; R16, Kahn report, 11/19/35.

78. Ibid.
79. R48, Nathan Katz to Hyman, 2/2/38.
80. 48—Gen. & Emerg. Romania, general, 1938–39, 4/28/38; report of Kahn and Schweitzer on meetings in Bucharest.
81. Ibid., for correspondence with the State Department in June and August 1938. See especially 5/27/38, memorandum by Paul Baerwald. Executive Committee, 5/19/39, Hyman's report.
82. Ibid., memorandum re legalization of social welfare activity in Romania, 3/1/39.
83. Ibid.
84. R11, memorandum of December 1938.
85. WJC submitted a sharply worded memorandum to a subcommittee of the League of Nations that was supposed to investigate complaints regarding the treatment of Jews in Romania, 3/1/39.
86. Speech by Joseph C. Hyman at the JDC National Council, 9/18/38.
87. 48—Gen. & Emerg. Romania, general, Troper to JDC, New York, 1/13/39.
88. JDC report for 1933.
89. R46, reports for January 1939. The population statistics are taken from Erno Laszlo, "Hungary's Jewry: A Demographic Overview, 1918–1945," in *Hungarian Jewish Studies,* ed. Randolph L. Braham (New York, 1969), 2:157–58.
90. 41—Gen. & Emerg. Lithuania 1937–41—report, 10/1/37.
91. In 1937 JDC spent $24,824 in Lithuania.
92. See *Farn Folks-Gesundt,* (Kovno, 1937), published by OSE. OSE's income decreased by 27 percent between 1932 and 1935, with corresponding decreases in expenditure; but a JDC report in 1935 reported 40.5 percent anemic and undernourished children, as against 33.5 percent in 1932 (R16, May 1935).
93. R16, Kahn, on 11/19/35. There were a ritual murder accusation and a pogrom in 1935 (at Telsiai). See *Jewish Chronicle,* 4/19/35, 10/18/35.

CHAPTER 6

1. Herbert Rosenkranz, "The Anschluss and the Tragedy of Austrian Jewry, 1938–1945," in *The Jews of Austria,* ed. Josef Frankel (London, 1967), p. 486.
2. Ibid., p. 480.
3. Ibid., p. 481.

4. 14–51, report, 2/7/34; 8–18, report, 2/28/34, and other material in that file; see also R62.

5. For the significance of the term "parasite" as applied to the Jews by the Nazis, see Alexander Bein, "The Jewish Parasite," *Leo Baeck Yearbook* (London, 1964), 9:3–40.

6. Julius Streicher, the notorious anti-Semite, published a lead article entitled "Madagaskar" in the January 1938 (no. 1) issue of his *Der Stürmer,* together with a cartoon of a Jew being driven from the world under the caption "DAS ENDE" (The End).

7. 38—Germany, reports, 1937–1944, report for October 1937.

8. Ibid., Nathan Katz report of 8/25/38, where he says that there were seventeen to eighteen hundred such victims. Rosenkranz (op. cit., p. 488) says the victims mentioned were prominent Jews who had been blacklisted and arrested within two days; they were sent to Dachau on May 30. It seems that Katz was referring to the same group. As to the figure of twenty thousand emigration applications, a report of 8/31/45 (Saly Mayer files 16), apparently written by Löwenherz, puts them at forty thousand by 5/20/38; Rosenkranz, p. 491.

9. 8–21, Baerwald to Wise, 3/16/38.

10. Ibid., Baerwald letters, 4/6/38 and 4/19/38.

11. Executive Committee, file, Budget and Scope Committee, 9/18/38. Morse, op. cit., p. 205.

12. 8–21, Baerwald to Wise, 3/16/38.

13. R11, C.M. Levy, report on a trip to Vienna, 12/1/38–12/8/38.

14. R55.

15. JDC's total expenditure in 1938 came to $4,112,979.

16. Germany—"G," institutions and organizations.

17. Sources: *Fortnightly Digest,* 24/25 and R28, 1938 report. The relief problem in Austria had some troublesome implications. In "old" Germany the government was at that time still supporting Jewish relief to the extent of about 600,000–700,000 marks monthly. In Austria, JDC and other foreign organizations were expected to foot the bill. If they did, the Germans might demand that they do it in Germany as well; if they did not, the Jewish poor would starve and be deported to concentration camps as "asocial elements." The upshot, of course, was that JDC paid.

18. Germany—ICA, Troper memo, 12/26/38.

19. Helmuth Krausnick, "Judenverfolgung," in Martin Broszat et al., *Die Anatomie des SS-Staates* (Olten and Freiburg, 1965), 2:341.

20. CON-48, Jaretzki report, 7/3/38.

21. Ludwig, op. cit., p. 75.

22. Ibid., p. 76.

23. Ibid., p. 82, footnote 1. Ludwig says (p. 83) that there were three to four thousand Austrian Jewish immigrants in Switzerland before April 1.

24. Ibid., p. 84.

25. Morse, op. cit., pp. 203–4.

26. Wyman, op. cit., p. 44; Michael Mashberg, "America and the Refugee Crisis" (M.A. thesis, City University of New York, 1970).

27. 9–44, memorandum on White House conference on refugees, 4/13/38; see also Morse, op. cit., p. 204.

28. 8–21, meeting of 3/28/38.

29. Executive Committee, 4/20/38.

30. The official protocols of the Evian Conference are kept in 9–28. Winterton said, 7/15/38, on Palestine: "Il est apparu indispensable, non pas sans doute l'interrompre l'immigration juive—ce qui n'a jamais eté envisagé—mais de l'assujetir à certaines restrictions d'un caractère purement temporaire et exceptionnel, ayant pour but de maintenir, dans les limites raisonnables, la population dans les rapports numeriques actuels, en attendant une décision définitive . . . relativement à l'avenir politique du pays"—a clear foreshadowing of the British move away from the partition proposal of 1937 toward the 1939 White Paper on Palestine. See Morse, op. cit., pp. 212–13; Wyman, op. cit., pp. 49–50; and Mashberg, op. cit.

31. 9–27, Brotman to Laski, no date [July 1938?].

32. See note 30 above and Ludwig, op. cit., p. 84, footnote 1.

33. 9–28, and Wyman, op. cit., pp. 49–50.

34. 9–28, Brotman memo, 7/16/38. According to Brotman, who represented the British Board of Deputies, representatives of governments were apt to be more liberal privately than in public speeches.

35. *New York Times,* 7/9/38.

36. CON-2, Warren to Chamberlain, 7/9/38.

37. For a fictionalized but essentially true account, see Hans Habe, *The Mission* (New York, 1966).

38. See note 31 above; Brotman added that Winterton's secretary was "doing her best to tell Lord Winterton that all Jews are not like those at the conference." The remark reveals the Briton's anti-Semitic instincts and the British Jew's feeling of inferiority rather than the failings of the Jewish organizations.

39. 9–27, informal meeting, 6/3/38.

40. Ibid., McDonald to Baerwald (telephone), 7/14/38.

41. Ibid., Katz to Baerwald, 8/9/38.

42. Morse, op. cit., pp. 218–19; Wyman, op. cit., pp. 51–52.

43. Executive Committee, Kahn to Budget and Scope Committee, 9/18/38.

44. R28, fortnightly digest, 10/15/37.

45. R62, meeting in Paris of 3/27/38.

46. R47, Comité pour la Defense des Israelites en Europe Centrale et Orientale, 3/24/39.

47. See below in the text, p. 243.

48. Morris D. Waldman, *Nor by Power* (New York, 1955), p. 82, quoting a report to the American Jewish Committee, 11/6/38.

49. Andrew Sharf, *The British Press and Jews under Nazi Rule* (Oxford, 1964), p. 171.

50. Ibid., p. 168.

51. Saly Mayer files (SM), VSIA-2.

52. Ludwig, op. cit., pp. 86–87.

53. Ibid., p. 90.

54. Saly Mayer's declaration at SIG in February 1938, SM, VSIA-2.

55. Ibid.

56. This was repeatedly stated in appeals to JDC from March 1938 on.

57. SM, VSIA-2.

58. Ibid.

59. 9–40, Baerwald to Kahn; and Administration Committee files (AC), 8/24/38.

60. SM, VSIA-2.

61. 9–38, for all the material on Luxemburg quoted in the text.

62. S. Adler-Rudel, *Ostjuden in Deutschland* (Tübingen, 1959), p. 166.

63. Ibid., p. 153. Raphael Mahler, "Ringelblum's Letters from and about Zbaszyn" (Hebrew), *Yalkut Moreshet* 2 (May 1964): 14 ff.

64. Germany—refugees in Poland, report: "The Activity of the General Aid Committee for Jewish Refugees from Germany in Poland, 11/1/38–7/1/39." The total collection was 3,543,299 zloty, of which JDC contributed 721,149, and other foreign sources, 539,725.

65. 29—Germany, Polish deportations, Zbaszyn, report by Giterman, November 1938.

66. Ibid., quoted by Hyman to Paris JDC, 1/20/39.

67. R10, report by Troper and Smoler, 12/2/38.

68. 44–3.

69. 44–21, Committee on Poland and East Europe, 2/8/39.

70. 44–29; Adler to Hyman, 2/9/39.

71. 14–39; report from Galicia.

72. 44–21, Committee on Poland and East Europe, 2/8/39.
73. 44–29; Troper to Hyman, 2/14/39; 44–4, memo on Poland, 5/1/39.
74. 44–3, Baerwald to Kahn, 1/28/37.
75. Executive Committee, 4/20/38; and confidential information given this author.
76. Broszat et al., op. cit., 2:94–95. According to Broszat, there were about ten thousand Jewish internees in each of the main camps at Dachau, Buchenwald, and Sachsenhausen. In his report (see note 78 below) Troper mentions an identical number of internees. Estimates by other sources are much higher, and are most probably incorrect.
77. E.g., Broszat et al., op. cit., 2:333 ff.; Gerald Reitlinger, *The Final Solution* (London, 1968); Morse, op. cit.; and other sources. Morse, by the way, is quite mistaken regarding the origins of the pogroms; he seems to think that they were organized by the SS, whereas in fact the SS "only" supervised security and arrested the victims; as a matter of fact, the whole affair was organized by Goebbels and the Nazi party. Cf. also Hilberg, op. cit., pp. 23 ff.; he puts the figure of the arrested at twenty thousand; but his sources are very doubtful (affidavit of an SS oficer in 1946 and a statement by Heydrich in a discussion with Göring). The figure quoted in the text is based on a report by Dr. Best in December 1938.
78. CON-2, Troper report, 11/30/38.
79. Broszat et al., op. cit., p. 335. Also: RGB (Reichsgesetzblatt), Verordnung zur Ausschaltung der Juden aus dem deutschen Wirtschaftsleben, 11/12/38.
80. Executive Committee, 11/28/38.
81. Executive Committee file, Budget and Scope Committee, 10/31/38.
82. R12, draft of public statement, 3/3/38.
83. Hyman at Executive Committee, 3/22/39.
84. R11, report on a visit to Germany, William Bein, 12/6/38.
85. R55, 12/14/38–12/15/38, meeting in Paris.
86. RV report for 1938. In May 1938 there were sixty-eight public and seventy-two private Jewish schools. In these private schools there were 9,844 pupils. An additional 10,156 pupils went to German or Jewish public schools. In July 1939 there were still 16,350 Jewish children in the age group six to fourteen in "old" Germany. I am indebted to my colleague Dr. Yosef Walk for these details.
87. 28–3, 1939 Arbeitsbericht.
88. Sources: Executive Committee, 4/19/39; 5/22/39; 9–19. The Jewish population of Austria was about one-third of that in Germany. The

figures above show how much further the pauperization had gone in Austria than in Germany.

89. Shaul Esh, "The Establishment of the Reichsvereinigung der Juden in Deutschland and Its Activities" (Hebrew), in *Yad Vashem Studies* (Jerusalem, 1968), 7:19–38.

90. Sources: R12; R21. The figures do not always tally. For Germany, for instance, a brochure entitled "Aid to Jews Overseas" (R9) gives the figure of $981,200.

91. AC, 2/2/39; Germany—AFSC, 2/9/39.

92. Sources: R21, 1939 draft report; R54, Troper letter, 5/16/39 (he puts emigration from "old" Germany in 1938 at 34,369); R10, newsletter, 6/15/39; R12.

93. 31—Germany, refugees 1939–1942, Hyman to David L. Podell, 3/30/39.

94. R11, November 1938, report by Noel Aronovici on a visit to Czechoslovakia.

95. Karel Lagus and Josef Polak, *Město za Mřížemi* (Prague, 1964), p. 334.

96. Livia Rothkirchen, *The Destruction of Slovak Jewry* (Hebrew) (Jerusalem, 1961), pp. 9, 14 (English summary, pp. vii, xiv).

97. 11–2, report, 2/3/39; CON-2, report by Marjorie Katz, 2/12/38; and R11, see note 94 above.

98. See note 94 above.

99. 11–4, 10/24/38 report.

100. Executive Committee, 2/26/39. According to JTA, twenty-seven hundred Jews were finally taken out from no-man's-land by Hungarian and Slovak authorities (1/23/39).

101. 11–2, 6/8/39, memo on Czechoslovakia.

102. R59, Troper letter, 6/16/39.

103. 11–2, exchange of letters and cables, 6/15/39–7/21/39.

104. R60, introduction to the March-April 1939 report.

105. 11–5, Smolar report, 6/9/39.

106. 11–5, Troper cable, 6/15/39.

107. Hyman at Executive Committee, 3/22/39; see also Executive Committee, 1/26/39.

108. R59, Troper letter, 5/16/39.

109. R46, January 1939 report.

110. Ibid.

111. R21, draft 1939 report.

112. 15–2, meeting in Paris, 6/4/39.

113. R12; R21, report for 1938 and 1939.

114. R12, 1938 report.

115. AC, Troper report, 3/31/39.

116. R21; 30—Germany, refugees in Belgium (Bruxelles); the figures in these two sources are contradictory; file 30 has a figure of $94,000 for JDC expenditures in Belgium in 1938. The discrepancy might possibly derive from the inclusion of JDC's support for the Belgian HICEM in the higher figure.

117. For Holland, see Executive Committee, 4/19/39; R46, January 1939 report; 34—Germany, refugees 1935–41, 1938 report. These are also the sources for the next paragraph in the text. Mrs. van Tijn reports (R52, 3/23/39 meeting of refugee committees) that the date of the closure of the Dutch border was December 17. I have not been able to clear up the discrepancy.

118. Ludwig, op. cit., pp. 94–151.

119. SIG, op. cit., p. 35.

120. Ludwig, op. cit., p. 164.

121. VSIA files, SM files.

122. 51—Switzerland, 1944; in a communication to this author dated February 5, 1970, the JDC office gave the sum spent in Switzerland in 1939 as $477,000. The difference, $7,000, was probably not given to VSIA but to other organizations in Switzerland.

123. R10, Troper memo on talk with Myron C. Taylor, 2/15/39; R55, report, 1/8/39.

124. Rosswell McClelland, interview (H).

125. *Hansard Parliamentary Debates,* House of Lords, vol. 111, no. 13, col. 463, 12/8/38, speech by Lord Dufferin.

126. R21, 1939 draft report; 12–22, report, 1933–43.

127. See, for example, *Sunday Pictorial,* 1/20/39: "Refugees Get Jobs; Britons Get Dole."

128. Joseph L. Cohen, *Salvaging German Jewry* (London, 1939).

129. 14–60, Kahn cable, 11/14/38.

130. Hyman at Executive Committee, 1/26/39.

131. 31—Germany, refugees, 1939–42, 2/21/39, Adler to Borchardt.

132. Germany file, movement for the care of children; and "Movement for the Care of Children," first annual report (London, n.d.), pp. 3–9.

133. Sources: R21, draft report 1939; 9–27, Kahn report, September 1938; "refugee countries" were France, Holland, Belgium, Luxemburg, Switzerland, Italy, and Czechoslovakia.

134. 9–30, 6/26/39, Warburg to Hyman.

135. George Backer at Executive Committee, 9/29/38.

136. James N. Rosenberg at JDC annual meeting, 12/20/38.

137. Executive Committee, 2/13/39.
138. Wyman, op. cit., pp. 53–56; Morse, op. cit., pp. 241–48; Raul Hilberg, *The Destruction of European Jews* (Chicago, 1961), p. 97. All these authors rely mainly on official document publications such as *Foreign Relations of the United States* (1938), 1:871–74; (1939), 2:77–87, 102–24, 95–98; *Documents on British Foreign Policy, 1919–1939,* 3rd series (London, 1950), 3:675–77; and *Documents on German Foreign Policy,* series D, 5:753–767, 780. Some unpublished State Department material is also quoted. See also Mashberg, op. cit.
139. *New York Times,* 2/14/39.
140. R46, January 1939 reports.
141. Ibid.
142. R55, 3/17/39, Baerwald statement and discussion.
143. 9–27, 5/4/39 memo.
144. Executive Committee, 6/16/39.
145. Morse, op. cit., pp. 270 ff.
146. CON-3, 6/27/39, Hyman to Baerwald.
147. Agar, op. cit., p. 85, footnote 4.
148. Command Paper 6014 (London, 1939).
149. Yehuda Bauer, *From Diplomacy to Resistance* (Philadelphia, 1970), pp. 11, 19–24.
150. For example, Executive Committee, 5/22/39, when Baerwald "deplored the slighting reference to British Guiana" in a letter by Henry Montor to JDC. There were to be other comments of this kind.
151. 30—Germany, proposals of settlement in other countries, British Guiana, 6/22/39, report of Robert Pell to the secretary of state.
152. Executive Committee, 6/5/39, 6/16/39.
153. AC, 6/26/39.
154. Executive Committee, 7/17/39; 9–30, 6/17/39 meeting.
155. 9–30, 6/7/39 memo (by J. C. Hyman).
156. Ibid.
157. 9–30, 7/15/39 cable by Jaretzki and Hyman to Linder. See also Adolph Held's letter to JDC, 7/12/39, in 9–30. Held thought that "before giving our consent to the Rublee plan, which is but a modified version of the notorious Schacht plan, we should at least try to find an answer to the most burning question of the day: Where will the emigrants, supposedly helped by the Rublee plan, go?"
158. 9–30, text of communique by Lord Winterton after a meeting of ICR, 7/19/39.
159. *Documents on German Foreign Policy,* series D, 5:927.
160. Hilberg, loc. cit.

161. Broszat et al., op. cit. pp. 340–45.

162. Wyman, op. cit., p. 56.

163. 31—Germany, refugees 1939–42, letter to Lord Samuel, 2/10/39.

164. Morse, op. cit., pp. 248–49.

165. Yehuda Slutsky, *Sefer Toldot Hahaganah* (Tel Aviv, 1963), 2:528–29. There were 360 passengers, but 50 managed to land without being noticed by the British.

166. R16, monthly bulletin, nos. 1 and 2, 3/6/35.

167. Slutsky, op. cit., 2:1036 ff.

168. Kahn material, file 1939/40, 6/15/39.

169. R55, Troper letter, 3/2/39.

170. 9–27, meeting of ICR directors with JDC and HICEM, 7/25/39.

171. R10, 5/29/39, Kahn note for Baerwald; R55, 5/11/39 report; 42—Palestine, emigration to Palestine, 1937–39.

172. For a list of the ships see 29—Germany, "Panic Emigration," 1938–39, 3/30/39; Executive Committee, meetings between December 1938 and July 1939; R9, "Aid to Jews Overseas" (pamphlet); also R56 and AC meetings during this period.

173. Cable of 3/15/39, quoted in Hyman's report to the Executive Committee, 3/23/39.

174. AC, 3/15/39.

175. A detailed list of the countries and the numbers of refugees in each was submitted to the Executive Committee meeting on 7/20/39.

176. A good example of this in Latin America was the secretary of the government of British Guiana (the proposed Jewish homeland). This worthy man wrote a letter to the British Guiana Information Bureau in New York (see above, note 172, 29—Germany) on December 13, 1938, in response to a request for an entry permit by a Jewish refugee. The refugee was told that anyone who had 50 pounds in his wallet could land. However, there were some small snags: there was no work and no employment; generally speaking, refugees would be well advised not to come. "It would be most inadvisable for your family and you to consider coming here. . . . You are strongly advised not to migrate to this colony."

177. R52, current reports, 10/12/37.

178. Executive Committee, 2/24/38.

179. R55, cables 1/12/39, 2/1/39.

180. R10, 3/19/39, Hyman memo to Backer.

181. R47, 3/22, unsigned. "One can also be of the opinion that it would be more worthy of a Jew to go to a martyr's death than to perish miserably in Shanghai. The first choice would be a matter of *kiddush*

hashem, the second merely a failure of Jewish emigration policies" (trans. from German).

182. R10, memo of 9/11/39; 44–4, Troper to Baerwald, 8/29/39.

183. JTA, 4/7/39.

184. 44–24.

185. R55. The creation of a Polish Central Committee was apparently discussed with Sachs in talks with Kahn in Warsaw in late 1937 (Sachs's letter to Kahn, 44–3, 9/15/38).

186. CON-2, Troper report, 11/30/38.

187. 44–4, 3/4/39.

188. 44–4, Troper at the Committee on Poland, 4/11/39: "Some of the men [at the Warsaw office] feel that Giterman's situation is not satisfactory from the JDC point of view."

189. 44–4, memo by Schweitzer, January 1939.

190. 44–3, Sachs to JDC, Paris, 2/28/39.

191. 44–21, Kahn at the Committee on Poland, 7/7/39.

192. 44–4, report by Schweitzer, 3/23/39.

193. 44–4, A. Kahn to Troper, 7/11/39.

194. 44–4, memo by Giterman, 7/17/39.

195. 44–4, Troper to Hyman, 6/10/39.

196. R55, Troper report, 3/5/39.

197. 44–4, "Interim Report," July 1939.

198. 44–4, cable of 9/2/39.

CONCLUSION

1. Based mainly on R21, draft 1939 report.

Bibliography

The historical literature dealing with the 1920s and 1930s is, of course, very large. However, only a small segment deals with specific Jewish problems. Some of this latter consists of memoirs, pamphlets, and one-sided descriptions. To list all these would burden our bibliography uselessly. The selected list given below therefore includes only those items that were either directly quoted in the text or provided immediate background material to the story.

Adler-Rudel, Shalom. *Ostjuden in Deutschland.* Tübingen, 1959.

Agar, Herbert. *The Saving Remnant.* New York, 1960.

Bein, Alex. "The Jewish Parasite." *Leo Baeck Yearbook.* Vol. 9. London, 1964.

Bentwich, Norman. *They Found Refuge.* London, 1965.

Bernstein, Herman. "The History of American Jewish Relief." Ms, JDC Library, 1928.

Blumenfeld, Kurt. *Erlebte Judenfrage.* Stuttgart, 1962.

Braham, Randolph L., ed. *Hungarian Jewish Studies.* 2 vols. New York, 1969.

Broszat, Martin et al. *Die Anatomie des SS-Staates.* Olten and Freiburg, 1965.

Cohen, Joseph L. *Salvaging German Jewry.* London, 1939.

Documents on German Foreign Policy, series D.

Esh, Shaul. "The Establishment of the Reichsvereinigung der Juden in Deutschland and Its Activities." *Yad Vashem Studies.* Vol. 7. Jerusalem, 1968.

Feingold, Henry L. *Politics of Rescue.* New Brunswick, N.J., 1969.

Foreign Relations of the United States. 1933–1939.

Grossmann, Kurt R. *Emigration.* Frankfurt a/M, 1969.

Handlin, Oscar. *A Continuing Task*. New York, 1964.

Hilberg, Raul. *The Destruction of European Jews*. Chicago, 1961.

Lagus, Karel, and Polak, Josef. *Město za Mřížemi*. Prague, 1964.

Lestschinsky, Jacob. *Crisis, Catastrophe and Survival*. London, 1946.

Lowenthal, E. G. *Bewährung im Untergang*. Stuttgart, 1965.

Ludwig, Carl. *Die Flüchtlingspolitik der Schweiz seit 1933 bis zur Gegenwart*. Zurich, n.d. [1957].

Mahler, Raphael. *Yehudai Polin bein shtei Milchamot Olam* [Jews in Poland between the two world wars]. Tel Aviv, 1968.

Melchior, Carl. *Ein Buch des Gedenkens und der Freundschaft*. Tübingen, 1967.

Morse, Arthur D. *While Six Million Died*. New York, 1968.

Proudfoot, Malcolm. *European Refugees*. London, 1957.

Rosenkranz, Herbert. "The Anschluss and the Tragedy of Austrian Jewry, 1938–1945." In *The Jews of Austria*, edited by Josef Frankel. London, 1967.

Rosenstock, Werner. "Exodus, 1933–1939." *Leo Baeck Yearbook*. Vol. 1. London, 1956.

Rothkirchen, Livia. *Churban Yahadut Slovakia* [The destruction of Slovak Jewry]. Jerusalem, 1961.

Sharf, Andrew. *The British Press and the Jews under the Nazi Rule*. Oxford, 1964.

SIG. *Festschrift zum 50-jährigen Bestehen*. Zurich, n.d. [1954].

Simon, Ernst. *Aufbau im Untergang*. Tübingen, 1959.

Slutsky, Yehuda. *Sefer Toldot Hahaganah*. Vols. 1 and 2. Tel Aviv, 1963.

Szajkowski, Zosa. "Budgeting American Overseas Relief, 1919–1939." *American Jewish Historical Quarterly* 59, nos. 1–3.

———. "The Attitude of American Jews to Refugees from Germany in the 1930's." *American Jewish Historical Quarterly* 61, no. 2.

van Tijn, Gertude. "Werkdorf Nieuwesluis." *Leo Baeck Yearbook*. Vol. 14. London, 1969.

Waldman, Morris D. *Nor by Power*. New York, 1955.

Wischnitzer, Mark. *Die Juden in der Welt*. Berlin, 1935.

———. *Visas to Freedom*. New York, 1956.

Wyman, David S. *Paper Walls*. Amherst, Mass., 1968.

INDEX*

Abyssinia, 16
Academic Assistance Council, 140
Adler, Cyrus, 11, 17, 55, 56, 95, 206, 249
Adler-Rudel, Shalom, 121
Advisory Committee on Political Refugees, 232
Africa, 233, 249. *See also* countries by name
Agriculture et Artisanat, 141, 151, 153
Agro-Joint, 59–104
Agudah, 31, 33, 53, 182, 222, 294, 296, 300
Ahavah home, 121, 122
Albania, 270
Alexander I, of Russia, 60
Alexander I, of Yugoslavia, 152
Allenstein (Olsztyn), Prussia, 226
Alliance Israélite Universelle, 139, 265
Allied Jewish Appeal, 42
Alsace, 264
Alsberg, Henry G., 13
Alter, Victor, 45–46, 48
Altreu, 129–30
American Committee for Aid of Jews in Galicia, 203
American Federation of Polish Jews (AFPJ), 194–95, 248, 282
American Friends Service Committee (AFSC), 16, 126–27, 259, 263, 269, 272
*Prepared by Kay Powell

American Hebrew and Jewish Tribune, 52
American Jewish Committee (AJC), 3, 5, 6, 20, 22, 52, 53, 66, 106, 108, 142, 145, 194, 206, 227, 232, 233, 249, 277
American Jewish Congress, 232, 276, 282, 283
American Jewish Joint Distribution Committee, *see* JDC
American Jewish Reconstruction Foundation, 36, 42–48, 197, 215, 251
Central Financial Institution, 197, 296
loan *kassas,* 15, 23, 36–37, 42–45, 75 ff., 94, 100, 114, 118, 131, 196–99, 212–18, 221, 296
American Jewish Relief Committee (AJRC), 6, 7, 12, 35
American Red Cross, 16, 20
American Relief Administration (ARA), 9, 10, 14, 57, 59
American Society for Jewish Farm Settlements in Russia (AMSOJEFS), 65 ff.
Amur River, 90
Anglo-Jewish Association, 140, 290
Anglo-Palestine Bank, 15
Angriff, 134
Antwerp, Belgium, 172, 266
Argentina, 27, 92, 120, 144, 145, 233

345 : *Index*

Marshall, James, 107, 116, 155
Marshall, Louis, 5, 6, 16, 17, 22–23, 24, 26, 27
Marxist party (Austria), 224
Mayer, Saly, 173, 176, 177, 240, 241, 292
Melchior, Karl, 109, 110
Menorah Journal, 26
Mensheviks, 69
Merezhin (vice-president of COM-ZET), 74
Mexico, 287
Middle East, 15, 164. *See also* countries by name
Mikolajczyk, Stanislaw, 181
Minśk Mazowiecki, Poland, 183
Mirkin, J., 74
Mittwoch, Eugen, 125
Moffat, Pierrepont, 107, 278
Moldavia, 14, 51, 210, 212, 215
Montefiore, Leonard, 139–40
Moravia, 14, 259, 260, 262
Morgenroit Institute, 49
Morgenthau, Henry, Jr., 107
Morgenthau, Henry, Sr., 3, 4, 142, 232
Morris, Leland, 228
Morse, Arthur D., 231
Mortgage and Credit Bank, 161
Moscow, USSR, 66, 90, 98
Moses, Siegfried, 129
Moskowitz, Henry, 54
Movement for the Care of Children from Germany, 272
Munich agreement, 260, 262, 270
Munkács, Czechoslovakia, 219

National Conference of Jewish Social Workers, 122
National Coordinating Committee, 255, 289
National Front (Switzerland), 173
National German Jews, 132
National Refugee Service, 289
Naumann, Max, 132
Nazis and Nazism, 30, 97, 166, 212, 217, 228, 229, 230, 238, 263, 267
Arbeitsfront, 113, 137
in Austria, 224–25, 275
in Czechoslovakia, 185, 229, 251, 260–64, 292

in Danzig, 177–78
definition of a Jew, 113, 114, 179, 220, 228
in Germany, 54–56, 104 ff., 152, 163, 168, 174, 180, 183, 194, 195, 244, 252–58, 260, 284–85
in Hungary, 219
in Poland, 187, 188
in Romania, 216
in Switzerland, 173
Nazi Teachers' Association, 133
NEP (new economic policies), 59, 61, 70
Neuendorf, Germany, 120
Neustadt, Leib, 203, 298
News Chronicle (Britain), 150
New York City, 194, 297
New York State, 27
New York Times, 105, 106, 142, 154, 194, 214
New Zlatopol, USSR, 104
Nice, France, 269
"Night of Crystal," 252–53
Nikolaev, USSR, 84
Norman, Montagu, 275
Norway, 270
Nuremberg laws (1935), 117, 133–34, 136, 153, 171, 214

Odessa, USSR, 82, 84, 85
Olympic Games (1936), 137
ONR (Poland), 181
Orduna, the, 289
Orinoco, the, 287
ORT (Organization for Rehabilitation through Training), 49, 53–54, 63, 78, 85, 121, 201–2, 256, 265
Orzech, Mauricy, 298, 300
OSE (OZE), 34, 49, 50, 53–54, 141, 264
Ostrog, Poland, 189
Oualid, William, 237
Oungre, Edouard, 237
Oungre, Louis, 36, 44, 45, 47, 95, 139
OZET, 60, 63, 83, 87
OZN (Poland), 181–82, 184–85

Palästinaamt, 114
Pale of Settlement, 59, 100
Palestine, 3, 15, 25, 61, 101, 102, 111, 121, 153, 161, 165, 182

348 : *Index*

349 : *Index*

Temple Israel

Minneapolis, Minnesota

In Honor of the Bar Mitzvah of

JOEL FINK

by

Mr. & Mrs. David Fink